IN DEPTH SPORT PSYCHOLOGY

In Depth Sport Psychology: Reclaiming the Lost Soul of the Athlete is a unique exploration of the vital archetypal elements and themes that emerge when considering elite sport psychology through a depth psychological lens. It provides athletes, young people, coaches and clinicians with ways to harness the self, placing athletes on a path towards personal growth and sporting excellence by reconnecting their spirit to their sport.

Burston's multidisciplinary and inclusive approach details the importance of spirituality and other unmeasurable factors, such as emotional recovery, when investigating sporting potential. Incorporating research from classic mythology and the Greek sports academies, he traces sport back to humanity's animalistic and traumatic origins, explores the rise of the Olympic movement and compares archetypal identities that are shared with athletes today. Relating this to today's financially driven and technological sporting climate, he considers the roots of play, examines the difference in the psyche of team sports and individual players, discusses the crucial, clinical welfare of young people and dedicates a section to sportswomen. *In Depth Sport Psychology* emphasises how awakening an athlete's unconscious spirit can positively improve their performance, and offers an applicable methodology for athletes and teachers to use to better understand themselves and achieve brilliance.

Uniquely exploring the connection between Jungian depth psychology and sports, the accessible tone of *In Depth Sport Psychology* will be key reading for analytical and depth psychologists in practice and in training, sport psychologists and other professionals working with athletes. It will also appeal to athletes and sportspeople interested in exploring a new perspective on sporting excellence.

David Burston, PhD, M.F.T., is a psychotherapist in Los Angeles, USA, spending part of his time working as a UK chartered clinical and sport psychologist consultant with a Premier League football club in London. Initially a professional actor, 15 years ago David began using his experience to help athletes perform, integrating those ideas with Jungian depth perspectives.

IN DEPTH SPORT PSYCHOLOGY

Reclaiming the Lost Soul of the Athlete

David Burston

Routledge
Taylor & Francis Group

LONDON AND NEW YORK

First published 2019
by Routledge
2 Park Square, Milton Park, Abingdon, Oxon OX14 4RN

and by Routledge
52 Vanderbilt Avenue, New York, NY 10017

Routledge is an imprint of the Taylor & Francis Group, an informa business

© 2019 David Burston

British Library Cataloguing-in-Publication Data
A catalogue record for this book is available from the British Library

Library of Congress Cataloging-in-Publication Data
Names: Burston, David Huw, author.
Title: In depth sport psychology : reclaiming the lost soul of the
    athlete / David Burston.
Description: Abingdon, Oxon ; New York, NY : Routledge, 2019.
Identifiers: LCCN 2018036553 (print) | LCCN 2018050240 (ebook) |
    ISBN 9781315144078 (Master Ebook) | ISBN 9781351386791
    (Abode Reader) | ISBN 9781351386784 (epub) |
    ISBN 9781351386777 (mobipocket) | ISBN 9781138500969
    (hardback) | ISBN 9781138500983 (pbk.) |
    ISBN 9781315144078 (ebk)
Subjects: LCSH: Sports--Psychological aspects.
Classification: LCC GV706.4 (ebook) | LCC GV706.4 .B84 2019
    (print) | DDC 796.01--dc23
LC record available at https://lccn.loc.gov/2018036553

ISBN: 978-1-138-50096-9 (hbk)
ISBN: 978-1-138-50098-3 (pbk)
ISBN: 978-1-315-14407-8 (ebk)

Typeset in Bembo
by Swales & Willis Ltd, Exeter, Devon, UK

This book is dedicated to a bird, a dog and a lion. They all know who they are . . .

CONTENTS

The ending   **165**

PROLOGUE

Before the beginning, meet depth sport psychology

Football is a big business for the peoples of this world. As I write this book the World Cup Finals of 2018 are in full motion and countries around the world are facing heartbreak or joy, depending on the result. Life is not a foregone conclusion for anyone and neither is this competition; the great can fall and the smaller nations can take some pride. Many psyches around the world are now deeply connected, yet the worlds of clinical psychology and sports often seem separated. It is understandable that they are so different; one take place inside a room and one outside on a field, one is analytical and the other an act of pure expression. Those of the two cultures do not often share the same ground. Athletes once had no interest in psychology, which may represent some kind of gap we can usefully explore and hope to fill here. This book is about what happens when these distinct spiritual disciplines join forces.

This section and brief introduction is a bid to orientate the uninitiated to the subjects and terms discussed in the chapters ahead. This chapter will also provide the reader with a sense of the different perspectives that will be encountered when considering sport from a depth perspective. The mission of this book is to relate a multidisciplinary approach, which means this work incorporates and seeks to integrate subjects such as anthropology, sociology and literature to achieve a deeper and richer understanding of sports and the psyche of sports.

In her book *Remembering Dionysus*, analyst and author Susan Rowland (2017) discussed the limitations caused by a culture of unnecessary 'turf wars' and divisions of epistemological thought and learning that have closed down synergistic possibilities when knowledge is shared: 'Disciplines that could be regarded as helpfully allied, such as literature and psychology, were firmly dismembered by the demands of the earlier 20th-century academy' (p. 99).

This book will take an inclusive approach, incorporating research from the original Greek sports academies as well as from physics, chemistry and astronomy. We are all in this together. Inclusivity is a positive value at the heart of depth psychology and sports, and this book will seek to explain why. This is a relatively new approach, forged as a response to these times, perhaps as a way to help alleviate the new pressures arising on young people. Depth sport psychology is now making a unique footprint on the well-trodden highway of elite sports. This book will outline our Jungian mark in the mud. We really can retrace many of our footsteps, so to speak, and that past will be the beginning of this book.

As well as individual and group psychotherapy, my work is also dedicated to 'applied psychology'. As 'psychological scientists', we have a desire to share our knowledge with others (particularly the young), who can then go on and use new knowledge with a more informed sense of the mind. This is so often a failing of modern science in that it becomes remote, or becomes used for ideas related to destruction – war and violence – or pure finance. In keeping with the original Greek storytellers, this book aims to be accessible to as many readers as possible, and has been written in such a way. This was once the way with all knowledge, and it was through storytelling that we once learned important lessons for life.

Depth psychology is a branch of clinical psychology, and this relatively obscure term has to some extent replaced the older name 'analytical psychology'; however, the aims and focus remain the same. Depth psychology is a science that in part incorporates the unconscious element of the mind, as in the work of Sigmund Freud and others at the turn of the last century. It is a science that takes into account unconscious processes in order to provide an interpretation. This premise accepts that if we have an unconscious, we are in relationship with something – even if we cannot immediately know what it is. Jung's contribution was the drawing together of truly universal themes and patterns within us humans that form archetypes we can identify and therefore understand better.

At the beginning of the last century, Freud, Karl Marx and Sherlock Holmes all had one thing in common. They demonstrated that what appears on the surface might not be in reality what exists beneath; one must simply know where to look. With a rigorous methodology and enquiry, perspectives can emerge that closer define the truth of something, whether that be the proof of the unconscious, the proletariat or who committed the crime. This was also a hallmark of Socrates, and in keeping with Freud's contemporary Carl Jung, we shall be referring to terms such as 'spirit' and 'soul' that may be unfamiliar in a science book. Jungian psychological approaches include an understanding of what were once called 'the classics', meaning mythology and, in particular (though by no means only), Greek mythology.

Soul and spirit might appear to be ethereal terms, but all elite sportsmen and women have a relationship with these elements as vital components of excellence. Science must grasp this nettle, and this book aims to do so. Spirit is a term often used in sport, for example, the notion of 'team spirit'. What does this term actually mean? What about the spirit of the individual, and how does this relate to team spirit? These are vital questions for an age where these things might not seem to matter, a time of progression and regression.

'Emergency' has meanings of urgency and emergence wrapped up within it. This book hopes to show what happens when even a whole nation is forced into a form of emotional recovery. The author Michael Novak was also interested in the deeper essences behind sporting performance; in his book *The Joy of Sports*, Novak (1993) suggests that 'sports are creations of the human spirit, arenas of the human spirit, witnesses to the human spirit, instructors of the human spirit' (p. 158). In a world where an extra 1% of improvement can be of inestimable value, there is, and always has been, a practical advantage in knowledge of the emotions, the sprit and the soul. They cannot be weighed, but that does not mean that they don't exist, or cannot be usefully investigated. Spirit cannot be measured, but its lack can always be seen in demoralised players and teams.

This book aspires to approach sport using a different, wider lens. That means here to hold a conscious space for the ethereal, historical and diverse. In fact, when considering the psyche of a performer – or any human being – experience suggests we must embrace the ineffable and the unmeasurable as a valid model for our investigations. If we do not, we run the risk of failing to accurately reflect the subject of the investigation. Paradoxes such as this are important to understand, and they will be investigated as this book unfolds. Jung once warned against being too 'schematic'; this book will seek to take some risks, which in life is often where things can get interesting. But this will involve some use of the Shadow, and that can be risky!

My work in sports has been primarily in the academies of Premier League football in London, and my work has been well received in my home in California. In the USA, I am a full-time licensed psychotherapist and clinician in Los Angeles. This book will also include contributions from other depth psychologists working in a range of sports and countries. The emphasis of this book is what the relational – in my case, Jungian – depth psychological sciences can share with sports people. My experience shows that our science can make a positive contribution, which is, is my estimation, needed.

First, it is important to consider the development of us as a species. The science of play will be investigated, and how it is fundamentally crucial for all of us, as well as for the welfare of young people in sport. A separate section will represent my humble research relating to women in sport. This book will consider the psyche of teams and individuals such as sprinters and golfers, who must primarily rely on themselves on the field of play. Like the original dragon-slayer St George, we have to slay dragons if we want to find the Holy Grail.

All sportsmen and women must do battle with external as well as internal opponents, and this book will outline a possible methodology an athlete or teacher can benefit from knowing and sharing. The aim is to help individuals better understand themselves and to provide an approach to tackle their own inner demons – the kind that haunt us all. That is the Hippocratic Oath for the psychotherapist, and ours is an optimistic, integrated kind of perspective that I hope the reader will enjoy learning more about.

For any clinician readers, there will be plenty of pit stops at those places where psychotherapy and sports converge. Our science has much to offer this world, which is so often a stranger to psychology. I do not know whether Jung or Freud supported a football team, but they would surely have appreciated the beneficial effect such support has for society. Technology is providing the fortunate recipients of its favours new and important ways to measure and see the world more clearly and accurately. However, there are so many sources it is hard to know which to trust. Things we cannot measure might not sound trustworthy, but this book will testify to their value.

Some current perspectives of scientific rationalism propose that we are all essentially computers. Clinicians recoil from this kind of idea because it serves to objectify the human, which is always degrading. And while this may seem like a modern issue, it is not a new debate. In ancient Greece, Plato was an energy- and spirit-based philosopher who believed in 'vitalism', a sense that there is an energetic base to the universe. This theory vied against Democritus, the 'atomist', who believed that everything was grounded in form, or 'atoms'. The clashes of materialism and objectification have perhaps always struggled with the drive towards spiritual enlightenment and co-operation.

Tragically, Socrates was forced to kill himself in 399 BC after the powerful of Athens became tired (and anxious) of his constant questioning and desire to see the other side of things. His genius was the first in the West to ask such questions as 'can you have too much of a good thing?' In India, the Buddha Gotama Siddhartha was reaching similar conclusions, suggesting that craving was at the heart of unhappiness. At the time of Socrates, Athens was craving and at war with Sparta. One can bet that Socrates had things to say about that; he was eventually accused of corrupting the young and following 'new demons'. There was a polarity then, as now, and Democritus and Plato might well have been arguing the same points today.

As well as a capacity for logic and analysis, the Greeks had a foundation of mythological characters and stories that helped them to navigate the vicissitudes of personal life. To use a modern idiom, this is a good time to iron out something regarding mythology. It is a misconception that if something is a myth, it is not true. Myths are stories that have remained with us so long because they represent human truths. They can be quite direct with their meanings and are not ethereal, obtuse narratives. They often say, 'if you do this, this will happen'. Irrespective of technological progress, our inner experiences remain human, the human animal inextricably bound to our past. The depth traditions refer to these patterns as archetypes. Sports have central archetypal themes and identities that the depth traditions are well-placed to consider. This book will relate those.

There is a core trinity that every serious athlete must adhere to in order to succeed. An athlete must prepare, face their challenge on the field, and then face the challenge of emotionally repairing after the result, finding a way to come back and fight another day. Every competitor or performer must find a way to repair and come back to fight another day. It was the same for our ancestors, and will remain a trinity to be mastered for all time. Emotions are very real emanations and a sign of humanity; we as humans are able to realise higher interpersonal capacities such as empathy and love.

Traditional portrayals of psychopaths often show robotic figures with no emotions. For three years, my work involved interactions with such people. My experience was that emotions such as empathy are not at all accessible for them, and this book will explore why this is important for sport psychology. Emotions and the deeper aspects of the psyche challenge us in modern times because they are not visible, concrete entities; however, we are all aware of how real they can be.

For an athlete, these are forces that, when consciously harnessed, will help them to realise their potential. Self-realisation and good sport psychology go hand-in-hand. Elite sports environments are worlds where 'many are called, but few are chosen'. There are real psychological issues or capacities that can make the difference between success and failure. Professional elite athletes are the chosen few. They have reached astounding levels of competence, but what can they teach us? In my experience, most elite athletes would relate the importance of psychology and a strong mindset. What do they mean? The lucky few athletes are challenged to find new paths for improvement. Just as our ancestors had to create new paths, it is the very stuff of neuroscience to see life as a journey to locate new avenues and possibilities. This is a principle of personal growth and one of the goals of psychotherapeutic progress.

You can put a brain in a jar, but you cannot bottle a mind. A mind is made of invisible and visible elements that need to be coaxed and tended and, yes, sometimes in life, *ordered* to improve! We are in an age where the power of data is becoming a greater and more insidious influence. We are all routinely tracked, graded and evaluated in ways we are mostly unaware of. Now even once-quiet side streets are transformed during rush-hour traffic; why? Because traffic navigation systems are suggesting short-cuts. In New Jersey, residents have had enough and are reclaiming the streets and banning rush-hour traffic from their neighbourhoods.

We can all sense that the current political and social polarities within Western societies and cultures are rising. We are living in a time the original medieval alchemists called *solutzio*, a time of dissolution and change. I detect today a real sense of dissolution and great uncertainty for the future. We are beginning to see more and more data-influenced sports analysis, even a computer that chooses the 'man of the match'. But what of the 'non-data' world? The natural world is different from the natural sciences, and, as it happens, this natural world includes our subject too, the realm of the sports performer. A tablet or smartphone cannot yet be taken onto the field; it remains a human-versus-human encounter.

The mission of this book is to look for the soul of the athlete. When one looks for intangibilities like the soul, numbers and rationalities become less relevant. The great philosopher and phenomenologist Hans-Georg Gadamer (1900–2002), in *Dialogue and Dialectic* (1980), wrote: 'no one could seriously contend that the ability to think correctly is acquired only through a detour through logical theory' (p. 5). Gadamer and his contemporaries sought to understand people in non-linear ways, meaning not just the things about that are measurable. But in order to go here we require some structure within science, not a rejection of logical theory. It is in these areas that our science has found a language, and where in life can be most interesting to observe.

All of the authors cited in this work have records in grounded scientific methodology, including the 1981 Nobel Prize winner Roger Sperry (1913–1994), who might define this book as a more 'right-brained' exercise. Indeed, we shall seek to investigate that dichotomy of left brain versus right, and what it means for the sport performer. My last book, *Psychological, Archetypal and Phenomenological Perspectives on Soccer* (2017), was a phenomenological enquiry indicating that these issues were crucial for understanding sport performance. This is where we study the inside, the 'erlebnis', of a subject – in my case footballers. Jung said: 'A psychology that wants to be scientific can no longer afford to base itself on so-called philosophical premises such as materialism or rationalism physical premises. It can only proceed phenomenologically and abandon preconceived opinions' (Jung, 1949, pp. 523–4).

For our athletes to truly thrive, I suggest and emphasise that they must learn to look beneath the obvious. My call to the athlete would be to become open, and remain teachable, to be willing to grow and evolve as an individual, and this book suggests how to find that path. Without willingness, most learning and growth is not possible, so how can we measure willingness? It is a spirit we must summon, and the calling for it begins here.

Fearing they cannot muster willingness in others, many leaders of the past have chosen force or deception as a way to motivate. This book speaks of the power of spirit, not force, in sport. Sport is partly an art form. The Greeks were the first to blend poetry, storytelling and sport, creating new human experiences which would soon become universal, and which we still follow today. They would no doubt appreciate that most good stories have a beginning, a middle and an ending. This section is *before* the beginning.

For the real beginning we must reach back, beyond the origin of sports competition in Greece, to the true beginning for humans.

My handshake with you, before the whistle blows

Psychotherapy has a primary virtue which is of the same value in all the elite sports cultures I have known and worked within – and there have been a few. Within the word confidentiality is the word confide, or what it is to place one's trust in another human being. In my 15 years of professional sport experience, I have been graced with many great confidences, which I am sure I could profit from sharing. But I will not. This is why this book contains no names and rarely uses anecdotes or references that could identify anyone I have ever worked with in English football, the world that the Americans call soccer. I work with many who should be national heroes and legends, but they stay quiet and dedicate themselves to making their athletes and apprentices better, just as the psychotherapists I work with do.

This way, we all benefit. If you can understand this principle, you will be much nearer to understanding the meanings in this book, and in my humble estimation on your way to greatness – in whatever form that may take for you.

References

Burston, D.H. (2015). *Psychological, Archetypal and Phenomenological Perspectives on Soccer.* London and New York: Routledge.

Gadamer, H. (1980). *Dialogue and Dialectic: Eight Hermeneutical Studies on Plato* (P.C. Smith, trans.). New Haven, CT: Yale University Press.

Jung, C.G. (1949). 'Foreword to Adler: Studies in Analytical Psychology', *Collected Works, volume 18: The Symbolic Life: Miscellaneous Writings.* Princeton, NJ: Princeton University Press.

Rowland, S. (2017). *Remembering Dionysus.* London and New York: Routledge.

The beginning

1

'THE KNOWLEDGE'

Stone tools to video chat in 30,000 years

In keeping with the spirit of depth psychology, in this section we can take a moment to look over our shoulder and explore our shared past as a species. After all, gathering information about our past is a natural way for humans to learn more about each other. Learning about our past helps us provide a context for someone or something. We are in an age when history and similar forms of knowing don't make much money, causing them to become marginalised or deemed unimportant. They are not 'the knowledge' right now that perhaps best describes the realms of information technology and the Internet. For depth psychology, the past is important. Depth psychological traditions are like most other counselling modalities, in that an analyst will normally ask a client about their past in order to get a better sense of them. An old adage suggests that 'if you want to know where you are going, you have to know where you have come from'.

This is not always the case for therapy; other 'postmodern' modalities of psychotherapy such as 'positive psychology' allow just one session for discussing the past and then explore positive 'now and forward issues'. Perhaps this really is the way to progress, but in the case of trauma there is an ethical imperative to allow healing to take place by, in part, 're-visiting' so we can 're-member' and 're-cover'. People need space in order to repair and get help. Denying this kind of reality might be a case of 'epistemological violence', a cultural phenomenon we shall explore later.

Our history as a species has seen much trauma – perhaps *mostly* trauma. It has been a rough journey and the challenge for us is partly to avoid denial. Coming to terms with our past is always a challenge, but this is a book about sport, which is part of the wonderful story of how we got from stone tools to video chat in 30,000 years. We are incredible beings with amazing capacities and a positive genius for survival. Our ancestors endowed us with temperaments forged in a furnace of suffering and loss. This section explores some of the mechanisms and perspectives that humans developed or harnessed in order to deal with a sometimes frightening and cruel parent we now call the Earth.

To be a taxi driver in London it was once a requirement that you had 'the knowledge'. This meant you knew the streets of London intimately and how to get around – fast, if you had to. It was the same for our ancestors, who needed knowledge and experience that could help navigate nature and one another. We currently live in a great age for the spirit of enquiry. For the lucky recipients who can access it, the Internet has enabled instantaneous education, information and entertainment which can make us better informed on any subject – that is, if we can wade through the mirage of infomercials and the wide diversity of alternative facts and truths available online for us to choose. The truth is out there for a discerning user at a time when facts become opinions and opinions can be facts.

This next section will endeavour to relate a timeline of how our common minds have been inspired, wired and shaped by our experiences as a species. I suggest that this history is a big element of our sporting story, and by looking back as a species we can explore why this knowledge is important to understand. As a result, we might increase our chances of capturing the elusive athletic soul that history suggests we have lost touch with to some degree.

Current cosmological science states that the Big Bang and the birth of the universe happened nearly 14 billion years ago, marking the beginning of time as we know it. The Earth was formed much later, 4.6 billion years ago. Molecular life forms emerged 3.8 million years ago and then went through many dramatic cataclysmic upheavals to get to us. Life fought for survival and adapted all of the way.

We ride a volcanic magma crust of tectonic plates that have moved, convulsed and drifted since the beginning. Another important big bang happened 66 million years ago, when an asteroid impact dug out the massive Chicxulub crater in the Yucatan Peninsula in Mexico. It may have been this that led to the elimination of the Dinosaurs, giving our particular species a chance to evolve and exploit the gap they left behind.

For 50 million years we went along our evolutionary path becoming primates dwelling in rich Amazonian-like forest canopies with social lives, wants and needs, as we do now. Science is not certain exactly why, but 5 million years ago we left our chimpanzee and bonobo relatives in the trees to follow a new path on the ground. We relinquished the protective canopies to face a much less certain future with new dangers, challenges and hazards.

The current understanding is that we left the trees because of declining forestry, but that may not be the entire story. I'm grateful to the author Yuval Harari, who points out in his excellent book *Sapiens* that this might have been the result of the remaining chimpanzees and bonobos kicking our ancestors out! This is a salutary reminder not to go jumping to conclusions when looking into the deeper past.

Whatever the reason, evidence shows that our ancestors faced a steep learning curve out there, exposed in the open. There is evidence that around 2.5 million years we began to use stone tools in limited ways. Around the same time or later came the first controlled use of fire. Early hominids were beginning to try to control nature in order to live better. Our ancestors had to adapt to new conditions and discover new ways to survive and thrive while contending with new challenges. Fire making was an important 'knowledge', and those with it will have had influence. Adaptability is an important principle for all life forms that survive on earth. The climate on earth has swung wildly at times and is, after all, constantly changing. Twice in the history of the earth has the entire planet become a snowball, at which times most life existed only in the depths, as bacteria lying deep within the rocks of the subterranean planet.

Change is a part of the permanent landscape and such a paradox remains for us today. A primary truth for existence on Earth is that our ancestors needed to use intelligence, flexibility and adaptability in order to survive 'the wild'. The Internet will not prevent this need; some can deny it, but future climate issues will escalate and it is the poorest on the planet who will suffer the most. As a species at every level we will need to be flexible, as life on Earth dictates that those who cannot be flexible will be the very organisms to die out. Earthquakes, floods, volcanoes, fire storms, ice, aridity and broader climactic changes over time have forced our ancestors to fit in, leave or die. Our predecessors, and all the beings who ever existed on Earth before us, had been helpless to these natural forces around them. Ours was the species that was different.

In 2017, the population of the world was stated as 7.5 billion souls. In 2005, it stood at 6.5 billion. Population growth is often a natural strategy for an organism in order to maintain survival, and this might indeed be a winning strategy. Rats and cockroaches may be able to survive a nuclear holocaust, but it seems that humans could not. However quickly our population is currently expanding, for most of history we were few in number.

About 40,000 years ago, *Homo sapiens* emerged out of Africa, spreading out in five directions across the world. *Neanderthal* hunters, built for the colder climates, were absorbed or driven away by these more adept new humans. At the end of the last ice age, 12,000 years ago, it was with the northward movement of large prey such as the mammoth that the *Neanderthals* were finally extinguished, leaving only us.

Hunting in small bands, the numbers of *Homo sapiens* on Earth remained limited until, as Stephen Pinker puts it, a 'population explosion after the invention of agriculture about 10,000 years ago' (p. 143). Before that, humans existed in bands of 20–30 individuals. Due to the need to find new mating partners, we can expect that early groups had some form of communication and relationship with one other.

In their book *The Extraordinary Story of Human Origins*, Angela and Alberto Piero add that life was short:

> It is estimated that the average life span of hominids on the African Savannah between 4,000,000 and 200,000 years ago was 20 years. This means that the population would be completely renewed about five times per century assuming that infant mortality has already been accounted for. It is further estimated that the population of hominids in Africa fluctuated between 10,000 and 100,000 individuals, thus averaging about 50,000 individuals.
>
> *(Piero and Piero, 1993, p. 194)*

This is not a large figure and we can be in no doubt that life was routinely tough and contained many trials. These small groups had to be interlinked – in which way, we do not know. Inbreeding will have been a liability so there were real imperatives for groups to communicate in their own way.

Perhaps in defiance of nature, and as a consequence of our helplessness to it, we have since sought to master and protect ourselves from it. We do this through education, medicine, arms, finance and building walls. But before walls and cities it was an obvious fact that our early species for a long time presented a comparatively meaty and juicy bundle to its predators. As well as predating upon, we have also had to deal with being predated. This has had its implications.

The Argentinian sport psychologist Ricardo Rubinstein (who features later) puts it so:

> Whether it was to seek food or to protect oneself from the threats of the environment, it became necessary not only to be able to run, swim and hunt, but also to fight, climb and fish. For this reason a period of training must have proceeded in order to achieve these goals. The acquisition of such skills benefited a person in the fight for survival and gave them advantages over the less fit. In this context, games would have been associated with competition with other men, and rules would have appeared that were accepted by the group. This constituted a further step in evolution.
>
> *(Rubinstein, 2017, p. 2)*

Meat is an important part of the human story as it was the crucial factor that gave us the rich protein diet that went on to build us a bigger brain. Meat and brains were important commodities then as now. Evidence shows that there was a lot to be afraid of. While hunting was not the whole picture for our ancestors, it must have constituted an important tribal reality. There were very practical reasons for being good at hunting and the topic will have been relevant to everyone in a tribal group, including those who could not participate. Animals of value would not necessarily be 'around the corner', so stamina to travel far and fast for the collective would be invaluable. If a group of hunters travelled from base, those individuals left behind could only wish their hunters the best, and wait for them to return. Some human preoccupations and pressures are very old.

Travelling far was probably one of the earlier forms of 'the knowledge'. Those that had travelled had experience of the world and will have known how to travel more safely. Stanislav Grof (1988), one of the founders of transpersonal psychology, writes about the relationship of early hunters in his book *The Adventure of Self-Discovery*. Grof suggests that the act of hunting itself required a need to identify and embody the prey that was hunted by early humans: 'They were able to tune into them and identify with them so fully that they got to know intimately their instincts and habits. Following this experience, their success in hunting increased considerably, since they were able to switch from the consciousness of the hunted animal and outwit their prey' (p. 55).

The primary responsibility in a tribe for connecting to the animals will have been left with its specialist, the Shaman. When we imagine an archetypal priest in the West today, we might naturally envision a pastoral and gentle kind of person, not a wild figure in a kind of animalistic trance, as may have once been the case. Shamans embodied the spirit of the animal, then transmitted it to the hunters. Generally, we do not connect theological traditions to hunting – but saving souls (or catching them) is a tough business, just like hunting. All animals will demonstrate that if attacked, they would much prefer to stay alive. Some will scream, kick, bite and fight in order to prevent themselves from being eaten – if possible, killing the attacker in the process.

My clinical experience tells me that clients also have negative systems alive within them that avoid change. Clients need courage to tackle these, as well as to fight emotional trauma from abuse. Many never succeed. Courage was required for early hunters, and we can assume that it was rewarded with kudos. Even though early humans cared for each other, medical attention was obviously of the intuitive kind and comparatively rudimentary. However, we might still be surprised at the earlier standards of homeopathic medicine, which will also have been an important knowledge. Our ancestors may have known more about some plants and their potential for healing than we do now. It is an axiomatic truth that injury was to be avoided, but also had to be risked, as hunting was by no means a gentle pastime.

Effective hunters of larger animals worked in teams supporting one another. Being social animals, this was only natural. Just by listening to a modern soccer team we can hear sounds and shouts with a lineage going back to the beginning. We do not know the real status of hunters in pre-history, but it would likely have been similar to today's athletes. Similar to the lions and wolves once roaming the plains, co-operation was a natural and necessary way to maximise efficiency as well as to stay safe. The lion is the only cat that works in teams, and we will explore the deep significance of this later. Today's lions are finished if they pick up a serious injury, but our ancestors were different. Healing is a crucial phenomenon for humans, as is the maternal energy that so often nurture and restore us.

Injury and healing remain a mystery for many modern athletes. We can assert that injury can ruin a career now, as it surely did for the hunters of pre-history. The internal psychic effects of injury tend to get ignored and subsumed into only physical concerns or displaced into suggestions of somatic conditions. It is the archaeological evidence of unearthed bones that prove our protection and care for each other. The discovery of some badly broken bones have shown extensive healing, demonstrating that their owners were protected and cared for. In all elite sports a supreme level of concentration is required, reflecting a crucial demand for, among others, physical safety.

David Rock (2009) uses modern analogies to illustrate points relating to neuroscience. Our ancestors had to find ways to create a mental mindset ready for hunting and maximise their chances of success and minimise their chance of injury. These 'group energies' are perhaps related to our modern propensity to enjoy collective shock, horror, dance, prayer, singing and watching sports. Emotional regulation is a key component of performance, that is, if one cares about being sharp and focused. Rock's research concluded that the balance of the neurotransmitters dopamine and norepinephrine represented a critical relationship of ingredients for maximum brain efficiency. Rock describes dopamine as representing desire and norepinephrine relating directly to our level of fear. For athletes, the balance of these neurotransmitters requires a conscious act of will to procure, particularly in challenging phases of competition.

This is why rigorous commitment and attention must be given towards effective preparation before a performance. Later, we shall explore these balances on a deeper level and how they relate to different kinds of play within us all. Contact sports are dangerous and a lapse in concentration might mean a broken bone or at least a lost opportunity. For the athletes of the ancient past, it may have been catastrophic. Teams will have been forced to find new hunters, or to bring in a young new player.

Hunting was a skill that required dexterity and a combination of physical and mental capacities that could make or break a band of hunters. Mastery over these things was key and such skills will have been nurtured and developed. As Rubinstein suggested, school and education were far from unimportant considerations for a pre-historical community. There were certainly places where their own forms of culture could evolve. Amongst many other examples, the 15–20,000-year-old cave paintings at Lascaux in southern France, and those in Altamira in the south of Spain, are perhaps the most well-known pre-historic art. This was the 'Magdalene' period, a time in history when, according to Leakey in *Origins Reconsidered*, 80% of such paintings were made (1992, p. 322). At this time humans appear to have been portraying and representing themselves and their surroundings in new ways. These paintings certainly show that the ancient human relationship with animals was substantial and significant enough to be worthy of artistic depiction.

Archaeologists suggest that caves most likely had a ritual function, possibly as a place to initiate the young into official adulthood. (My own research has shown that initiation is a significant emotional experience for all young sports people and we shall explore the significance of this in depth later.) Cave paintings also portray shapes and dotted lines in circular vortexes. The dotted lines may be impressions from images witnessed while in an altered state of trance, later represented pictorially by the Shamans for the others in the community.

These cave paintings also depict important figures known as 'therianthropes'. These are half-human, half-beast figures that have been identified in numerous locations. The Shamans, with their mesmeric incantations, helped the hunters 'join the dots' – and perhaps they were, if for a brief time, immersed in the world beyond normal existence.

The ages of animism and scientism

Anthropologists suggest that during early pre-history we lived more psychologically attuned mythological existences, wrapped up in the experience of living intimately immersed within nature. 'Animism' ascribes spiritual life to all material things of nature; even the stones and mountains are alive and have a spirit. Animism may be the antonym of 'scientism', which was initially inspired by Democritus and the belief that everything is separate, rational and only of form – an object. Animism is the mindset that best represents how life was experienced by our ancestors. Dismissed by the rational and the scientific approach to the world, it now seems to be making a comeback. In 2016, German ex-forester Peter Wohlleben released a bestselling book, *The Hidden Life of Trees*, describing how trees 'talk to each other, have sex and look after their young'. This built on research that already established evidence that trees communicate alarm about disease or threats via an Internet of connected microfibres.

Animism can be upsetting to some modern minds. Wohlleben's work irritated scientists in Germany, who formed a petition against his theory because he used words implying feelings and human emotions – many suggested that his work was a 'fairytale and wishful thinking' (Brown, 2007). Humans do not have the mediators that we used to; the language of animism now vies uneasily with its polar opposite, scientism. As described earlier and from what we know now, the communal focal point and representative for that other spirit world was the Shaman. Anthropologists suggest the part-human therianthropes described above may have been themselves depictions of the early Shaman. It was he or she that entered into an altered animal state, seeing visions and visiting spiritual realms. We do not know for sure, but Richard Leakey suggests that 'a more convincing argument is that they represent shamans or hunters dressed in animal skins, sometimes wearing horns or antlers' (1992, p. 334).

The part-animal, part-human beast represents an early archetype that we can see had meaning for many of our earliest ancestors. One of the earliest myths in Greek culture came from the Minoans, at around 4,000 BC, and still survives today. This is the therianthrope story of the Minotaur. The Minoan world will have been naturally mystical and surely at times terrifying. What would our ancestors have made of a rainbow, an eclipse, lightning, a tornado, a shooting star or torrential rain? Naturally, they could only conceivably be made by supernatural forces and deities in motion.

Now we can seek and find rational explanations to explain almost all things – apart from where we come from or where we go after death, that is. Or what happened before the Big Bang. Or why it happened. There is an awful lot we don't know. Our ancestors will not have had the same psychological processes as our current existentialism. Theirs was a life immersed, not as separated beings, distinct from other life and the world around (and at the same time within). Understanding the natural world rationally, as we do now, is a recent phenomenon.

All is not lost – we have still retained a connection. Animals and flowers will have 'spoken to' our ancestors as they still do now. Earthly emanations for our ancestors represented special powers or spirits bestowed by the gods, or the gods themselves in motion. Evidence from caves suggest that the representation of animals through art was not one-dimensional or just about hunting and prey. A new appreciation and visceral connection to nature was being replicated and we have every indication that the experience created 'awe' for the viewer.

Wonder at the world may not seem to be a very scientific experience, but it was evidently worth pursuing for our Palaeolithic ancestors. Citing the well-known anthropologist Claude Levi-Strauss, Richard Leakey recounts how he 'once observed of art among San and Australian Aborigines, that certain animals were depicted frequently not because they were "good to eat" but they were "good to think". The question is about what the thinking was about' (1992, p. 320).

Evidence shows that we have always been drawn towards the animal kingdom. We know the early Egyptians believed that animals such as birds could perform feats such as flight because they were endowed their special skills by the gods. Unknown to them, of course, birds were the eventual lineal descendant of the Dinosaur. Their avian lineage symbolised a principle for Egyptians – that of 'seeing the bigger picture'. This was embodied in form by the bird-headed god Horus. Birds must have originated from the world beyond, or even represented a message or clue how to be.

Disconnection or connection to our own nature is a significant theme when considering our relationships to ourselves and the planet. Deliberate pollution of the natural world as we do today may have seemed abhorrent to our more 'primitive' ancestors. Pollution would have been regarded as an insane, criminal or just plain stupid thing to do. It could only mean the gods of the Earth would take offence and cut such arrogance down to size. Now, the industrial superpowers have arrived at a paradox. We have the greatest powers of mastery over natural forces while at the same time we are increasingly disconnected from them.

We shall later explore a very early African Kalahari myth – that of 'The lion and the hunter'. This myth warns us we should not avoid facing and coming to terms with our inner animal and spirit. This is a powerful universal archetype for us humans. Animals hold an archetypal presence that continues to resonate within the human psyche because perhaps they are an intrinsic part of us and always have been. Jung declared that his inner guide, Philemon, told him that 'thoughts are like animals in the forest' (1961, p. 183). We cannot escape these thoughts; we can only ignore, repress or rationalise them away. But that does not mean they will therefore accede and go away. Today we can readily see the 'animal helper' as a part of religious and film iconography.

Classical Eastern and Indian religions often portray their deities as accompanied by an animal such as a deer. Animal helper stories in contemporary America include Lassie, Flipper, Champion the wonder horse, the real-life warhorse 'Warrior', Ed the horse, Greyfriars Bobby, Tin Tin – and even in computer form in the movie 'Star Wars', incarnated by the 'robot' R2D2. *The Wizard of Oz* is a modern illustration of the classic archetypal story; the hero Dorothy has Toto, the small dog who accompanies and defends her. In 2017, the Disney film 'Moana' had the rooster Hei Hei as its animal helper. In the phenomenal film and book series *Harry Potter*, these animal helpers were represented by the 'Patronus'. Renowned mythological expert and student of Jung Marie-Louise von Franz (1974) had this to say about animal helpers:

> the animal plays this way and that, from an ethical standpoint, but if you go against it you are lost. This would mean that obedience to one's most basic inner being, one's instinctual inner being, is one thing that is more essential than anything else. In all nations and in all fairy tale material I have never found a different statement.
>
> *(p. 146)*

Marie-Louise von Franz is a major figure in Jungian psychology who suggests that we are lost without our inner animal. I am grateful to the analyst and author Donald Kalshed for his work on this subject, for pointing out another related example in the Hollywood film 'The Golden Compass' (2007). Author Phillip Pullman's book *The Amber Spyglass* was the first children's book to claim the auspicious Whitbread Literary Prize – his second book *Northern Lights* became 'The Golden Compass' (2007) starring Nicole Kidman and Daniel Craig. A central feature of the film was that the cast of characters was accompanied by inner animals throughout the film. Some had powerful animals, such as the hero, and some villains merely had insects on their shoulders. Inner animals were referred to by the cast as 'daemons'. In depth psychology these inner animals are also called daemons. The arch-villain of the film is a polar bear, whose inner animal is merely a rag doll he clutches. It is a fine portrayal of an ancient and familiar portrait of the soul, rarely explored because perhaps we as a species also have a propensity to fear and mistrust the animal within.

The German philosopher Arthur Schopenhauer (1788–1860) wrote that 'Compassion for animals is intimately associated with the goodness of character, and it may be confidently asserted that he who is cruel to animals cannot be a good man' (Schopenhauer, 1840). Cruelty or negligence towards nature can still be asserted as of 'bad character' even to the extent of England's Royal Society for the Protection of Animals, founded in 1824. At this time in England, many – even most – urban children worked under conditions of slavery, abuse and the bondage of child labour. The Abolishment of Slavery Act was in 1833. This curious fact alone demonstrates that a profound and instinctual relationship is alive within us that is best embraced, or else, as evidence shows, we can suffer. Much of the good work done in psychotherapy relates to embracing and integrating this vital and living part of us, which defies definition.

In Jungian depth psychology we also refer to this side of ourselves as the 'Shadow'. It was Jung who initially identified these elements, defining a sharper portrayal of these archetypes within us in motion. Here another paradox reveals itself. Experience shows that it is our less rational, more creative, unruly and sometimes wayward behaviours that also help us to develop our psyche more fully. Even the Bible refers to the 'wayward mind', acknowledging in paradox that there is a vital element of the psyche we must hold and grapple with. 'Those who are wayward in spirit will gain understanding; those who complain will accept instruction' (Isaiah 29:24). Some part of the human psyche seems to revel in deviance.

The Shaman was the conductor or connector to the wayward Shadow spirits. But this was not entertainment; there had to be some purpose for this role. One of the most authoritative authors on pre-historical mythology is Karen Armstrong, who, in her 2005 book *A Short History of Myth*, discusses the cultural and anthropological basis of our myths and archetypes. 'The very first myths of ascent date back to the Palaeolithic period, and they were associated with the shaman, the chief religious practitioner of hunting societies. The shaman was a master of trance and ecstasy, whose visions and dreams encapsulated the ethos of the hunt, and gave it a spiritual meaning' (Armstrong, 2005, p. 12). Armstrong suggests the Shaman had a community function and also a direct responsibility for helping hunters prepare, develop and hone their intensity and drive to hunt.

He or she was the specialist, the representative and holder of the animal space they were about the enter. Hunters had to hunt, they did not have the time to focus on other worlds and altered planes. That was the job of the Shaman, who held the role for everyone by embodiment, transmitting a deeper message and state for the others to use. For us that means in sporting environments it is up to the sport psychologist to read the books, discover 'the knowledge' and share it with his or her charges. In order to teach mediation, you have to be a meditator. If you speak about 'heart', you have to live with heart.

Anthony Stevens and John Price, in their book *Evolutionary Psychiatry*, described the Shaman's role in this way:

> Central to the charismatic experience is the ecstatic merger of leader and lead in the form of *participation mystique* which assumes religious intensity. The inspired figure is always one who stands apart, completely focused on his innovation. This sets him on a level above that of ordinary humanity. It means that he speaks with the conviction of being 'higher authority', which puts the followers in awe of him.
>
> *(2001, p. 149)*

Very few people get to be experienced with 'awe'.

Rather than this figure being the sport psychologist, I would argue that in elite soccer this a place and Shamanic space held by the coach or the manager. The coaches and managers are the conductors, charged with mobilising a group or an individual to reach new heights. Part of their job description is the capacity to give an inspirational halftime team talk for positive change. In elite team sports environments, it is they who the athletes should be in awe of. I would suggest that it is the job of a sport psychologist to help athletes be in a psychological condition that can exploit it. Performance for our athletes is also a *participation mystique*, a time when disconnection (from the outer, wider world) and connection (to the inner world) happen at the same time. The Shaman replicated this union and had a role in helping hunters realise and embody this balance when immersed in the hunt.

Women are top cats

Pregnancy, birth, life and death all began to hold increasing meaning for our ancestors as we began to psychologically evolve and also attach meaning and devotion to things that were precious. Natural processes such as the day itself are greater than us and have a rhythm, and we were all once subject to them. To these we can add the interior cycles and patterns that are a part of our bodies, quite unconsciously in motion. As well as natural circadian rhythms, our ancestors will have noticed that females ovulated every month, in rhythm with the moon. As well as being the source of creation this will have enhanced reverence for the feminine and the female, who, research suggests, was a primary figure in early communities.

Our ancestors were aware that the seed goes in the ground and into the darkness. Then, miraculously emerging, it is transformed into a new form of life and into the light, just as the newborn from the mother. It is perhaps not a coincidence that in modern stadiums players come from the depths out into the light. Initiation and birth represent a new beginning and were celebrated by our ancestors, who will have also appreciated that the young represented their future. One of the earliest objects ever found is the 'Venus of Hohle Fels' unearthed in Germany and dated between 35–40 thousand years old. It was discovered by the University of Tubingen in 2016. The 'Venus' series of stone artefacts are the earliest known and all depict often rotund, pregnant females. The choice of name was controversial at the time of discovery, but their gender was not.

In her book *The Goddesses and Gods of Old Europe*, Marina Gimbutas (1997) wrote 'In contrast to the Indo-Europeans, to whom earth was the great mother, the old Europeans created maternal images out of water and a divinity such as the snake and bird goddess. A divinity who nurtures the world with moisture, giving rain, the divine food which metaphorically was also understood as mothers milk, naturally became a nurse or mother' (p. 142). We can see the primacy of women in the earliest images and carvings, which evolved over time and became even more reifying.

Remembering the therianthrope Shaman described earlier, we can see the genesis of new expressions in form and figure emerging in the more familiar deities of the later Egyptian culture. 'When the old European civilisation reached its cultural peak around 5000 BC there emerged the sophisticated image of the bird and snake goddess. She is now either an exquisitely shaped vase wearing a mask or a lady wearing an elaborate dress and mask' (Gimbutas, 1997, p. 136). At this point we should add that no one has any real idea whether the deities and figures were created by women in the first place. But it appears for our predecessors that the Earth was our natural mother and the giver of life, and a symbol of creativity and healing, and it seems she was considered to have the value of being like a bird, seeing the bigger picture.

The journey from the chasm of empty darkness into the light is a familiar archetypal portrayal of the creation. Describing the beginning of everything, the opening passage of the Bible begins 'let there be light' (Genesis 3:3, NIV). Our predecessors were immersed in the realities of new beginnings, middles and endings, with the beginnings represented by birth and the miracle of reproduction they could see in motion. Researchers suggest that the caves of Lascaux and Altamira may have been special locations where humans could recreate the act of birth by leading initiates in, and then, after a ceremony of some kind, out of the cave reborn. Historically, comets were also interpreted as representing a new birth or change. The birth of Jesus was represented by a star appearing in the heavens; we know that stars had already long been regarded as auspicious bodies.

The new knowledge: the star

Over the course of any year, stars were predictable, but the planets, as the Greek *asteres planetei* implies, were 'wanderers' along different courses. Humans began to focus more on them as practical points of reference, enabling travel over longer distances – the seas in particular. We know that migrating animals detect the magnetic waves of the earth in order to get direction, but we cannot; we needed another way, and this was it. A knowledge of the ready-made map of the stars enabled early humans to begin journeying on the seas and oceans with more certainly and safety. There is a good argument to suggest that the regions of the world with clear skies and close islands will have been those most able to benefit from this knowledge, such as the Polynesian and Cycladean islands of Greece.

New capacities for predicting time and orientation were now possible – no small matter at sea. This became the new 'knowledge' and those with it could roam, trade and profit. For many hundreds of years, travel was by the stars alone – until the invention of the seaman's 'Harrison Two' clock in 1740s England by pioneering English clockmaker John Harrison. This was the first time humans no longer depended on the stars to know their location at sea. Knowledge of these subjects was important and we can see a human interest in stars and their relative positions depicted on many of the earliest temples we know of, apart from Gobleki Tepe.

Those with this knowledge will have been regarded as having special powers which later ages would even come to mistrust. In medieval England, the much-feared and demonised Arabs were often portrayed as astronomers with turbans gazing out to the stars. By identifying disparate objects found in burial sites and even rubbish dumps we can see that 10,000 years ago there were wide trade links between the East and West. Communities emerged who were able to profit from the journeying traders hauling and exchanging objects, materials or spices. The relevance of the stars and the importance of this knowledge will have increased exponentially as did man's capacity to exploit this knowledge, resulting in profit, wealth and the consequent need to consolidate power.

The new male gods of the sky

In keeping with the idea of the new reification of the star instead of the animal, we see the new 'astronomical knowledge' represented in one of their earliest images we know: the 'Ghassulian star', a cave painting discovered in Jordan in the 1930s. The familiar animals had been replaced by a large star, surrounded by assorted small symbols.

Evidence indicates that early tribal communities were not war-based. The majority of arms finds relate to hunting, not weaponry. Even early fighting swords buried with the dead show little signs of actual use. It is at this time that we can imagine a possible conflict as the role of the astronomer may well have competed with and subsumed the role of the Shaman as primary authority or influence. The new sun gods and archaeological finds confirm that stars had become important considerations for early peoples. In Europe, four tall ceremonial gold hats, like the one in Figure 1.1, have been discovered, worn by a king or a priest with 'the knowledge'. These hats date back to 1200 BC, all with astral shapes on them. They curiously resemble more recent portrayals in contemporary culture of a wizard's hat.

FIGURE 1.1 Bronze Age gold hat with stars worn by a tribal leader or priest.

Credit: Jaroslav Moravicik/shutterstock.com.

Another ancient archetype we will explore later, known as 'Merlin', wore a hat with the image of stars on it. In the Disney film 'Fantasia' (1940), we see how America's divine child Mickey Mouse puts on the wizard's hat and gets into deep trouble. The historical allegiance to the hunter's moon had become converted into a new fidelity for the sun. For humans it was perhaps a plausible and natural direction to follow. Our ancestors could naturally appreciate that it was the sun that created daylight and gave energy and life to the plants we needed for food. It was the sun that gave warmth and energy. The old moon could now become the realm of the dark, cold and dangerous. But there was a cost.

Once the global population grew in size, economic necessities were inevitably created as a result. Issues such as food quantities could not be ignored as there was a new imperative to organise and feed increasing numbers of people. Dependence on the weather, and tension relating to the quality of the weather in a season, increased. Appeasement of the new sky god became more important. Storage of food became a greater issue, and its protection became imperative. The pressures to feed growing populations created a new urgency for labour on a daily basis.

A surplus of men, women and children was now available to work in agriculture or to defend property, agriculture and livestock. As the agricultural revolution of the eighth century BC progressed, reverence for women seems to have ebbed away. They were replaced by more patriarchal systems where women became more like possessions or property. At this time, large trading communities were forming, based in the tidal plains of the Euphrates, the Ganges, the Yellow River and the Indus River in India.

As human capacities to make and store this new wealth developed, so did another need. This was the need to account for what was being accumulated. Accumulation was a limited option for highly mobile peoples, but the chance to stay meant the chance to collect – and, therefore, an axiomatic need to count things. Counting things is what gave rise to the modern job title 'accountant'. In the book *Sapiens*, Yuval Noah Harari writes that the first ever known recorded name was written on a clay tablet in 3400–3000 BC; it was not a spiritual god or animal, but an accountant called 'Kushim' (2011, p. 139). Writing had become the new 'knowledge', known only by a few, and only for transactional purposes.

The capacity to count enabled human beings to regulate and more concisely approach things, including planning for the future. In turn, this consolidated the creation of a new division of labour determined by agriculture for food. If you grew crops you needed to protect them, and therefore sections of land would have needed to be partitioned and patrolled. A system of measurement was needed and had to evolve. Having more things accumulated meant moving them around. By 5500 BC, the wheel had been invented for hauling and, crucially, new possibilities for trade and weapons of war.

Humans now had to contend with a different kind of society. More of us had to live closely together than ever before, and eventually new rules formed. Formalised laws needed to be maintained so governance was required and 'civilisation' made an important step. This is conventionally regarded as an age of progress and civilisation for humans, and for some it surely was a good deal. Wealth needed not be distributed in the same old way and property meant a sense of entitlement, justified by new laws maintained by owners. This was not animism. Even in recent history we know that some Native Americans were confused by Western ideas of property. For these early agriculturalists, archaeology indicates that their health and strength declined. Anyone who has ever been on a farm knows it can be relentless hard labour all year round.

The emphasis on the softer energy of the hunters' moon was replaced by the less forgiving energy of the sun. The sun grew the crops and was the new source that mattered. More men became rich by being organisers, staying at home, and the role for women declined. The conditions for bondage and slavery had now been established and we can only guess at some of the tyrannies that might have been in store for the miserable recipients. Armies now emerged in the world, battling in new ways for territory, women and property. If perhaps safer for some, life may not have necessarily become happier. There were rules in order to get one's daily bread.

The first ever Brexit

In perhaps a Neolithic equivalent of Brexit, some Northern European cultures in fact appear to have opted out and resisted the move towards collectivised change. In 2015, researchers used bead ornaments as a cultural indicator of attitudes and lifestyle across Neolithic Europe. In a collaboration between France's National Centre for Scientific Research (CNRS) and New York University, their research demonstrated that in Northern Europe this switch to agriculture and counting did not go down well with some hunter-gatherer populations. It appears large groups resisted change towards the agricultural trends. 'If cultural artefacts are an accurate indicator, Northern European populations remained foragers for centuries after the introduction of farming. Their apparent aversion to agrarianism has yet to be fully explained' (Dussault, 2015).

Perhaps it is understandable to naturally view collectivised human life as progress, as superior to hunting and gathering. The fundamentals of colonial thinking perhaps began here. Why would anyone prefer a life travelling through the world in the open rather than the security of living behind a big wall with their possessions? The Shamans might have had established loyal followers, and taking one look at the new town dwellers might have been enough to prevent adherence to this new way of life. Any young professional soccer player in England will tell you that after hard work, battle and struggle, to face defeat and then win is the perfect preface to a good party.

Musical instruments are amongst the oldest artefacts to have ever been found. In Chapter 4, we shall speak more on the primacy of music for humans. It is deeper than one might imagine. After a good hunt there is no reason not to believe that life would have been very enjoyable for those early peoples who could relax with enough to last for days. Eat, drink and be merry you can wake up late tomorrow and make pink jewellery. But now, for increasingly many, there was only the daily grind.

Andrew Cooper has also written on spirituality, sport and our connections to our inner natures. He cites the author Peter Nabokov's visceral observation of American-Indian runners who were capable of astounding feats of endurance and skill.

> Indian runners relied on powers beyond their own abilities to help them run for war, hunting and sport. To dodge, maintain long distances, spurt for shorter ones, to breathe correctly and transcend oneself called for a relationship with strengths and skills which were the property of animals, trails, stars and elements. Without the tutelage, the beneficence of one's potential could never be realized.
>
> *(Cooper, 1998, p. 112)*

Even though the world is changing rapidly there are some messages and meanings that have not changed. These are the archetypes within our nature, and this book is going to explore them. These strands and identities are vital elements of what it is to be human, now as much as it was then. They are the clues for progress in the aspiring athlete. That is, if they can step back and look within. To do this we must look over our shoulder one more time, but with some finer detail. As a later myth will show, we can now trace the soul of humans back to Africa. However, we can only discern the soul of the athlete by first considering the Greeks. They created sports as we know them, and they knew how to play to win.

References

Armstrong, K. (2005). *A Short History of Myth*. Edinburgh: Canongate Books.

Brown, M. (2017). 'Trees Talk to Each Other, Have Sex and Look After Their Young, Says Author', *The Guardian*, 31 May. Online. www.theguardian.com/environment/2017/may/31/trees-talk-have-sex-look-after-young-peter-wohlleben-hay-festival (retrieved 5 July 2018).

Brown, S. (2007). 'Animals at Play'. YouTube. https://m.youtube.com/watch?v=iHj82otCi7U (retrieved 1 December 2017).

Burston, D.H. (2015). *Psychological, Archetypal and Phenomenological Perspectives on Soccer*. London and New York: Routledge.

Cooper, A. (1998). *Playing in the Zone: Exploring the Spiritual Dimensions of Sports*. Boston, MA: Shambhala.

Dussault, J. (2015). 'Did North Europeans Resist the Rise of Agriculture?' *Christian Science Monitor*, 8 April. Online. www.csmonitor.com/Science/2015/0408/Did-Northern-Europeans-resist-the-rise-of-agriculture (retrieved 10 September 2017).

Gadamer, H. (1980). *Dialogue and Dialectic: Eight Hermeneutical Studies on Plato* (P.C. Smith, trans.). New Haven, CT: Yale University Press.

Gimbutas, M. (1996). *The Goddesses and Gods of Old Europe 6500–3500 B.C.* Berkeley, CA: University of California Press.

Grof, S. (1988). *The Adventure of Self-Discovery*. Albany, NY: State University of New York Press.

Harari, Y. (2011). *Sapiens: A Brief History of Humankind*. London: Vintage.

Jung, C.G. (1949). 'Foreword to Adler: Studies in Analytical Psychology', *Collected Works, volume 18: The Symbolic Life: Miscellaneous Writings*. Princeton, NJ: Princeton University Press.

Leakey, R. and Lewin, R. (1992). *Origins Reconsidered*. New York: Doubleday.

Novak, M. (1993). *The Joy of Sports: Endzones, Bases, Baskets, Balls, and the Consecration of the American Spirit* (rev. ed.). Lanham, MD: Madison.

Piero, Angela and Piero, Alberto (1993). *The Extraordinary Story of Human Origins*. New York: Prometheus.

Pinker, S. (2002). *The Blank Slate*. London: Penguin.

Rock, D. (2009). *Your Brain at Work*. New York: HarperCollins.

Rowland, S. (2017). *Remembering Dionysus*. London and New York: Routledge.

Rubinstein, R.A. (2017). *Sports on the Couch*. London: Karnak.

Schopenhauer, A. (1840). *On the Basis of Morality* (E.F.J. Payne, trans., 1903). Oxford and New York: Berghahn Books (1995 edition).

Stevens, A. and Price, J. (2001). *Evolutionary Psychiatry*. Hove: Brunner Routledge.

von Franz, M.L. (1974). *Shadow and Evil in Fairy Tales*. Boston, MA: Shambhala.

Wohlleben, P. (2016). *The Hidden Life of Trees: What They Feel, How They Communicate. Discoveries from a Secret World*. Vancouver: Greystone Books.

2

THE GREEK LEGACY OF SPORT

The Axial Age and the birth of a sporting world

Competition sports as we know them today were created by the Greeks. It is the Greeks who will lead us toward the next chapter and the current business end of sport, and what could happen in the future. If we are looking to our past with a telescope, then this is the last and perhaps most relative place we have to focus on in this beginning. The Greek nation had true genius encoded in its national psyche, which has also to some degree now become our universal human code. It was a nation of competitors, triers and doers with a commitment to enjoy beauty and harmony in order to live the good life.

For the early Greeks, there was always trauma and constant strife to contend with, and as a result it appears they had to evolve the minds capable of solving these problems. Much of the early Greek philosophy that we understand today originated around 800 BC with the writings of two men, Homer and Hesiod. Homer created the *Odyssey*, the story of a hero who had to overcome his inner demons as much as the outside world.

Hesiod coined a philosophy of 'good strife' or 'bad strife', which in many ways symbolised the creed of the Greeks. Good strife was to compete with a neighbour, plough the best field or make better pots than the competitor, to do one's best whatever the task, make it better, faster, nicer, cheaper – sound familiar? At this time, human evolution was at a cusp, what the German philosopher Karl Jaspers (1883–969) first called the 'Axial Age'. From this time would come the great thinkers Gotama Siddhartha (the Buddha), Confucius and a Western genius, Socrates.

Other rival worlds such as Persia and Egypt had vast irrigated areas producing significant quantities of grain and livestock they could now sell and trade. Unlike the Fertile Crescent of the Middle East, the Ganges, the Indus Valley and the Yellow River, the mainland of Greece was a mountainous world surrounded by sea. Greece could not compete with the scale of farming or grain production possible in the agricultural states and in the powerhouses forming around them. Under leaders like Darius and Xerxes, Persian culture was also a force in its own right, with unique expertise in science and astronomy.

But Greece was the location where the Titans had 'thrown down the stones', being just a set of rocky islands with no pastures. On the surface, there wasn't much going for the place. But the Greeks had intelligence and good ideas to compensate. The word 'idea' itself is the same vocal expression now as it was then, meaning a 'form'. The Greeks would get up early, sail boats, travel and trade things. If they didn't have something, the Greeks showed from the earliest times that they would make it. The human genius for the function of imagination had found a new role as a tool for wealth and power. They designed unique pottery, and had one secret weapon bestowed on them by the Goddess Athena, which remains an iconic Greek product today. Homer called olive oil 'liquid gold', and it was in olive oil that the country found its faithful friend.

Greek cultures were the first to develop widespread writing and the use of language as we know it today. It may have been 'Kushim' who was the first

FIGURE 2.1 The original Greek therianthrope, the Minotaur.

Credit: Bagrin Egor.

accountant, but the ordinary people of Greece were the first to use words for creative purposes such as poetry and storytelling. Homer's *Iliad* and the Indian *Vedas* were written in poetic form, as they could perhaps be remembered better that way. In the eighth century BC, the Greek answer to its shortcomings as an agricultural state was Homer and Hesiod, and historical evidence suggests their works became required reading (or listening) for Greek children. Failing that, one could go and listen live in the streets, where many travelling poets recounted stories and poems they had learned by heart. Like actors and sportsmen, the best will have known how to embody the emotions behind the story, using their hearts to convey themselves with passion. Maybe it was all they had, but it was a good start.

The birth of science as we know it

None would truly revolutionise the world of olives or the wider world itself quite like the peoples who lived by the original Meander River in the Greek city of Miletus. By 600 BC the well-established city had wealthy and creative inhabitants who were experiencing their own trauma, a life-threatening natural disaster for the river traders that could extinguish the life of the city. It wasn't the Persians – who invaded later – but the river feeding the city was silting up and receding. Today, the word 'meander' is what remains from the original Meander, which is now as much as six miles away from the original site of Miletus, a desert town, now abandoned. The original and brilliant philosopher scientist Thales (625–545 BC) lived there, as well as the later Anaximander and Anaximenes, who all contributed to the development of science as we know it today.

Later would come the colossal genius of Archimedes, but before him Thales changed everything by describing a compelling argument for rational understanding, as a conscious departure from mythological thinking. But crucially this idea did not interfere with or jeopardise their fidelities to their Gods. This wasn't a threat to the state; it showed more promise as a way to strengthen the state with the new power of *logos*. As the inescapable fate of the people of Miletus unfolded and the Meander receded, Thales convinced locals to focus on the fact that the natural world was shifting and encouraged them to measure and learn more about it.

This was not the guilt-driven response of most other cultures to the occurrence of a bad event. Usually after a negative event, a culture might sacrifice its most valuable assets – often even its children – in order to placate the gods, who must be angry. But here, in true Greek style, this became an opportunity and an invitation to learn the laws of nature and to try and become their master. As if by an act of individuation, the Greeks had become a nation able once again to transform and see itself in a new light.

This was the new paradigm: that there were laws of nature, and not only the whims of the gods in motion. *Logos* held implications for deeper understandings to become possible. In 456 BC, Democritus would realise his theory of 'atoms' as a result of Thales and his deductions. Physical matter could be understood as being in states of aggregation. One element in the river soon became another, and indeed all matter changed eventually. The Greeks were able to reconcile this with their gods and the emergence of the 'hero'.

This idea reflected the notion that individuals could glimpse a sight of the divine, whoever they were. As with all key moments in understanding, this was a breakthrough, where the science of measurement could be understood in its own right, a revolution for humanity. There was a practical side to all of this. Thales went on to invent machines that could more effectively process olive oil, enabling Greek culture to produce a product with a unique level of efficiency, and thus profit. As Egyptian culture began to decline, the Greeks became the future, and Thales was a new star for the world.

The Greeks valued history and held onto their knowledge. They always had an ear for those who went before them, and the most conspicuous mathematicians in Thales' time were the Egyptians. We know that Thales knew about the pyramids, even having studied them. The Greeks appreciated architecture and form, and many of them must have looked at the distant Egyptian feats of construction with awe. Thales was thought to have been inspired and trained by Egyptian priests, who had inherited the astronomical knowledge of their forerunners. They were the original masters of geometry and early mathematics and their knowledge served Thales well. He became the first human to successfully predict a solar eclipse, on 28 May 585 BC, a feat which may in later times have caused his execution by fire – after science had been destroyed or forgotten by the Church of Rome.

By breaking away entirely from mythology, Thales was embracing a perspective and way of looking at the world we now call *logos*. This became the new 'knowledge', and a school of science was later consolidated by Athens, with many great thinkers assembling there. Thanks to *logos*, those Greeks who came after Thales began to appreciate the benefits of science; his theories were later developed by Pythagoras, Archimedes, Plato and Aristotle (and his student Alexander the Great). The Greeks took pride in their intellectual capacities and traditions. It was common for Romans to send their children and leaders to Greece to be educated. The Greeks were evolving. King Philip II (359–336 BC) even referred to himself as the first 'Philosopher King' – and with some justification.

After a period of dissolution, it was Philip II who once again drew together the disparate city-states into one coherent country. Sadly, he met a tragic end. For some unknown reason, he was murdered by his servant. Out of this family trauma, his son took over and came to be known as Alexander the Great (356–323 BC) He also died in mysterious fashion when he was just 33 – possibly poisoned by a rival.

Before his death, Alexander had become one of the most successful war leaders in history, spreading the Greek empire over vast areas and continents. Alexander colonised countries and consolidated his gains by offering something worthy in return, as the Romans later did; under Alexander, there was better trade and security and, more often than not, new colonies accepted his rule. He regularly developed relationships and married local women in kingdoms to solidify personal connections and get them 'in the family'.

Later, the famed Carthaginian leader Hannibal would name Alexander as his inspiration. Alexander was a sophisticated winner, a prodigy modelled by his father, mentored and schooled by Aristotle and taught to fight by the Spartans, perhaps the greatest warriors in history. He was nurtured in the spirit of care that was no longer casual with the lives of Sparta's young progenies, represented by the growing class of *ephebe* – the young person protected and allowed to grow strong.

In his 1998 book *Playing in the Zone*, Jungian analyst and author Andrew Cooper suggests that 'Excellence, *arête*, is not just the aim of the athletes striving; it is also the moral basis of that striving, for in excellence is found freedom. A sport is a structure in which the truth of this is lived out and imprinted on the soul. For this reason, a sport is, like any craft, an object worthy of care' (p. 134).

Alexander was a different kind of leader, a thoughtful man who sought peaceful takeovers in preference to bloodletting. Like a knife through butter, he stretched his kingdom all the way to India and to the foot of the Himalayas, for some there becoming a 'Priya', or beloved one.

In 1200 BC, there had been a serious and potentially terminal collapse. This was a period of global trauma and decline, labelled in Greece as the 'first dark age', and happened for reasons we don't entirely understand today. Scientists are now mostly suspecting climactic rapid change as a chief suspect. Parts of Greece had indeed been invaded by the Dorians, but more importantly this was a global phenomenon. It was perhaps the first global economic crash in history. Historians also refer to this time as the 'Homeric age'. The polytheism of before remained intact, assisted no doubt by the traditions of Homer's storytelling and poetry. This disaster was a time where the ruling elites suffered most, and life had not changed drastically for ordinary merchants and traders. The Greek recovery period after 800 BC is regarded by archaeologists as a kind of 'people's recovery'. Evidence shows that the lives of the original smaller communities and villages had remained intact and carried on.

After the dark ages, new possibilities for ordinary people were emerging and the good times looked like were returning for everyone. Agricultural communities and farming methods were maturing globally and trade was consolidating the growth of the Middle East, China and Egypt. More trade was possible and this was naturally a boon for the Greeks and played into their strengths as traders. Greece, a nation of sailors, was well-suited to exploit this situation; the wine was beginning to flow freely again. While it looked good, there was, however, an elephant in the room.

All the good times, promises and riches ahead were never enough to stop continual violent outbreaks between regions and communities. The word 'draconian', meaning harsh and punitive, was a Greek term that came from the Athenian leader Draco (600–650 BC), who issued a decree that punished even small crimes by death. This approach vied with more liberal and democratic approaches to society in Greece for hundreds of years, inspired by Solon (640–558 BC), who implemented the democratic principle that even normal working people could make decisions for the state.

Yuval Harari points out: 'The problem at the root of such calamities is that humans evolved for millions of years in small bands of a few dozen individuals. The handful of millennia separating the Agricultural Revolution from the appearance of cities, kingdoms and empires was not enough time to allow for an instinct of cooperation to evolve' (2011, p. 30). As we can still see today, like a pendulum Greek city-states swung back and forth between liberality and democracy, at times even getting draconian on crime.

As recovery unfolded in the eighth century BC a normal and perhaps inevitable atmosphere of competitive mistrust between the rival Greek city-states smouldered away. And from their perspective, why not? After all, wasn't it all about Hesiod's good strife? Who would be the richest, have the biggest army, the best thinkers? It was a re-run of the same old story, and some Greeks were conscious that all could be lost again, and this time forever. While Persia was trading and making wheat, all the Greeks could do was fight each other. It was a recipe for disaster at the very time they had just recovered from the last one. Wiser heads might have remembered the myth of Icarus and a need to keep their feet on the ground. The future of the Greek family was at stake and thankfully the parents of the time could see the writing on the wall.

Particularly with the nascent Persians, any senseless conflicts could be regarded as a form of national suicide. But what could they do? This was not a time for a hippy peace movement party on the Elysian Fields. That would have to wait until San Francisco in 1970. The country needed capable warriors and sailors, and a lot of them. Something new had to happen, and that thing was the Olympic Games. Being an opponent was something the Greeks had learned how to do. The games would certainly be worth watching.

Harmonia, the Olympic love child of a shotgun wedding

The first Olympic Games in 776 BC must have been quite an occasion. It is also regarded unofficially as the birthdate of Greece. As with the nascent Italy, what has been called Greece in previous chapters was a collection of different city states, but the Olympic games brought them together. Mount Olympus was already the established home of the Gods and the place of the oracle. Gifts and shrines had already made the area wealthy, which is why it could perhaps afford to hold such an auspicious event. The games were dedicated to the principle deity, the god of the sky and lightning, Zeus. This was no small matter; laws were initiated to protect anyone travelling to the Games, and to rob them was to rob Zeus, which could only mean a sticky fate!

The original Olympic stadium was situated near the town of Elis, where races and games were thought to have already been held for hundreds of years. According to legend, Heracles (who would go on to have a bright future with the Romans as Hercules) created the stadium after he had completed his famed '12 labours'. This is especially relevant, as Heracles is an example of 'apotheosis', which means being part-god, part-human – an earthly human kind of therianthrope more commonly known as a 'demigod'.

It was the Greeks who were the first to have gods with human problems, emotions and responses like ours. No longer necessarily part-animal, the gods were themselves portrayed as human, and consequently also as part of us. The big difference for the gods was they needed not suffer the consequences of their actions. But in this Olympic way, ordinary mortals could also be in touch with the gods, for a brief moment anyway. Fortuitously, citizens could all see sport happen in the stadium there at Olympia, the home of it all.

The mythological union of Aphrodite, symbolising beauty, and Ares, the god of battle and warfare, is a fitting emblem for the ideals of sport. In mythology the marriage of combat and beauty produced an offspring called Harmonia. Harmony is an aesthetic sensibility, a subject that fascinated the Greeks. Aesthetics as a form could be experienced by onlookers who joined with the performer and shared the experience. The struggle that is recreated by competitive sport and performance is a magical property that we can witness and join. Greek athletes wanted to achieve their optimum altered state for sport; a place they called 'arete' is what athletes often today call 'the zone'. The contest was as compelling as a Shaman was to earlier peoples.

By their own account and efforts, a man or woman could achieve public fame, which the Greeks called 'kleos', through their own labour and skill. The gods had smiled upon the athlete, and the athlete's labours would be rewarded with glory. This wasn't totally new for humans; we can imagine our ancestors of prehistory regarding and lionising the most successful hunters. The word 'athlete' is an ancient Greek word that means 'one who competes for a prize'. This was related in turn to the Greek words 'athlos', meaning 'contest', and 'athlon', meaning 'prize'. Later, the Greeks did indeed give prizes, but originally athletes would compete only for the prize of 'the laurels' and the grace of Zeus. Competitors ran races, rode horses and wrestled. They threw the discuss and javelin – all of course related to warfare and combat, just in case.

This was a new idea, but in keeping with the Greek ideal of the 'good strife', that hard work was an end in itself. The philosopher Herodotus was another fascinated by the Olympics. He gives an account regarding the lack of material reward in the prize for the contestant. 'When the Persian military officer Tigranes heard that the prize was not money but a crown (of olive), he could not hold his peace, but cried, "Good heavens, Mardonius, what kind of men are these that you have pitted us against? It is not for money they contend but for glory of achievement!"' (Herodotus, 1920, 8.26.3). This was a new kind of high, and athletes worked hard to get there. Like the cocoa leaf, the laurel leaf was a mild stimulant, and this is related to another kind of 'high'. This was the birth of the true cult hero, but, remembering the Shaman from earlier, replicated a need for leaders we could adore with our projections.

Heracles was eventually raised up and went to live permanently at Mount Olympus. There were image rights of a kind even then, and his were inviolable. Jung (1950/1990) discusses the role of the 'cult hero' in the essay 'Concerning Rebirth', where he describes the sacred Greek ritual, the 'Metamorphosis of

Apuleius', as an illustration. This ritual also has an element of public performance: 'The initiate, an ordinary human being, is elected to be Helios; he is crowned with a crown of palms and clad in the mystic mantle, whereupon the assembled crowd pays homage to him' (Jung, 1950/1990, p. 128). We can thank Baron de Coubertin for initially resurrecting the games for us in 1896 after studying in England. There he learned about the Hellenistic ethics of competition embodied by some public schools as 'Muscular Christianity', a term introduced by the concept's chief advocate and headmaster of Eton, Thomas Arnold.

Certainly, the original ethics of the Greeks were ideal for a consolidated British Empire that needed recruits to run the colonies in a 'fitting way'. After a few failed attempts, the first international Olympics in the current form originated in London in 1908. This was essentially a middle-class endeavour watched by the working class. Working peoples were not involved much in public sport, which was initially the purview of the educational elites of Eton and Rugby. Note that later these Eton soccer teams would face working-class teams created from the factories, and they would lose.

We cannot be simplistic here, as some race and gender issues have remained as barriers to sports. But now is not like 1908, and there is more accessibility to sports endeavour than before, and theoretically anyone in the West can 'make it'. Modern athletes really are 'stars' paid homage by the media and, as is often the case now, the subscribing fans. Certainly, English professional soccer players are often normal men 'raised up', who achieve widespread adoration and fame. This is often the ultimate destination and goal for the elite athlete immersed in their sport: longevity.

Sport is not all about glory and for many it remains a simple healthy form of shared experience. For other sportsmen the issues may be very different. For Kenyan athletes, for example, more likely it reflects a way of life inspired not by fame but by a simple need to feed and clothe their family. But for some athletes it is all about winning alone, and sport psychologists have to help all kinds to get there. It can be a heady business. Echoing all that has been discussed so far, Pindar writes on the original Olympic experience for the athlete:

> Creatures for a day! What is a man?
> What is he not? A dream of a shadow,
> Is our mortal being. But when there comes to men,
> A gleam of splendour given of heaven,
> Then rests on them a light of glory.
> And blessed are their days.
>
> *(Pindar, 1997)*

This new Olympic celebration and form of theatre must have produced an extraordinary emotional release for many Greeks who had at times only ever known pain, strife and conflict. We will share more on the value of losing in this book but it is important to know something about Greece. There was no Olympic silver or bronze medal on offer. Winning was the only thing and everything, and there was a reason. Second-place for the young Greek nation could only mean ultimate destruction and death for the country as a whole. Treading water, so to speak, for them was like drowning; they had to get better and be better. And they *were* the best, for a time.

I'm grateful to Phil Cousineau, who cites the historian Will Durant, who wrote about the power of this event in his book *The Life of Greece*: 'Religion failed to unify Greece, athletics periodically succeeded . . . Under the rubric of athletics we find the real religion of the Greeks—the worship of health, beauty and strength' (Cousineau, 2003, p. 33). For a thousand years, until outlawed by Theodosius in the fourth century AD, these contests would feature in Greek life. Along with the *logos* of Thales and later the ever-questioning Socrates, a new cultural seed was thrown in the ground that would keep on growing to be what sport is today. Now it has reached even greater heights than the Greeks could have imagined.

The Greeks absorbed Egyptian knowledge of mathematics and geometry and made it their own. In a letter to Robert Hooke, the genius English mathematician and physicist Issac Newton wrote 'If I have seen further it is by standing on the shoulders of giants' (Newton, 1675). Early Greek democracy was of a more exclusive membership compared to today. For example, the early Olympics only allowed male contestants from Greek states. Women could not even watch the games. The men competed completely naked. Amidst this new-forming world, a new identity for a person, the athlete, had been created – one we could all identify with and follow if we chose to. As democracy was just a fledgling notion, so too the games had to be nurtured. It is evident that the Greeks wanted it badly enough.

During the sixth century BC, a sports festival and competition existed for women called the Heraean Games, dedicated to the goddess Hera. Some historians have speculated that the games were initiated because Rome's young women could freely compete and attend their athletic games and public contests. For the Greeks that couldn't be right, and the women's games were established. Initially, competitions were foot races but in time chariot races were held, and the winners were able to inscribe their names in the temple of Hera. Records suggest that initially Spartan women were the most successful and later, in a section dedicated to women's sports, we shall explore more specifically why.

The Greeks had discovered a sustainable, new way to make sense of themselves and their world. The human capacity to produce the best throw, make the best move, run the best race in the best time and possess the most needed skill was highly valued, and worth watching – but such a skill was only truly 'divine' if an athlete could deliver it at the right moment. Winning the games for a particular region would have been quite an accomplishment for 'a boy or girl from Thebes', for example. This was something new to aspire towards. The Greek poet and philosopher Pindar (522–443 BC) wrote this regarding the status of athletes at Olympia: 'whosoever, by being victorious with his hands or with the prowess of his feet, gaineth the greatest prizes by courage or by strength. The brazen heaven he cannot climb; but, as for all the bright achievements which we mortals attain, he reacheth the utmost limit of that voyage' (Pindar, 1997, 10.22–29).

The passage to stardom, what is considered by the Greeks a kind of journey, often starting with nothing. It remains an archetypal truth today that the 'hero's journey' has a vital component of Homerian truth, that at one point for the hero, all seems lost. It must have felt so for those trying to bring Greece together. But one way was through Hesiod and Homer. Homer admired sports and was conscious of their importance for the development of character. In his book the *Odyssey*, one of the characters makes a comment that bothers the sensitive hero Odysseus. Euryalus says to him: 'Ah, well, sir, I would not put you down as a fellow who goes in for games' (Homer, 1938, VIII). Feeling upset and a little wounded by this comment, Odysseus becomes inspired and goes on to prove his strength in throwing a discus.

The Olympics provided a channel for young people to direct their energies peacefully whilst still maintaining their acumen. In Chapter 4, on play, we can explore more about how latent kinetic energy is expressed and used at these times. This was a healthy way to keep young men and women 'out of mischief'. Many of the brutal *Conquistadors* that decimated South America were Spanish civil war veterans who were afterwards hanging about on the streets with nothing else to do. With all that energy they were given their blessings to go off and be 'over there', spending all that energy finding gold and creating new lands, no doubt to the relief of the Spanish monarch.

The deal: do the gods, or the gods will do you

The philosopher Epictetus (50–135 AD) was once a slave who naturally understood that good psychology is intrinsically about a kind of interior freedom. Flexibility with perspectives means that insightful reappraisals can happen, which is why there is power in such knowledge. Epictetus could have been a pioneer of cognitive behavioural psychology when he wrote his well-known statement in the *Enchiridon* (trans. Carter), suggesting 'men are not disturbed by things but by the principles and notions which they form concerning things.' It is not what happens to you, but how you react that matters. We know for certain that Epictetus was interested in attending the Olympic Games, as sadly he died watching one. We can see from his advice to the aspiring athlete that times have not changed much.

> You say, 'I want to win at Olympia'. If you do, you will have to obey instructions, eat according to regulations, keep away from desserts, exercise on a fixed schedule at definite hours, in both heat and cold; you must not drink cold water nor can you have a drink of wine whenever you want. You must hand yourself over to your coach exactly as you would to a doctor. Then in the contest itself you must gouge and be gouged, there will be times when you will sprain a wrist, turn your ankle, swallow mouthfuls of sand, and be flogged. And after all that there are times when you lose.
>
> *(Epictetus, 1865, Discourses 15.2–5)*

The disciplines for an athlete as he describes them reflect a simple deal. It is true that progress for the human psyche can often be a bargain with oneself, and the gods, named or not, who hold the space for the unknowns in us. The principle of 'good strife' laid out by Hesiod was an ethos. It's a meaningful ethos, and the same one that inspired the 'American Dream', a belief that the life of a Republic and the life of an individual can flourish by the collective good labours of its citizens. Life, liberty and the pursuit of happiness are ancient goals of inclusivity for a people. The Greeks saw ethics as a form of excellence, and for all Greek intellectuals and philosophers they mattered. Hippocrates (460–370 BC) would, among other things, develop the first ethical code for doctors. We all know this as the Hippocratic Oath: that 'thou shall do no harm'.

Olympic Odyssey author Phil Cousineau (2003) related a discussion he had with cardinal Jungian author and philosopher Joseph Campbell. It is not commonly known that Campbell was a high-level athlete when he was younger. He told Cousineau: 'You have to channel all the energy or they'll burn your cities down. I don't know what I would have done without athletics when I was a young man. It gave me discipline for a lifetime. I still swim forty-four laps a day, meditating on a different tarot card during each lap' (p. 61). Campbell resonates with the inner values of sport, the inherent qualities that can help any individual become an individual. 'Life's tough. Running taught me how to pace myself in everything I've done in my life. It takes real guts to make your way through this world. The discipline you can learn in sports can give you that' (p. 61).

Ethics are different from the law, which dictates what you 'must do'. Ethics are related more to what you 'should' but do not *have* to do, not just hard work, but also the right kind of work, where you put yourself second to the cause that is bigger than you. Psychotherapy is also necessarily an ethical practice and profession with many years of training in the subject. It has a rich potential to help the athlete but remains often ignored as a routine requirement for success. It's a big subject; in ancient Greece, training environments were also places where lectures were publicly delivered. 'Aristocratic and educated men also visited them daily for physical and intellectual exercise. Sports enthusiasts such as Socrates were known to visit the "Academy", and after Plato established his philosophical school there those who studied with him were called Academics' (Cousineau, 2003, p. 80).

'Academy' remains the title for all centres of soccer (and most other team sports) for those who have apprenticeships in the West. I can testify that the academies currently producing the top young soccer players in England can be very much like the old Greek centres of philosophy and personal development. In 2006, Carol Dweck published her book *Mindset*, which related to education and learning in the young. She proved that students with a work ethic can incorporate and interpret failure as an inevitable part of growing and development and will therefore learn more and faster. This contrasted with more egotistical 'talent cultures' which were more egotistical and produced less growth. We will focus more on her important work later. This research proved a kind of general 'Anamnesis' exists and remains a feature of our culture today. We are simply learning a knowledge we already once knew. This kind of thing intrigued Socrates and Plato.

Paradoxically, there can be an urgent requirement for patience! The Greeks lay a special emphasis on developing young people they called 'ephebes'. This was a way of ensuring the strength of the country as well as the quality of its young people. For much of my professional life, for fourteen years, I was an actor. After that career ended I had an experience watching a nervous soccer player and realised a great empathy for that young man. I was a nervous actor myself when I was young and, like the nervous player, I was playing in the professional realm and the big leagues. I realised in that moment that I could help him and others in 'the field'. That began an intuitive understanding I had that soccer and acting were the same principles in motion. Only later did I discover that the Greeks also felt this way, calling all actors and sports people 'agonistes'.

The lost soul of the performer

The path you tread as a public performer is the same for actors and and all sports performers, as the Greeks understood. On 2 February 2014, the Oscar-winning actor Phillip Hoffman was tragically found dead in his home in New York, apparently from a heroin overdose. During his life, he often made connections between acting and sport:

> I don't understand people who are actors who don't love sports. I think it's the same thing. What it takes to be a great athlete is the same thing that it takes to be great actor, I think that kind of concentration, that kind of privacy in public and that kind of unselfconscious kind of experience are very similar, and that kind of pressure of the people watching, and finding privacy.
>
> *(Hoffman, 2014, online)*

In the sports world today, having a background of psychotherapy can be helpful. The capacity to follow the advice of Epictetus and bite the dust, feel pain and then after all that to lose and come back is surely a graphic reflection of life itself in motion. But it is a difficult thing to do. To be defeated in ancient Greece might have been just as painful an experience as it is now. They had their mythological 'underworld', which was for everyone after death. We all went down there; only the heroes like Heracles went 'up'. It was Christianity that sent the bad down *there* and the good up *there*. The very bad in Greece ended up in Tartarus.

Many athletes today have been sadly lost to emotional injury, depression and self-hatred. If your soul has been touched by the power of Zeus, perhaps the rest of your life really may be a disappointment. Many pass on unnoticed and die obscure and in poverty, their past life experiences much like some kind of dream, their current lives a kind of nightmare, often tainted by the epidemic of pain killer abuse aided by negligent physicians. For some, or even many, this is because they have not had ethical mentors around them, as their sporting inspirations might have done.

Epictetus alludes to the coach as a mentor, another Greek word meaning 'mind maker' – before Odysseus left for his mission he left his son Telemachus with the aged Mentor. Life has always been difficult for us humans and perhaps, while it may be more convenient, life is not getting any simpler or easier. Then, as now, life was not straightforward or easy. However, Alexander the Great showed what was possible when you taught people 'the knowledge' and combined physical and mental energies.

Philosophy, inner balance and physical exercise are mutually linked and not exclusive, as the Yogis in India always tell their Western students. In *Olympic Odyssey*, Cousineau suggests a need for more what he calls 'philosopher coaches'. These are men and women who have life experience, and can model emotional and spiritual maturity as well as wiser approaches. This is such an important and ancient relationship that cannot be taught online remotely, but we can expect growing pressures to do use exactly that route. In the next chapter, these modern cultural pressures and conditions will be explored in more detail.

I know that performance worlds tend to foster intimate relationships of emotional trust. Coaches have to help their charges through times of defeat and struggle, more often perhaps than victory. Icarus was told to not go too high, but he was also warned not to get too low. The origin of the word 'sport' comes from the medieval word 'desporten', meaning to be 'carried away'. Like the Goddess Nike, Heracles was able to go and live up in Mount Olympus, redeemed, which predated the rise to heaven of Jesus. It was Nike who gave laurels to the victorious on the battlefield, using her bird wings to fly around anointing the brave and victorious. Now if you look for her online you will only see the sports clothes brand, but nevertheless the goddess Nike is still with us. Her symbol will be the logo on many sports shirts this year, but does it have any remaining meaning for us beyond that?

The ultimate prize of victory was as important to competitors then as it is now. But in being victorious, the Greeks wisely understood that they were not the gods themselves. Perhaps past experiences had informed them this was the case. The likes of the Roman Caesar Caligula would later get that confused with psychopathic narcissism (and suffer for it). But athletes, along with all peoples, need to keep their feet on the ground with humility (in Greek, 'aidos') and also an appreciation of the divine favour (in Greek, 'charis') that they possess such a gift in the first place. This is the Greek spirit forged out of loss and tragedy that was at times irrepressible. The Phoenix coming from the ashes of the ancestor is a central Greek idea. We still say 'ashes to ashes' as we say goodbye to one phase and go onto to another.

Athletes have to 'un-learn' things, and this task of unlearning is the substance of this book. Tragically, for a while at least, the leap back required for us in the West maybe too big a request. The remorseless machinery of commerce and trade is moving into a new age and, as we saw before, this force stands for no woman and no man. Today that can mean unpopular and expensive commodities like time and patience and, more than that, an actual human being to teach things. Computers will not replace the human connection but commerce may yet try.

In 1976, Julian Jaynes, a Princeton University professor, wrote *The Origin of Consciousness and the Breakdown of the Bicameral Mind*. He was interested in the early developments of the human mind and capacities for thought and behaviour. He contended that consciousness as we know it is only 3,000 years old. 'If our research has been correct, it is perfectly possible that there could have existed a race of men who spoke, judged, reasoned, solved problems, indeed do most of the things we do, but were not conscious of it at all' (p. 47). The implicit idea is that Homer's *Odyssey* reflected a turning point for humanity and that humans since then have developed a new sense of self-consciousness, which in turn would influence the systems of society for good or bad.

As described earlier Albert Camus was very interested in the expression of the soul in all its forms, resisting outside imported influences and experiences. He was seeking a more complete, honest form of human expression, which he found in soccer. Camus and the French existentialists all believed that we have been corrupted by our governments and institutions to some degree and we have lost part of our soul. Socrates also was perhaps referring to this in *Apology* with his admiration for the poet. Also, this issue was starkly drawn by Nietzsche, who was primarily concerned with what would fill the spiritual hole in the Western psyche living without a god of any kind, in an isolated form of congregation disconnected and surrounded by urban jungles.

Part-animal, part-computer

Now we live in an age where the animal appears to have gone underground and the materialistic engine of *logos* rules ever more over the planet. It has a language of its own, expressed by what we call 'data'. There is a new media 'Sky God' in the world, one that controls the airways, and it is to this world where we must go next. The new 'knowledge' is data. Along with all the other developments and leaps that humans made and that have been described, here we have another. Through digital Internet technology we can witness the influences beginning to change and determine the nature of sport itself. Depth psychology contends that it is our undefinable, interior elements that make us human, feed our soul and give our lives meaning. Now looking behind us we see a conundrum for humans: how are we to become part-human, part-computer?

Do we see this reflected by the new diagnosis of OCD and ADHD? What effect are computers having on us? It is difficult to say. From what I can see in America and England many people in public seem to have their heads down looking in their smart phones or computers – me too sometimes. Is something happening or not happening? Now in order to solve a domestic issue you are likely to speak to someone at a call centre who responds with a rehearsed script as if part of them is indeed a system, a human computer. The airline I use has a real computer and no person for a large part of the call. Think of the famous British comedy show with the character sitting behind a computer who blankly tells the customer 'computer says no' to every request. Computers are now in many objects and integral elements in our lives, if something goes wrong, we will be on our own.

I'm grateful to the author Robert Romanyshyn, who has informed much of my work. He has explored this disconnection in his book *Technology as Symptom & Dream* (2004). He cites the and novelist and psychiatrist Walker Percy's observation in 1983 that, 'Every advance in our objective understanding of the Cosmos and in its technological control further distances the self from the Cosmos precisely in the degree of the advance – so that in the end self becomes a space-bound ghost which roams the very Cosmos it understands perfectly.' Romanyshyn then goes on to summarise that 'Nevertheless, the self in its retreat from the world is forced to carry the experienced world inside itself either as illusion or as something very subjective' (2004, p. 69).

We cannot always escape into a computer. These are new gods, and man or woman cannot depend on 'data alone'. If you want a meaningful emotional life it is also a business of the heart, which defies systemisation. Psychotherapy remains the healing art and a science that must be shared. This is the world that has the lexicon and language to help in a data-driven age. Both our psychological ways of seeing are made to work together but technology can make life a difficult business for humans with a heart. Socrates famously said 'the unexamined life is not worth living' and a Buddhist monk I know adds, with a joke: 'the unexamined life isn't worth examining'! The challenge for the modern athlete with a soul is an age-old question that only they can ultimately answer. Are they willing to look for their soul? There are now real models available to help us join the dots and I will share some of them with you.

My experience suggests that as well as utilise empirical sciences and statistics, a progressive athlete will do well to look to the past, our ancestors, psychology, the arts and the animal spirits. Author and clinical psychologist Iain McGilchrist, in his aptly titled book *The Servant and his Master* (2012), describes the relationship of left and right brain as this: 'The right hemisphere underwrites breadth and flexibility of attention, whether left hemisphere brings to bear focused attention. This has the related consequence that the right hemisphere sees things as a whole, and in that context, where the left hemisphere sees things abstracted from context, and broken into parts' (p. 27).

Most successful athletes learn to protect their inner animal, make it tough and, like the Greeks, find a way to win. So far, this book has concentrated on the philosophy of the Greeks during the Axial Age and their unique contributions. But this must not imply that the Eastern traditions of the Buddha and Confucius are not vital for us to include. They are also philosophies that can light up the sometimes jaded and systematised Western psyche and create real chemistry and change. They all happened at the same time. This joining together of Eastern and Western philosophy was one of Jung's primary contributions to psychology. Confucius suggested 'wherever you go, go with all your heart.' What that journey of the heart constitutes is the remaining essence of this book.

Vive la France, **plus Coubertin**

As I write the closing part of this section I am still moved by a recent sporting occasion that exemplifies all that has been described above. Traditionally, there have been uneasy tensions between France and England on all levels, probably ever since the English Channel formed and initially separated them. Soon after a terrorist atrocity in Paris where 130 people were murdered, the two national soccer teams were scheduled to play a 'friendly' match at Wembley Stadium in London. French officials and the public alike were surprised by a spontaneous gesture by the English fans. Before the match began, in unison, they sang the French anthem 'La Marseillaise'.

On 13 June 2017, the return match was played at the Stade de France, in Paris. As a gesture of solidarity the French military band played a song by British band Blur. After the routine anthems, spontaneously again the French supporters sang the English anthem 'God save the Queen' and the English fans again sang 'La Marseillaise' in return. Few politicians could have ever prompted in a lifetime what happened that night for the relations of the two countries. Both populations were under strain, struggling with endemic terrorism, and this was their answer, to express their connection through sport. I visited Paris soon after that and was struck by what an amazing world cultural centre it really is, and what marvellous people live there.

This is a timely reminder of what the Greeks discovered in sports – and the awesome power it has to transcend, unite and inspire. While there is a passion behind it, our athletes want to be at the heart of winning, and as long as there are races and sports this will not change. Now is an age the Greeks might have appreciated. Thanks to the new 'Sky God', sports are again on the rise as a form of entertainment and thus an opportunity for connection. The Greeks understood that a crisis can be an opportunity, an invitation for the human spirit to coalesce, producing new harmonies at the most difficult of times. But the Greeks also foresaw the dangers of a rise during the recovery period around 800 BC and had the wisdom to be careful with and look after their young 'ephebes'.

So with a new data Sky God rising alongside the rising tide of sports and global media, what kind of world are our young children and athletes getting into?

References

Cooper, A. (1998). *Playing in the Zone: Exploring the Spiritual Dimensions of Sports.* Boston, MA: Shambhala.

Cousineau, P. (2003). *The Olympic Odyssey: Rekindling the True Spirit of the Great Games.* Wheaton, IL: Quest.

Epictetus (1865). *The Enchiridion* (E. Carter, trans.). Boston, MA: Little, Brown and Company.

Harari, Y. (2011). *Sapiens: A Brief History of Humankind.* London: Vintage.

Herodotus (1920). *Histories* (A.D. Godley, trans.). Cambridge, MA: Harvard University Press.

Hoffman, P.S. (2014). 'On Acting: An "Exhausting" And "Satisfying" Art'. Online. www.npr.org/2014/02/03/270954011/philip-seymour-hoffman-on-acting-an-exhausting-and-satisfying-art (retrieved 8 February 2014).

Jaynes, J. (1976). *The Origin of Consciousness and the Breakdown of the Bicameral Mind*. New York: Houghton-Mifflin.

Jung, C.G. (1990). *The Collected Works of C. G. Jung*, Vol. 17. Princeton, NJ: Princeton University Press (original work published 1951).

McGilchrist, I. (2012). *The Master and his Emissary: The Divided Brain in the Making of the Western World*. New Haven, CT, and London: Yale University Press.

Newton, I. (1675). Letter to Robert Hooke, 15 February.

Pindar (1997). *The Odes and Selected Fragments, Pythian 8* (R. Stoneman, trans.). London: Everyman's Library.

Romanyshyn, R. (2004). *Technology as Symptom and Dream*. Hove: Brunner Routledge.

3
SPORT, HERE AND NOW

The modern global plume of sport

Looking into our past is an essential way to begin to know this soul we seek. Understanding our history has a paradox, in that it can much better inform us about where we are now. In doing so, this book will explore more about life for athletes today, especially the young. In my experience, most of the people working in a sport club are young. The Internet has already shown us that when commerce is involved, new possibilities and potentials emerge all of the time. The latest trend here in Los Angeles is electric scooters; they are everywhere, and used primarily by the young. They are dangerous, but when commerce is involved, future safety laws can be written in blood.

The welfare of children should ideally be different to how it currently is, in that we can learn from experience and help young people, rather than exploit them directly or indirectly. Preparation is an elemental skill for the elite performer. This is commonly understood. 'Fail to prepare, then prepare to fail', goes the old saying. Youth is a time when athletes and performers develop their skills and capacities for interior focus and the demands of a professional-grade performer. This is also true of bigger pictures, like the psychological development of children in general. In good cultures, evidence shows that everyone benefits from healthy practices, not just a few. But what are good cultures?

Having explored some of the historical origins and identities that reside within sport, this chapter will set the scene more on our current situation. We will then examine the current culture and see what is happening today. Experience suggests that Jungian depth approaches can offer useful and even timely ideas for any sports culture. Some of them, indeed, are actively searching for new approaches to old and, up until recently, hidden problems. This chapter will explore some of the modern cultural pressures and tensions that affect us all, and outline some of the solutions on offer using clinical models.

As for the Western world at least, evolution and technology have afforded us comparative safety from nature. But evidence suggests that better insulation and science cannot protect us completely. The question remains: are we safe from our own natures? The Internet is an amazing highway connecting us with limitless communication opportunities related to education, commerce and entertainment. What we cannot see is that it is nevertheless influencing, tracking and researching us, whether we are aware of it or not. Dangers exist; the modern dichotomy of organised sport is that it can represent the promised land of fame and fortune for one and the road to perdition for another. If a teacher or coach turns out to be Dr. Jekyll, experience now shows that, in some clubs, a nasty surprise might be in store.

The development of the Olympics was a significant moment in human evolution as it created new possibilities for humans to express themselves in aggressive ways other than war. Greek sport demonstrated the capacity to transcend cultural differences in a shared celebration of beauty, power and harmony in action. Even then, sport was also adored by the more practical worlds of finance and commerce, who have constellated towards it ever since. Sports markets are now expanding on a global scale and the media corporations of today are paying incredible fortunes for the ownership of clubs, organisations and broadcast rights.

By 1997, the nascent Internet showed enough financial form to suggest it was to be a game changer for everyone. Futures-orientated market investment groups began to circle sports clubs and media channels as commerce awoke to the radical possibilities on offer as the Internet tracks were laid. In 2016, broadcasters paid $11.6 billion to the top four sports alone. That is twice the GDP of Somalia, which in 2016 was $5.71 billion. A dramatic groundswell is rising, and we clinicians might be the ones who should ask: what is the dark side of this mountain?

Depth psychology is the science that takes into account the unconscious within an individual as well as the collective. This financial largesse bestowed upon sport tells us that something important is happening for a lot of people, and the media moguls are assuming that people are willing to pay for it. In order to fully appreciate the psyche of modern athletes, we may be mistaken in separating them from the cultural conditions or history that contextualises us all. For the democratic cultures of the West, economics and trade have been the traditional way of creating wealth and consolidating institutions. Nothing has changed on this front, but, as with

TABLE 3.1 Financial deals in various sports since 1998

League	Billions ($)	Increase since last deal (%)
NFL	4.95	+60
Premier League	2.60	+71
NBA	2.60	+180
NLB	1.5	+100

our young scooter riders, there are dangers. Recent technological advances and innovations are happening so fast that even governments appear unable to respond, regulate or predict their influence.

Commerce is also driving the development of increasingly diverse sources of information, news and entertainment to an ever-expanding audience, including young children. The vision of a globally connected media highway is well under-way and accelerating, but where are we all going? Nobody seems to know, and this 'uber'-changing climate is all set amidst the rapidly shifting sands of global politics and radicalism. Many groups have also begun to utilise the Internet as a way to create influence, ideas, infomercials, theories and 'mindsets' of their own. Just as once with the Oracle of Greece, we all Google our questions away to the gods, but can we ever trust the answers? Today, opinions are facts, and facts are just opinions.

For many in the professional sports world in general, the future looks bright. As a form of entertainment, all organised sports in 2018 are still continuing to benefit from this media explosion and cash windfall. Regional sports such as American football, cricket, rugby and baseball are played in comparatively few countries, yet they can still command huge incomes for viewing rights, advertising and patron-age. American football has the richest league in the world, but not the biggest audience, which is reserved for soccer. The idea that a truly global, huge business was unfolding was confirmed in 2016/2017 when Chinese soccer clubs began to offer gigantic, record-breaking sums of money to lure the best professionals to the nascent Chinese league clubs of Shanghai and Beijing. Nevertheless, today the advent of e-sports may change all of that again. Later, we shall explore more about this new kind of performer.

Most of my experience working in soccer has been in the Premier League, which is a league table competition played in England and Wales, and at this time regarded as the richest and best soccer league in the world. At the end of the sea-son the top team is hailed as the champion and, along with the three clubs below, qualifies for another lucrative competition – the European Champions League. For those clubs in Europe that qualified in the 2016/2017 season, £1.1 billion was distributed as prize money. The bottom three in a Premier League season are relegated and fall into the division below, where they must meet their fate. This spells dramatically reduced revenues that can be a catastrophe for a club, sending it into a spiral that can end in decline and dissolution. Clubs can be just like people and families in that respect.

This is perhaps part of the public appeal and tension of competition that com-pels so many to watch. Players in soccer are now paid huge, ever-increasing sums for their patronage and skills, each with their carefully manicured Internet social media pages and live feeds. The Greeks would have surely appreciated the way players such as Cristiano Ronaldo (a Portuguese player currently contracted to Italian club Juventus) and Lionel Messi (the star player of FC Barcelona, perennial champions in the Spanish domestic league) become iconic pin-ups, legends even to themselves.

Cristiano Ronaldo is a truly magnificent player who, according to his agent Jorge Mendez, recently turned down an offer from China promising him a $105 million salary. The same player recently and notoriously erected a statue of himself in his garden. Along with David Beckham, he is a global star; both embody the Greek principles of masculine strength and beauty. Along with their Hollywood counterparts, they are adored by legions of loyal female fans, perhaps resembling the original followers of Dionysus, the maenads.

Jung suggested that everything with a substance creates a shadow, so in this case there could be a long one. Thanks to the child protection laws born out of the Victorian era in England, there are not many workplaces in the West where children still labour *en masse*, but football is one of them. All of the major clubs across the world have football academies created to develop and nurture the next star of the future, and of course the children work very hard towards that end.

Cultural pioneers, or the road to perdition and abuse

In a speech by President Nelson Mandela at the launch of the Nelson Mandela Children's Fund on 8 May 1995, Mandela declared: 'There can be no keener revelation of a society's soul than the way in which it treats its children.' Sports bodies and organisations are not separate from or above the realities of this wise observation.

Soccer academies in England today have many children in their care and they can be regarded as at the forefront of child protection and welfare standards. In England, children attend from the age of eight, all hoping to become the next Ronaldo or Beckham. They are not the only ones. Many agents and a loose affiliation of private entities may be invested in the fortune a child can create. As the finances build, so can the pressures on the children themselves as they try to repay the dedicated hours a parent must give to help them succeed. In England in 2017, soccer academicians under the age of 16 are required to attend three sessions per week, which for parents can mean a lot of driving, effort and sacrifice in the cold and rain.

But for many parents it still turns out to be a good deal. The elite football in England culture is used to being 'wanted' by the outside world, and in my experience coaches protect and care for their charges in earnest. Nearly all elite academy settings have child protection officers, doctors, physiotherapists, welfare officers, education officers and nutritionists all dedicated to the health of the young. All 'scholars' in an academy over the age of 16 have to maintain their education, continue with their studies and pass examinations. There is evidence to suggest that some elite academy cultures are providing a more well-rounded form of education than the comparatively poorer standard for the rest. In many ways the culture has unwittingly become a model of care for young people, who are more often the unwitting guinea pigs for this modern complex culture in the West. The way state education has responded to these changes appears in some areas to have been like the proverbial rabbit caught in the headlights.

Academy scholars have to stay fit, eat well and are comparatively shielded from the current drug epidemic on any normal campus in the West. Full-time scholars over the age of 16 in the UK are taught cookery, safe driving skills, finance, health and safety, and in my case life skills and performance psychology. My mere inclusion in the team environment demonstrates a commitment to psychology and the soul that is rare and somewhat courageous. Indeed, the psychology in this book has been developed in tandem with and as a result of working with soccer coaches. But the issue for the many ethical coaches in the game today is that ethical mentors are not where they are most needed. It is another paradox that someone like me is employed by the kind of people and cultures that may need my services the least.

The quality of a sports culture experience remains largely the responsibility of the coaches, managers or teachers that runs it. Sometimes the will to win 'at all costs' combined with egotistical, aggressive personalities can create cultures where militaristic ideas or bullying styles become normalised. Even in schools, rather than sources for inspiration, sports teams become cauldrons for the entitled and arrogant, breeding fear, hatred and antagonism. Ethical ideas evaporate and a more primitive culture devolves with values such as force and narcissistic power over real leadership and inspiration. Even if a club hires a sport psychologist in England, culturally it has been a misunderstood or poorly understood occupation. I have heard of numerous occasions that young people with emotional issues or crisis situations are referred to the 'sport psychologist' who has no training or background in counselling or therapy. Britain is ahead of America in many ways regarding youth protection, but this reflects a cultural shortfall – and now a legal liability – that many clubs are ignorant of.

Suffering for children is often the result of neglect, wilful or otherwise, and we now have precedents to warn us of where this can all lead. In educational settings, sports cultures can implode in on themselves, merely reflecting a primitive culture for those that can hit hardest or get the most favour. The killers at the Columbine High School massacre in 1999 called for the 'jocks to stand up first' (Adams and Russako, 1999) before they began their atrocity. Sports cultures are often 'worlds unto themselves', often hiring from within, often ignoring or suspicious of outside agencies. Like in any family these are relationships requiring trust and consistency and sensitive authority.

Without ethical, conscious leadership sports teams anywhere can become cultural dead zones where malevolent dangers lurk, predating on the young. Rather than 'living the dream', children can become trapped in a kind of nightmare. From 1994 until 2009, American football assistant coach Joe Sandusky sexually abused children attending Penn State University under his care as scholars. His position of power demonstrated how easily he could create arrangements where he could hold children hostage to his sexual desires, able to operate with impunity and secrecy, hiding under the cloak of 'team business'. It is a cultural reality for performers that wherever there are dreams to be made, there is a price to pay and for some children it can be with their lives. The organising bodies of sport in America must have hoped that this was a freakish occurrence, impossible to be repeated.

In November 2016, news broke of another bewildering sexual abuse case on a scale that defied understanding. Evidence began to accumulate relating to a highly successful professional soccer coach in England, Barry Bennell, who had sexually abused boys as young as nine in his care. For the first time his victims began to share publicly how his powerful influence over their football careers between the 1980s and 1994 had put them in an impossible trap. Britain was then still recovering from the shocking news that a national hero, fundraiser and wacky disk jockey Jimmy Savile, was a serial child abuser over six decades. He was a nationally famous figure and one of the nation's 'favourite sons'. He had an OBE from the Queen, and used his power and notoriety as a way of protecting himself from his comparatively less-connected and influential victims, who he would sue if they complained.

These victims found themselves in a modern celebrity trap of vice made good by expensive lawyers and calculated cunning sociopathy. Children were also caught in a self-perpetuating inner cycle of shame and silence. Like Sandusky and Savile, Bennell was a sociopathic gatekeeper predating on the dreams of children, like the mythical monsters many of them may have read about when they were young. Now that the truth is out, healing seems possible – yet the bad news continues. In January 2018, abuse was discovered relating to hundreds of cases over many years by 'sports doctor' Larry Nasser. Some of his crimes even took place while parents were present.

The longevity and widespread extent of these violations against children has indicated the dangerous culture trap that children can fall prey to. In England, as time passed, more and more information was collected by Operation Hydrant, a body set up by the police around 2015 to investigate these issues of 'historic' child abuse, ultimately revealing a beast with many heads. On 18 January 2017, the NPCC (National Police Chiefs Council) said the number of affected football clubs had grown to 248, up 100 since its December 2016 update. It said Operation Hydrant had received 1,016 referrals from the NSPCC (National Society for the Prevention of Cruelty to Children) and from police forces (up from 819), and had identified 184 suspects and 526 potential victims, of whom 97% were male, with ages ranging from four to 20 when the alleged abuse took place. As well as soccer, victims were identified in 22 other sports, including rugby, gymnastics, tennis, swimming and golf (Topping, 2017). It appears from the latest evidence that this issue relates to the dynamics of the inner relationships that are a part of sports and youth development. We as depth clinicians have the language and understandings to assist the sports world as it develops into a brighter, more open example of education and modelling in the modern era.

These are perhaps ancient issues for an old culture set in the modern world. For sport in the West at least that means they now must face these issues head on. Thankfully, we are now in a different climate, where the victims of abuse feel empowered enough to speak out. There is a momentum here that represents the bright side emerging out of the abuses of recent times. Thanks to the original players who were brave enough to speak out in December 2016, a new organisation was formed called the Offside Trust, providing a full-time resource for victims to share their experiences and receive support. For victims, sharing publicly in the way they did was indeed an act of heroism. These heroic individuals within sports culture are currently making a difference in the UK and USA. After recent sentencing it was revealed how Barry Bennell called himself 'the Pied Piper'. Later we shall investigate that myth and identify the real meaning of his self-imposed title.

Reconnecting with the soul of sport

To become a practising psychotherapist in Los Angeles is a long road that normally takes a minimum of five years. Many never get to be licensed. Humans are complex beings and the long path for a psychotherapist reflects the many demands on someone in order to practise at a consistent level. There is a masters degree, followed by a probationary supervised 3000 hours, plus multiple very challenging board examinations, in addition to studies in law and ethics. The profession is mostly poorly paid with sometimes dangerous patients and clients. One has to want to do this.

There are many rewards and it is a good life, but as with all careers there can be times of struggle. Vocations are difficult paths, 'callings' (taken from the Latin *vocare*). For a therapist, ethics is a crucial area of practice, and is a part of continuing education in the USA, a mandatory area of ongoing study. While this cannot ensure ethical conduct, it does demonstrate how the capacity not to exploit a situation can be taught, and for some this kind of learning is crucially needed.

The international governing bodies of football, such as FIFA (governing the world game) and UEFA (the European game) could do well in educating their staff about their own stated values of ethics. Too often, these have been catchphrases or lip service to virtuous principles. Some messages have become demeaned as if they were advertising slogans. In September 2010, Sepp Blatter, President of FIFA, pioneered the Respect campaign, endorsing important and inclusive principles by naming and promoting them. It was a great idea and a sincere initiative on his part. Soccer talked a big game, but behind the scenes the sport organisations who originated these principles couldn't deliver.

Every Saturday, football players in the Premier League walk out live on TV, watched by many millions, holding the hands of child mascots. Children are ubiquitous in sport and the symbolism the Premier League attaches to them is significant. The works of Jungian analyst Donald Kalshed will be explored later – he describes, reflecting Jung, the importance of that universal figure, the 'divine child'. This figure of innocence has always symbolised the inviolable principles of the spirit of the game. On 24 February 2016, a FIFA appeals committee upheld the dismissal of Sepp Blatter on charges related to financial mismanagement, along with many other senior officials and managers. Finances scheduled for the game in third-world countries and for younger age groups were some of the accounts apparently targeted by fraud.

The fortunes of corporations and governments might change, but what of the customers of sport? These are the people who ultimately pay for and fuel its existence and growth. In 2017, it appears that those enjoying sports together are still creating a booming market, and that people are having a lot of fun. Fun means business, and today live television and media events have helped create a social phenomenon that until recent times could have not been feasible. It has been fun for business people.

On both sides of the Atlantic it is now common for mixed-gender, all-age groups to gather together to watch particular matches according to their team. High street bars in America have discovered a new set of multi-coloured customers bedecked in their regalia and colours. It is an act of dedication. Like monks, they sometimes arrive at 4:30am to watch their soccer teams play live from England and Wales. Later in the day restaurants have discovered that the American Football crowd can follow, and then, no doubt, the supporters of the Ice Hockey leagues. It can be big trade, and restaurants and vendors can all profit by attracting customers to watch live events.

This is part of the reason that big financial commitments are being made for the future of this kind of entertainment. Big emotional affiliations also exist, making these events compelling for many. Inclusion or exclusion in a competition like the World Cup has very real implications for the economy. The US men's soccer team did not qualify for the 2018 World Cup Finals, which was lamented by many, including sellers of beer, food and entertainment. International soccer matches now connect nations together in a unique alchemical experience, sharing together thrills and spills as the game unfolds on the big screen.

This is a connection between peoples from all backgrounds and families that is quite distinct and numinous, for it is a joining to a body of people where the process is greater than the individual. As if all one big body in itself, a shared experience unfolds as countless millions of people suspend their lives and enter into the emotional experience of watching sports together. In the theatre we suspend our disbelief and forget that the set is nicely painted wood, and that the actor is not really Cleopatra. In sport, spectators suspend themselves for a time in a more anxious or ecstatic way even than in the theatre.

This has always been big business. Early Shakespearean theatres may well have had atmospheres like contemporary sports games. This is a numinous experience according to the Jungian lens, in that everyone gives themselves over for a time to something that is bigger than they are, in this case represented by the trials on show of their idols and heroes, their team and allegiance. They also perhaps give themselves over to some deeper tradition of expression, the fidelity to a team as a family. Sports is a big family, and many are watching.

Currently, sports coaches in England and America at all levels are using ideas and perspectives from clinical psychology. As mentioned before, academies have very young children attending, so good coaching staff are looking into developmental ideas and intelligence to help them get it right. One way of contributing to sports cultures is to educate the coaching staff, who commit to psychosocial 'age-appropriate learning' models. This is where the overall coaching style reflects the particular age and stage of transition a child reaches. When we consider our subjects carefully, new insights can emerge that can be for the benefit of everyone and in keeping with best practice, a modern term for an ethical approach.

Psychosocial stages and thoughtful cultures in sport

In my experience, the work of Swedish analyst and developmental psychologist Erik Erikson on child development (1952) is the most useful and well-respected psychological model – for soccer coaching at least. It is very helpful for us to have this model as it spans the age changes that occur for a child attending academy settings between the ages of eight and 25. I have been fortunate to have spent many years working with young children in sports (aged nine and up) and what follows are some useful models that I think can provide a useful road map for the coach or practitioner. Any athlete should also be aware of these models, as there are implications for them also.

Psychosocial stages are not just some clever idea thought up by a psychologist. These stages represent the physical biological human reality that comes along with growing older in society. When we are ten years old, our bodies, our minds and our life conditions will be substantially different from the next ten years. We do not need to recognise these stages, and many cultures do not. But, for developers and coaches in sport, it would be missing a trick to not do so.

Erikson referred to each stage as a 'crisis'. By this, he meant that each stage needs to be navigated and overcome. Like for any competitor, success means one thing, failure means another. These models indeed have implications as to the way we train our young people and the issues they may encounter. The eight stages Erikson created are listed in Table 3.2.

Working in this way reflects more consciously the changing needs of the child's psyche as they mature and grow into the world. As young children develop psychologically and therefore 'psychosocially' they have to inevitably face the difficult ordeal of becoming young men and women with all the complexities and new challenges that entails. That means your identity, where you are in the world.

TABLE 3.2 Erikson's psychosocial stages

Age	Issue to navigate
1 yr–18 months	Trust v mistrust
18 months–3yrs	Autonomy v shame/doubt
3–5 yrs	Initiative v guilt
5–13 yrs	Industry v inferiority
13–21 yrs	Identity v role confusion
21–39 yrs	Intimacy v isolation
40–65 yrs	Generativity v stagnation
65+ yrs	Ego identity v despair

Who am I in the eyes of others? Am I rich or poor? Am I in or out? Am I good or bad? These are all questions, issues and impressions that young people must encounter. This next section is about helping us adults be more attuned to these realities and therefore better able to deal with them.

We will now go through each of the relevant stages with implications for sports; please do not be too rigid in terms of ages, they can be flexible. In today's climate young people appear to be growing up faster – but do not lose confidence in the model's basic parameters. Children are still at school, for example, and are not like adults for that reason alone, so we can still stick to these principles. Also, all of the issues that are in contention are revisited throughout a lifetime.

Industry v inferiority (5–13 yrs)

If we think about developmental priorities in sports, this stage indicates that the primary virtue here is skills development. This does not mean that things like working in a team are not important; this is a question of emphasis. Children at this age need to learn skills, learn how to use tools in the world. In the case of soccer this means ball skills and technique. Children are beginning to look at themselves in relationship to others. This is often the basis of their comparison – can they do it or not? Issues like 'winning' are less important at this stage, however unpopular that might be with coaches. 'Win win win' cultures with young children are more to do with the egos of adults than the ego of the child. At the same time, 'losing' cultures can become demoralising for any group at any age, so there must be a way to win something. It is said that children who begin fishing but do not catch anything tend not to come back to try again.

The relationships between coaches and parents are crucial at this stage. At an early stage wise coaches see the parent as the primary relationship. Consequently, that means communication. Coaches should be in touch with parents at this stage as much as possible. As a child grows, this relationship changes. Ultimately, that means that Premier League managers do not generally need to be speaking to the parents after a game or a bad week of training – even though they might sometimes want to! Skills also have a psychological dimension and they can be developed with disciplines relating to behaviour and effort and ideas related to not giving up. We will explore more ways of working with children in Chapter 7.

Identity v role confusion (13–21 yrs)

As a child or young person matures into the world and approaches adulthood, new priorities take precedence over those of earlier times. One of them is 'who am I, in relation to you?' This can be a difficult time for a child, who may vacillate between highs and lows in five minutes. Puberty is now beginning to kick in, so the mysterious world of romantic love appears and all the complications that means. This can also be frustrating for a coach, who wants a child to be focused but has to be patient as it is often evident that they are not. The child is just being a child.

At this stage in my experience, small things can be big things for the first time. That means good coaches notice smaller details and engage a young person on their level. Gifted coaches have 'relatedness', which means a natural talent for connection to people of all ages. Disingenuous behaviours, it should be remembered, can be sensed by most children at most ages. Coaches have to model how to be 'genuine'. This is a time of great plasticity and flexibility. Recently, a rich seam of studies from the Netherlands has been very useful; Toering (2011) discovered that children who had a capacity for self-reflection had better chances of success. This is a learned behaviour practised by mentors and parents. Unless help is given here, young people's reflection is merely anxiety and obsessive worry. Or, in Erikson's terms, confusion.

Intimacy v isolation (21–39 yrs)

Now young people look and sound like adults – although, until they are 25 years old, evidence suggests humans are still growing and developing. These are the stages where certain ideals should be in place. If things have gone right, you have a young person who is more likely to be industrious and have an identity emerging. If these things are not in place then a young person may have a sense of inferiority and be confused. We might not think that a young person would get far perhaps in athletics, but they do. Young people often have inner strategies for coping with life but unfortunately these can become redundant and are deserted when life goes through another stage transition. This also happens with adults in their fifties, for example. We may never fully escape the challenges these stages represent.

Earlier, I mentioned the primacy of the parental relationship for young athletes. As children grow older, the important people in their lives change and significant people in society begin to predominate. Many parents don't like it much as an experience, but we all know that a young person or clinical patient has to one day fly the nest and make it on their own. For that transition they need mentors, an idea this book will never stray far from.

If trusting relationships cannot be developed for whatever reason, then most young people will suffer. Some young prodigies may be able to make it on their own, but I have not met any. Even genius prodigies need their mentors when young. Coaches cannot get around the fact that much of a child's early home relationships establish the pattern for what lies ahead. The best coaches are able to be flexible and approach each individual as a separate person.

Erikson's stages challenge us as mentors to assist young people in natural life processes: developing skills, gaining an identity and developing a capacity to realise relationships that can be intimate. Imaginative people developers are always conscious of these issues and tasks. If we mentors fail young people by abusing or neglecting them, we are more likely to see them dogged by inferiority, confusion and isolation. This might all seem irrelevant for what happens on the field of play, but my research suggests that this is the realm of the 'extra 2%' (at least) that coaches often communicate to their players.

One of the best books on Erikson is *Erikson on Development in Adulthood* by Carol Hoare (2002). It issues a timely reminder about the dangers of cultures like soccer and what can happen; 'He saw that identity, its evolving adult forms, cannot coexist with cynicism, isolation, and rejection' (Hoare, 2002, p. 113). Sports cultures can be in danger of being enemies unto themselves. In the next section we shall cover the climates that best encourage play – such an important word in sports. We can be sure that some sports coaches, however unconsciously, do the very things that stop play from happening. Hoare goes onto say: 'In keeping such defensive needs and mechanisms intact, Erickson saw adults to project their own fears and negative identities. In this way adults dominate youth and "colonialise" both their own vitality and children around them in an ongoing way. Originality, creativity, genuine play, wonder, abandon, and leeway are variously restrained' (2002, p. 114).

There is a real need for evolved, mature mentors and coaches to help young children navigate this world. This would also be in keeping with Phil Cousineau's call for modern 'philosopher coaches'. In *Olympic Odyssey* (Cousineau, 2003) he calls for more men and women who coach to have a sense of the interior and be able to reflect deeper human qualities. Much of my own work is with soccer coaches. They are the ones that naturally spend the most time with a player and have one of the primary relationships. My research indicates that young people inhabit a 'supra family' condition (Burston, 2015), where all kinds of different relationships are happening as children begin to become adults in the world.

But especially at early ages all mentors worthy of the title should be ethically capable of the 'unconditional approval for the client' present in psychotherapy and professional counselling. It is a reflection of a broader principle encoded within the Hippocratic Oath that we do no harm at all times. Jungian approaches take the myth and spirit seriously, as did our ancestors. They also had to face similar pressures, but then more for survival reasons and not entertainment. In my experience the spirit of self-sacrifice and nobility is alive and well in the organised soccer world. Our ancestors lived in more basic times but they too surely needed messages from those they could trust to help them. Now we have the experience of science to help, although it can surely only go so far. But then again, what if it is the wrong message from the wrong person in the wrong way?

David Rock is a consultant and business mentor who has written an excellent book called *Your Brain at Work* (2009); I am indebted to his great knowledge and insights. The following model has been very useful as a reference point when working with young children and adults. David Rock calls this the SCARF model, which relates to the climate that determines the efficiency of a learning environment.

For too long, little or no attention has been paid to this issue, but you will find that most of the best teachers are intuitively in accord with these principles.

S: status

For young people, status can be very important. teaching situations are often in the collective and as such there can be a large degree of self-consciousness in the room. Remembering Erikson's stages, young people are wired to worry about what others are thinking of them; it is an obsession for some. Therefore, you will understand that using young people as 'learning tool' can be very painful, humiliating and unhelpful for a child. Most people know the old adage that you remember how you felt in a bad situation even when you forget the specific details about it. This puts a coach's relationship with a student in jeopardy. In my earlier years, when I worked in lots of different clubs, young people would share with me times they had been wounded. I could see how initial shame and embarrassment then turns to disdain and disregard and a feeling of being let down. Unwittingly, coaches can create players who will one day happily see them fail; this is unhealthy for any team.

C: certainty

Certainty is being clear about the intention of your message, and making sure that you are fully being understood. When I address young people directly in classroom situations or on the field, sometimes I can see by the anxiety in their faces they think something is wrong or they have done something bad. When I was a child I grew up watching Monty Python, and sometimes I lapse and replicate one of their characters. One is the Colonel, who stops everything by saying 'too silly, too silly, stop that, stop that – knock some sense into them Sergeant Major!' in his clipped Eton accent. I think it's a hilarious moment, brilliant timing, the lot. But I have noticed that half the room is wondering what on earth is going on. It is not good teaching; it is a kind of narcissistic excess. Clarity at certain times is the way to truly honour the message you are sharing.

A: autonomy

Autonomy is a central goal of all education. It means that in developmental terms an individual will be able to think quickly in difficult situations, and be able to make a decision. This sounds easy, but actually is rather difficult, especially when the stakes are high. Unless parents want their children to be dependent on them all their lives they must establish autonomy in a young person. This is difficult for some. In practical coaching terms, this can be fostered by discussing a theme and asking a young athlete: should you have gone right or left? When the young person says 'left?' the coach can enthusiastically reply 'yes, you got it'. This means that young people can own their own learning process, and not simply be like a performing seal that responds to cues.

R: relatedness

Earlier, I mentioned my television habits when I was a child. I was just young enough to remember when television programmes for children were delivered very differently to now. Usually, a rather headmasterly, archetypical paternal BBC voice would introduce programmes and tell you to sit down; sometimes a younger presenter would speak directly to you as if you were an adult. These tones were very obviously different to me. News programmes for children had the quality of relatedness, a very subtle and nuanced quality. In therapeutic encounters, I am not casual, but at the same time I try not to recreate a person or figure of authority, as if I am the expert. Connections to people in education need to be caring and connected. If you seek to connect to a culture, then begin to care about it and watch the magic happen.

F: fairness

It is an interesting point of course to consider that when you are the leader, coach or teacher working with a group of athletes, there are sometimes 20 pairs of eyes upon you. Therefore, what happens to one person is seen by all of the others. If a coach or teacher is unfair, it can have a debilitating effect on others in the group. Effective teachers are always aware of the reality that they are always being observed. A capacity to sense the mood of a group, and by doing so not derail your own focus, is a kind of mastery in itself. It is a form of group consciousness and capacity that actors share with comedians, musicians and any contestant of whatever kind. As with status, if you see something happening to a friend, you won't want it to happen to you.

David Rock makes another significant contribution for our cause here by pointing out a fact related to the relationships of chemicals, or in our case neurotransmitters. As this book continues we shall be returning to this simple and elegant piece of science, of interest to any performer. Rock cites the work of Yale neuroscientist Amy Arnsten (Rock, 2009, p. 65) who researched important information regarding a critical relationship between two neurotransmitters, dopamine and norepinephrine. Dopamine provides the rush associated with desire, forward motion, motivation and getting your fix. Norepenipherne drives feelings of fear, anxiety, tension and running away.

If Picasso wasn't 'feeling it' one day at the canvas he could have perhaps gone off and had a cup of tea and a think about it. Athletes in competition do not have this luxury. These two neurotransmitters must be in a balance or there is a cost, and the elite athlete find must find ways to mobilise them at will.

We cannot measure these levels in an individual easily, But the point is that neuroscience and clinical science can make a crucial contribution to ideas that can help our young athletes organise their thoughts around those two lines. This is why the sport psychologist Mihaly Csikszentmihalyi (1990) identified that certain amounts of stress are important for athletes. Here we can see neuroscience endorsing something we already know, but this also describes our need to be able to access dopamine not when the situation demands it, but when we demand it. We shall meet these two chemicals later as we deepen our investigation into the psychology of performance.

Futures markets in sport

The sport of football remains a 'natural game' in that no smartphones or computers are allowed. Even if they were, they would not help. As I write this, I can see from my window a father in a park showing his two sons a neat soccer trick with a flick of the foot, as my father did for me when he was alive. The world is very different today, but some things remain the same – sport being one of them. Something runs deep within our collective psyche that is a real treasure for some in a world so bleak for so many.

On the streets, in corporation boardrooms and in the halls of government power we can also see it matters, but for different reasons. With the financial stakes outlined earlier, it is perhaps easy to foresee great soccer factories and ware-houses of the young, like battery hens repeatedly drilling skills. If this happens in the West, we clinicians will only have ourselves to blame. The conclusions of Carol Dweck in *Mindset: The New Psychology of Success* (2006) clearly show how children suffer or thrive depending on the cultural mindset they inherit. My attention was drawn to her work after a Premier League soccer coach in England visited her at Stanford to learn more. I have never read any convincing explana-tion of why these results have not been incorporated by all competitive cultures.

This chapter may have indicated at least some of the material reasons why. Sports environments can create cultures where everyone can win or lose. A Shadow kind of reality rarely discussed in organisational cultures is that of 'epistemological violence'. This is a condition in societies and cultures of all kinds and, put simply, is a space where the unconscious is not considered and 'feelings' ultimately do not matter. For example, this can be seen in prisons where offenders are more likely to commit crimes after the experience of being incarcerated.

Governments, corporations, teams and families will all continue to make their own choices and perhaps no one can entirely ever eliminate abuse. But evidence shows that we can stop it in its tracks with conscious safeguards, staff and good models for psychological care. The idea of epistemological violence may be an obtuse or difficult idea for some to grasp, but the time has come for the abuses described in this chapter to stop. Just like individuals of the past, corporations have vast legal budgets that can make cultural progress impossible.

By involving ourselves as clinicians we can share the healthy ideas we know from the Jungian world that can help young people organise their thoughts and culture themselves to maintain a healthier identity. Abuse relies on the opposite, the minimisation of the mind and soul as relevant or a priority. Another classi-cal feature also predominates, that of secrecy. Recent discoveries of abuse have unearthed survivors who in turn have become our own heroes. They stepped out of the shadows into the spotlight unashamed and we have to be proud and stand with them.

Recent evidence is showing that the sporting culture, in Britain at least, is under strain. On 6 October 2017, *The Guardian* newspaper released an article by David Conn relating to welfare issues for young people involved in particular in English soccer. The article reported how Premier League club Huddersfield Town FC had scrapped its academy for the 8–16-year-old age groups. They found that since 1999 no one had graduated into professional football and the operation had become an unnecessary expense for the club. The article went on to relay concerns over the emotional pressures on young people involved in academies who all had dreams to become professional. The article cites the concerns of Gordon Taylor, the chairman of the Professional Footballers Association, the oldest such organisation in the world. He says 'that of the boys to make it into the league scholarship program at 16, past P.F.A. researchers found that 5 out of 6 are not playing professional football at 21.'

The article goes on to cite the work of Chris Green, who in 2009 wrote a book called *Every Boy's Dream*, exploring the institutionalised disappointment that many boys taken into academies from a young age must face. His book calls for a greater knowledge and commitment on the emotional and psychological impact of the youth development system in England. This feels to me like a call to the clinical psychology community to step in and share its voice. In all likelihood, that won't happen. Huddersfield demonstrated, like any other business would, that they it does not provide a social service. If only it did. The tragedy is that such an opportunity for connecting to young people is now lost.

The David Conn article also includes a reference to Michael Calvin's *No Hunger in Paradise* (2017), which is an alarming critique of the academy system. My work shows that the answers are out there for many of these problems and issues. A proactive commitment to psychosocially conscious contributions for groups and individuals is possible. Depth psychological approaches include room for the consideration of emotions, psychosocial development and learning about the soul.

As stated previously, no doubt this chapter along with all of the others could be a book in its own right. The issues are huge and this is merely a glance at the surface at some kind of bigger picture. But, like any stage set, it is what we see before us. Behind the scenes there are many other forms of abuse, including physical bullying or verbal abuse by peers or coaches. The spirit of professional cultures can be tough. Learning difficult things may always be tough. The more support and education we can give the sports world over these issues, the better.

If there are children at school who just play the game for fun, or dream one day they are going to be a star, they must be free to do so. Later, if a child is talented and lucky enough to be considered or wants to try to get in a team, they will ecounter 'the deal'. They have to give themselves over to something greater than they are, the game they play. And there is another essential word that actors and sports peoples have in common, which will define the next chapter. It's a crucial skill for an athlete, actor or child, and an activity that predates humans by billions of years. It is the very primal substance of sport and drama, a humanistic force that we cannot escape.

Hamlet says 'The play's the thing, wherein I'll catch the conscience of the king' (Hamlet, Act 2, Scene 2), and it is to the spirt and soul of the play that this book next turns.

References

Adams, L. and Russako, D. (1999). 'Dissecting Columbine's Cult of the Athlete', *The Washington Post*, 12 June. Online. www.washingtonpost.com.wpsrv/national/daily/june99/columbine12.htm/ (retrieved 29 January 2010).

Albert Camus Society, UK (2012). 'Camus on Football'. Online. www.camus-society.com/camus-football.html (retrieved 14 November 2011).

Burston, D.H. (2015). *Psychological, Archetypal and Phenomenological Perspectives on Soccer*. London and New York: Routledge.

Calvin, M. (2017). *No Hunger in Paradise*. London: Random House.

Conn, D. (2017). 'Football's Biggest Issue: The Struggle Facing Boys Rejected by Academies'. *The Guardian*, 6 October 2017.

Csikszentmihalyi, M. (1990). *Flow: The Psychology of Optimal Experience*. New York: Harper & Row.

Dweck, C. (2006). *Mindset: The New Psychology of Success*. New York: Ballantine.

Green, C. (2009). *Every Boy's Dream*. London: A&C Publishers.

Hoare, C. (2011). *Erikson on Development in Adulthood*. New York: Oxford University Press.

Kagan, P. (1998) from Quirk, James and Rodney D. Fort (1992), *Pay Dirt: The Business of Professional Team Sports*. Princeton University Press.

Mandela, N. (1995). Nelson Mandela Children's Fund speech, 8 May, Pretoria.

Rock, D. (2009). *Your Brain at Work*. New York: HarperCollins.

Toering, T. (2011). 'Self-Regulation of Learning and the Performance Level of Youth Soccer Players', University of Groningen. Online. www.academia.edu/2588854/SelfRegulation_of_Learning_and_Relative_Age_in_Elite_Youth_ Soccer_International_versus_National_Level_Players (retrieved 20 February 2014).

Topping, A. (2017). 'More than 240 Clubs Now Involved in Football Sexual Abuse Scandal', *The Guardian*, 18 January. Online. www.theguardian.com/football/2017/jan/18/police-confirm-500-potential-victims-sex-abuse-football (retrieved 25 June 2018).

4

DON'T PLAY AT YOUR PERIL

We cannot be entirely done with the beginning unless we cover play. Plato (427–347 BC) is often attributed to have said 'I can discover more about a person in an hour of play than in a year of conversation'. How can this be? This chapter seeks to explain. Earlier, I described how Odysseus left his son Telemachus to be raised by Mentor. Most education in those times was an act of individual tutelage, as was that known by Plato. We can thank Plato for developing the first formal educational school setting in 387 BC, known as the 'Academy', located at the Grove of Hecademus in Athens.

Plato, a student of Socrates, was committed to learning. Like all of the great achievers in the ancient world, he was nurtured carefully and schooled in ethics. Both were fascinated by investigating the original 'form' or essence of things, their primary sources and states, as reflected in a book by Mike Brearley titled *On Form* (2017). Ultimately, this work is a journey to try and comprehend the origin of all forms, and whether we all came from (or indeed, form) the same place. Plato's quote above suggests we reveal something deep about us when we play, opening a window on our inner character. This chapter will aim to explain how a simple subject like play can be a window on the soul and how at the same time it can also reflect the interior character of sport.

Play is a powerful concept. It represents an essential demand for our sport players and also a kind of invitation. It is true that in one sense, perhaps, we really are played by the game. Earlier we explored how some experiences hold a numinous quality, and how some elements and principles of the world are 'bigger than us'. Play is another one of these cardinal paradigms where we must 'give ourselves over'. It is a dance that is bigger than humans and certainly older, as the animals of pre-history will have certainly played. In developmental terms, we know play has a central function within the psyche, helping with physical improvement and motor co-ordination.

Play will undoubtedly help create and support growing muscles required for action and mobility in the world. There are differing opinions in science regarding the purpose of play, which we will explore as the chapter unfolds. No doubt Plato and Socrates would approve as we look in depth at the form of such an ancient behaviour. Because of associations to children, play is often overlooked in the pressure-driven world of adult sport. If an athlete is struggling, play is a vital element that is also likely to be absent and at risk. Play falls into a rubric of developmental psychology and pathology, both essential elements of clinical understanding.

Play represents an instinct and an archetype. This means there are universally recognised themes and characteristics in motion which we can all identify. There is a distinct spirit to play, a medium which appears to weave naturally into the heart and soul of sport. This chapter will illuminate the different kinds of play that humans engage in, some healthy, and some less so. 'Re-creation' of course immediately gives us a clue as to the nature of what real play is. Play is refreshing, alive and colourful. Any observer of animals at play can see that it appears to please those that experience it. It has an identity, a happy feel to it. The etymology of the word also relates this connection to levity. The origins predate the tenth century, from the Middle Dutch *pleien* – to leap for joy, dance, rejoice, be glad. There is a motion and movement within play that has a distinct energy and feel to it.

We all know that, generally, children love to play, but is it the same kind of play for soccer ace Ronaldo and the players of the major leagues? Perhaps it is; I have heard senior players express with longing their wish to play as they did when they were children. We can all have a playful mood from time to time. There is a freedom, absorption and innocence to play that can become lost or eroded as we age. It is something we might have, but come to lose. People can get jaded in all sorts of ways. 'Cynical realism' is an occupational handicap that afflicts the seasoned professional in many vocational careers. This is perhaps why Jesus is quoted as having said 'Truly I tell you, unless you change and become like little children, you will never enter the kingdom of heaven' (Matthew 18:3, NIV).

A personal observation here: after a few years I noticed there was a common feature to all the psychotherapeutic clients I met on day one. They all had an inability to play. It was just an intuition at first, but in ten years of practising psychotherapy (not a long time) I can still say it holds true. One remembers the old saying, 'all work and no play makes Jack a dull boy'. Many male clients especially tell me they 'work hard and play hard'. Rarely has it turned out that they were really playing; they were on a drug or alcohol binge, which is something quite different. Intoxication there remains a better description and unlike play this behaviour often creates issues further down the line. This kind of depression does not like movement and it does not tend to play.

We naturally might think of children when we think of play. Therefore, it may be easy to relegate the topic as irrelevant, but evidence clearly shows something different. Children retain a central symbolic presence in organised sports today even though many never think to wonder why. Perhaps because of the innocent characteristics inherent in play, this symbolic representation is used. The un-self-conscious qualities that play demands likewise hold a virtue the young most often posses. Play is perhaps awkward for some adults because it implies the immaturity of a child, which for some may be a humiliating notion.

This is understandable, as all young adults want to be seen as distinctly different to a child. But does it ever leave entirely? Jung spoke about this link, suggesting that this core part of us remains alive, whether we consider it or not. 'In every adult there lurks a child – an eternal child. Something that is becoming, is never completed, and calls for unceasing care, attention and education. That is the part of the human personality which wants to develop and become whole' (1990, p. 286). This may help us come closer to understanding Plato and the soul of the athlete.

Play holds a fundamental key to the psyche that can unlock and release fluidity of motion. It is a primary form and dimension of what it is to be a human and an animal. Perhaps this is why some mistrust or deter it. Then again, very often play is dismissed as a form of immaturity, a kind of aimless doodling of the mind. Some people truly believe it to be a waste of time, period. Is it a choice? If we don't play, so what? Much play today by children will be done online. Currently, we do not necessarily live a playful era. We know that some parents actively discourage play from happening at all, ever.

Virgil suggested that "The gates of hell are open night and day; Smooth the descent, and easy is the way: But to return, and view the cheerful skies, In this the task and mighty labour lies' (Virgil, 1997, pp. 124–41). Hell on Earth happened for hundreds of Americans on 1 August 1966 in Austin, Texas, when Charles Whitman 'smoothly' (from a vantage point, without emotion) murdered 16 people and injured 32 with a sniper rifle. He was finally shot himself by police on the top of the university tower from where he executed his prey. On the surface it might not seem plausible, but it took a clinical psychologist to discover that this act had everything to do with play. His psychopathic rampage initiated a series of events that culminated in the formation of the National Institute for Play in America.

Psychopathology and play have an intimate relationship that, while not obvious, remains very real. Out of this horror came a step forward in psychology that revealed a deeper understanding of what play is, and isn't. This is an important understanding for those working or aspiring to work with an athlete or performer. The founder of the National Institute for Play, Stuart Brown, was initially commissioned to investigate Whitman's act. In a bid to learn more, he discovered that Whitman's father was rigid and unkind, ironically describing himself to police as a 'self-made man'. After visiting many other homicidal men in prison did Stuart Brown discover that they all had one factor in common. Their fathers also stopped and rejected any play, often interpreting recreation as laziness or effeminacy. Fathers would often respond to play with violence and cruelty, denying the child any right to continue.

We can note that Hitler and Stalin also had cruel fathers who beat them, a connection we shall make again later. As well as the physical benefits we have mentioned, Brown's research demonstrated that play was a crucial component of early social skills development. Researchers consequently discovered the nature of the difficulties that some children have with entering into a state of play, or, we could say, the spirit of play. Play here represents a psychic space and intermediary place, a kind of 'grey zone'. For young children in a playground one of the natural ways of getting to know each other is often the 'rough-and-tumble' kind of play.

In *Recognition and Destruction: An Outline of Intersubjectivity*, Jessica Benjamin (1990) writes more about this phase. 'This is the moment when we discovered "there are other minds out there!" And that separate minds can share a similar state' (p. 181). Whatever the reason, that 'similar state' was the issue to grasp for young children. Those who had problems most often overdid things, went too far and became overly aggressive or violent. Some could not join in at all. They often appear frozen on the sidelines. Physically on the outside they looked immobilised, but we can all understand their interior of course was very active. But for children the danger is of a vortex, a cycle of ever-decreasing isolated actions and thoughts. Many experience anxiety and a sense of being different, and new kind of public self-perception, shame.

Children often blame themselves deep down, experiencing profound guilt for their shortcomings. Whitman wrote a series of letters to his family apologising for what he was about to commit. It is a subtle but important distinction here that these are the children vulnerable to bullying, compounding their isolation and pain at not being able to join. I have met many patients in clinical settings who lament the painful experience of being 'teased' at school. Teasing wool is a form of separating and this is indeed an apt analogy. Without a relationship or culture willing to catch this early, some children become marooned and perhaps consigned to a future of psychopathology. Therapists have a good sense of this and try to 're-weave' children back into the skill of playing together.

Poets are the interpreters of messages that come from deep within. Socrates describes this as a way of knowing and being, like sports, utilising a kind of release as the primary virtue. Characterising all the great Axial Age thinkers, Socrates also liked to get to the 'story beneath the story'. He was curious about poets because of their capacity to ask for the material to come to them, to be able to 'receive' an inspiration which arrives. This was echoed by the later Roman philosopher Plotinus (204–270 AD) who talked of inspiration in his book *Enneads*: 'the gods must come to me'. 'Active imagination' is the term that Jung developed for this, which is the modern equivalent in the Jungian world. It is an altered state, allowing the imagination in and a capacity to interpret deeper intuitions that arise.

This is also a principle that all great hunters understand, that you can even make an animal come to you. Sometimes in life opportunities for gain can arise, and sports are no different. The capacity to take an opportunity when presented is often embodied by the characteristic known as poise. Poise is a kind of suspension. The Greek god Kairos was the spirit related to taking an opportunity when it comes your way. He is depicted as walking a narrow line, holding scales of justice. The British prime minister and statesman Benjamin Disraeli is often attributed as suggesting this was the secret of a successful life itself.

One can easily imagine Socrates would have been interested in what British poet John Keats (1795–1821) once said about creativity and another kind of poise. He was also interested in the 'grey zone' or neutral space that he experienced himself and identified in other creatives. He called this space 'negative capability', a necessary experience for the artist. He suggested a poet was 'capable of being in uncertainties, mysteries, doubts, without any irritable reaching after fact and reason' (22 December 1817). This can be a challenging idea for some people today. The psychic space that 'defies fact and reason' is in this case the space of play for the performer and for a professional, an essential realm to locate and master.

The poet Samuel Taylor Coleridge (1772–1834) died soon before professional soccer was played in England but he also had things to say about the process of creativity. He coined the term 'primary imagination', relating the mind to more unconscious processes such as dreams and intuitions and our capacity to respond to random things. He also referred to what he called the 'secondary imagination', which he believed was the domain of the poet. He saw this as a kind of fusion between unconscious and conscious processes, the seen and unseen, as they work together.

When working with a group of athletes I will sometimes show them a picture of a traffic light. Where, I ask, is the zone of the performer?

Next to red, we have 'DANGER – ALERT!'. Next to amber: 'NEUTRAL' and next to green: 'GO, GO, GO!' Not every athlete I ask gets the answer, but by now you may appreciate that Plato, Socrates, Keats and Coleridge – even Kairos – might suggest it is the neutral state, the challenging place, where we do not know what comes next. The traffic light is not just a performer's light; this is a light designed for all of us. It is at one time also a challenge and an invitation to use our judgement.

On the street every day, traffic lights ask us the question: 'do you stay, or do you go?' (Figure 4.1). If you want to drive a car, or wish to cross the road safely,

FIGURE 4.1 The world asks us every day: 'do you stay or do you go?'
Credit: Veniamin Kraskov.

then this is a skill you have to learn or you will get hit. In order to be safe we have to join a world that has uncertainty as a central principle and reality. Perhaps the dynamics and possibilities of creativity and play are likewise some kind of invitation to our your senses. Unless we retreat from life, as many do, it is difficult to avoid, and for our performers impossible. Anxiety is often the enemy of the performer and the capacity to tolerate uncertainty remains a key emotional capacity to master. It is life.

The experience presents itself to us in many guises. As clinicians speaking with clients we must also hold this kind of space for them, not knowing what comes next. As the saying goes, listening 'does not mean thinking of what you are going to say next'. It is also said that the best communicators are also the best listeners. It is a primal act of engagement and we are challenged as psychotherapists to listen more than speak. It is the same for sport psychology and all people-developers. Some of the most meaningful experiences for a teacher are in those spontaneous, unexpected moments when we grasp a thread or a comment and develop it. This is the spirit of Kairos, a refined human capacity to seize and develop a moment.

An athlete in sports must aim to be aware of the limitless possibilities emerging around them in the field of play. New options continually unfold as the game is played. The seminal psychoanalyst and founder of humanistic psychology Carl Rogers was also interested in play and the human capacity to join with something wholly.

> It involves discovering the structure of the experience in the process of living the experience. Most of us, on the other hand, bring a pre-formed structure and evaluation to our experience and never relinquish it, but cram and twist the experience to suit our preconceptions, annoyed at the fluid qualities that make it so unruly in fitting our carefully constructed pigeonholes.
>
> *(1961, p. 413)*

This is like all spiritual principles – essentially a call to be open and present.

A pigeonhole might shelter us, but it may also stop us seeing fully. This is the ethos regarding artistic creation that Coleridge and Keats were describing. An image that has boxes or walls is not very accurate when considering the ethereal mind of a human. I once intuitively shared with a nervous debutant soccer player the greatest martial artist Bruce Lee's advice to 'flow like water my friend, flow like water'. It gave him an idea that could help him connect to his body and organise his thoughts around. All Zen masters appreciate the paradox that 'less is more'. This is a paradox that every artist and athlete must also understand and master. As described earlier, the etymology of 'sport' comes from the Middle English word *desporten*, which comes from the Latin *des porto*, to carry away. Where is it we go, and what is the pulling power?

Whitman showed what can happen when we get 'carried away'. Later we shall explore the myth of Icarus and how this issue of high or low applied so much to his fate. Then again, Whitman had the air of a cold-blooded killer, quite remote from a sense of being carried away. His mind had become an empathetic dead zone driven mad by a deep rage that he could not express. It would be understandable to assume sport mindsets and criminal mindsets are quite distinct, but they are not. Much of pathology and sports meet along a fine line. The word 'conviction' is a key value in sport and it also relates to imprisonment. Commitment is another sport term, and also a term for being sent to an insane asylum. Famous English soccer player-turned-youth coach Stuart Pearce was also affectionately known 'Psycho' because he was so passionate and committed. Like play, they are singular forthright expressions, whether good or bad or high or low. They are also words that can fit to love.

The German phenomenological psychologist Ludwig Binswanger (1960) was a colleague of Freud and Jung who was interested in why it was that 'what must go up must come down'. What purpose does that serve? It is fitting to the myth of Icarus. The Buddhist author and monk Jack Kornfield wrote a book aptly titled *After the Ecstasy, Then the Laundry* (2000). Binswanger suggested that human beings live on a vertical as well as a horizontal plane, which is an idea many athletes might appreciate. There is a relationship between how high we can safely go, and how far we have gone on the horizontal plane in life.

Iain McGilchrist puts it like this:

> one needs to bring what one has learned from one's ascent back into the world where life is going on, and incorporate it in such a way that it enriches experience and enables more of whatever it is that 'discloses itself' to us (Heidegger's phrase) to do just that. But it is still only on the ground that it will do so, not up in the air.
>
> *(2012, p. 22)*

The young Icarus in the Greek myth fell to his death because he got 'carried away' and flew too high. Then again, he didn't have much experience. Binswanger's horizontal plane represented the ordinary passage of life, which in this case also implies a journey. The word 'journey' originates from the French *jour* (day), relating to how far one could travel in a day.

The Danish quantum physicist and 1922 Nobel Prize-winning scientist Neils Bohr was also the stand-in soccer goalkeeper for Denmark. His brother was the main goalkeeper. He said, regarding any mastery of a craft: 'an expert is a person who has made all the mistakes that can be made, in a narrow field' (1954, p. 62). Dweck's research revealed that children who could see experiences as challenges rather than painful assaults on the ego learned more and did better.

Playing for peace

There is a large and varied literature on play. This has in turn produced many theoretical models and philosophies we cannot entirely do justice to here. One of the main theorists on play is Brian Sutton-Smith (1997), who in *The Ambiguity of Play* discussed different types of play, as well as the 'rhetoric of play', relating to the ethics and rules of play. Another significant work is Richard Schechner's (2002), *Performance Studies*, which provides an introduction to major theories in the field of performance and ritual studies. Schechner is an academic professor with a background in performance arts who has explored in depth the internal dynamics of acting and play.

Schechner's book includes and exploration of the work of Gregory Bateson, who conceptualised the theory of the 'play frame'. This is a special ordering of time and space which allows animals and humans alike to signal that play behaviour is taking place. Play is a 'singular state' and, as such, is a form of language and a medium of expression. Evidence suggests much of this process and exchange of information is received and processed at an unconscious level. Bateson points out how time is ordered in its own special way and the perception of time also changes during play. It appears that when perception of time changes, it can be the hallmark of an equally unconscious element in parallel motion. If this were so, then one might expect to see unusual or strange events happen during play that might deviate from normal conscious behaviours and patterns.

In an interview with Phil Cousineau, Stuart Brown recounts one such example. He gives an account by an arctic scout who had witnessed a strange event in the extreme north. He was in charge of a group of Husky sled dogs who had just eaten and were settling down for the evening. A hungry polar bear suddenly appeared from nowhere and swiftly moved in for the kill, preparing to pounce on a blissfully unaware Husky settling in the snow. The Husky turned, seemingly too late, and instead of fear, for some unknown reason, gave a playful wiggle underneath the rampant bear. Instead of pouncing, the bear instantaneously relaxed and responded playfully in kind.

For a week the bear returned to play at the same time each night. Fortunately, a cameraman was present and captured the entire event. Pictures of the event and a description from Stuart Brown are all available online (Brown, 2007). This strange occurrence was apparently not unique; many rangers consequently contacted him to attest to witnessing similar experiences. It was also fitting as an illustration in keeping with the ultimate philosophy of the Institute for Play. Play as a medium of expression has unique propensities to disarm, unite and inspire. Sport has a real track record of uniting different groups in conflict, as the Greeks once us showed could happen for real. In 2018, the world saw a unique moment as North Korean leaders shook hands with South Korean leaders at the Winter Olympic Games in PyeongChang, demonstrating that the Olympic pulling power of shared play still holds moments and opportunities for joining together.

Another seminal author and contributor to the science of play is Johan Huizinga, whose classic book *Homo Ludens* (1955) explores many aspects of play and sport. 'Ludo' is a popular board game with its title taken from the original Latin word *ludere*, meaning relating to play or chance. Play need not be competition. Huizinga argues that play is a primary building block for the generation of culture. He suggests play acts as a developmental medium able to morph and develop into other expressions of life to be experienced later. Sport is one of them. It corresponds to a variety of different types of play, including vicarious audience play, risky or deep play, and our form, represented by sporting contests.

Roger Caillois (1913–1978) is another cardinal author and researcher on play. He was a French sociologist and contemporary of Albert Camus, who will feature a little later. Caillois' contribution was to distinguish and delineate different categories of play, providing a more concrete definition of forms and types. Below we can take a closer look at each kind. In each category we will also explore the relationship of the two previously mentioned neurotransmitters, dopamine and norepinephrine. They are worthy of note here as we can see there are variations in each type of play.

1. **Agon**. As described earlier, this is the world of the agonists, the 'should I stay or should I go?' conditions of the traffic light. It is the world of competition and the struggle to overcome exterior and interior opponents. Often this happens within a team where competitors are required to operate in a coherent, unified manner. It particularly defines individuals such as chess and tennis players who also live in the struggle and the agony of competition. Here we can measure the balance of stress and desire reflected in the presence of the neurotransmitters dopamine (desire) and norepinephrine (urgency). The primary element is the 'contest'. A balance of dopamine and norepinephrine seems to produce optimum psychic states.

2. **Alea**. 'Alea' was the name of a sailor who played dice on Odysseus' ship. This relates to games of chance and less of skill. Sport is to play as gambling is to Alea. Picture the lines of casino 'players' – more witness than competitor in front of their spinning wheels of fortune. Apart from gestural participation such as pulling a handle the player is an inert and passive participant, which may be part of the attraction. Computer gambling is most likely better suited to this category because of the sedentary nature of the player. Alea is more 'Ludo', the game of chance. While a gambler spending the last of their money may be producing plenty of dopamine, there is certainly not much norepinephrine or fear. Yet, competitors who might sneer at this form should remember that gambling can constitute play for the elderly! Significantly, this kind of play is often done alone. The primary element is 'chance'.

3. **Mimicry**. The form of mime most commonly associated with the Frenchman Marcel Marceau, who portrayed reality in the art of pretending. This form is characterised by the embodiment of a 'guise' – remembering the Greek symbol of drama was the two masks. The first drama can be traced back to the women-only festivals of Dionysus in Anthesteria, Greece, around 500 BC. Fantasy and the spirit of spontaneity characterise this style. Think of children playing at 'cops and robbers'. We can also visit a 'play' at the theatre where we must 'suspend our disbelief' and enter into the spirit along with the 'players'. For a performer in this world, the neurotransmitter balance, as with the other agonistes, is necessary for an effective performance – another reason why the Greeks called actors and sports competitors by the same name. This form can

be solo, but most often requires a team and a human observer. The primary element is 'disguise'.

4. **Ilinx**. The Greek word for 'whirlpool', which represents the thrill-seeking, rollercoaster riding extreme sports type of play such as high diving, snowboarding, surfing and the such like. There are real physical dangers here. Caillois also includes recreational drug highs from hallucinogens and drugs like ecstasy. This would constitute a desire for a lot of dopamine and not so much of the fear factor, norepinephrine. Evidence suggests we may have to trade one for the other. Drugs can effectively hijack our natural neurotransmitter balances, giving us materially based (i.e., from a substance) feelings of exhilaration and power, something that eventually wears off. Remembering the sage Kornfield, 'first the ecstasy then the laundry'. This kind of play is often solitary, much like Alea. The primary element is extremity.

Today, companies such as Red Bull are known to specialise in and sponsor extreme sports, currently gathering large followings as a subculture in modern sport. Red Bull Leipzig is a complete German soccer team owned and inspired by the organisation. The Olympics still serve today as a platform and introduction for new sports and expressions such as snowboarding. This is an Ilinx culture that has burgeoned in recent times out of another Ilinx, skateboarding. As we shall see with online sport peoples later, there is no reason why psychology couldn't help a cave parachute diver, for example, but perhaps the Alea of the fruit machine world is beyond our influence. But of course for them, patience must also be a virtue, so perhaps there is, after all, always something to be learned from sport psychology.

FIGURE 4.2 'Ilinx' or the 'whirlpool'; the thrill-seeking kind of play.

Play and prayer are the same

None of the above are mutually exclusive. In team sports, whenever there is an opponent on the field, mimicry and deception can always have a place. In soccer, a good striker is full of feints and plays, as is a quarterback in American football and a baseball pitcher. Play really does have within it the world of the dupe, the trickster and the court jester.

In my life I have had two useful psychological intuitions from dreams; one of them was that 'play and prayer are the same'. When I was young I had a toy tank and an 'Action Man' with a parachute that I threw out of the upstairs window. As I sprinted downstairs for all the world I was saving us all from a dark and menacing enemy. I was immersed, in one place, but is that a kind of prayer?

Caillois developed parameters and a delineation for what constitutes play. In this scheme, the world of professional soccer is ruled out at the first stage. We can see how play becomes a sport and then a business. But this doesn't mean it doesn't remain a feature of sports. For Caillois, play must:

1. be free without cost and not obligatory
2. be an activity separate from the routine of life, occupying its own time and space
3. have an element of being uncertain, so that the results of play cannot be predetermined and some kind of initiative is demonstrated by the player
4. not create any wealth; the game ends as it begins, economically speaking
5. have rules that suspend ordinary laws and behaviours
6. involve imagined realities that may be set against or beside 'real life'

Comparing each of the elements above we can now venture for the first item on the list that meditation or prayer is something you can do without cost, and is not something you can be forced to do. It has its own time and space, deliberately separated. We all remain subject to uncertainty as ordinary mortals and we cannot always control what we think of during meditation. The internal experience of each meditation will be different from one sitting to the next.

Meditation or prayer does not create any wealth, in that by the end we are not any richer by doing it. Ordinary rules and behaviours are suspended as to be done properly; mediation or prayer is not done while watching a movie or delivering a lecture. The last on the list, 'imagined realities that are set beside real life', could be a very good description for the values of spiritual practice. Now empirical science clearly proves that many aspects of life can be improved with a minimal practice of settling the mind from inner chatter, whatever name you call it by.

Immersion and being in your body

Perhaps the connection between prayer and play can explain why so many philosophers have been drawn to investigating sport and play in the past. One of Caillois' French contemporaries was the Nobel Prize winner Albert Camus, who was a seminal figure in the 1950s French existential movement. He was also a goalkeeper for his successful university soccer team, about which he said: 'After many years during which I saw many things, what I know most surely about morality and the duty of man I owe to sport and learned it in the RUA' (Camus, 2012). High praise indeed; Camus also suggests that when we gather together in this way, highly significant and meaningful potentialities are mixing together with powerful possibilities.

There is a chemistry in motion when teams work together and our ancestors knew this. Earlier, we mentioned the contribution of Karl Marx to thinking. It was he that realised that even on the macro scale, society can also be seen as a predictable formula and definable entity. In this way society can be viewed as a set of ingredients with predictable outcomes and institutions. In *The Future of Ritual*, Richard Schechner (1993) explored social dramas in this context in a chapter entitled 'The Street is the Stage', describing the celebrations leading up to the fall of the Berlin Wall. He suggests public demonstrations as one example of a human 'festival' where the outcome is unknown; demonstrations are therefore a form of play.

He likened this kind of immediacy to soccer; 'The excitement of such social dramas, not unlike what grips whole populations during some sports matches, especially those like the soccer World Cup where team and nations are closely identified—is rooted in the tension between known patterns of action, stunning instantaneous surprises, and a passionately desired yet uncertain outcome' (1993, p. 97). He correlates the spontaneity and caprice of play in crowds as a powerful possibility for change –for good, as well as the dangerous kind of change incarnated in the mob.

In tune with some of the archetypal connections made earlier, Schechner (1988) also connected performance, play, sports, rituals and other types of performances to our past as hunters. He suggested these various energetic kinetic forms of play and ritual have their origins in the need to practice skills useful for hunting. Hunting requires long periods of stealth, sudden outbursts of energy and lots of practice. Remembering that an animal will defy the hunter any way it can, this is a skill that takes much preparation and schooling. In the animal world, Schechner emphasises how species that play the most also expend the most energy in sudden bursts. Those animals engage in activities that demand kinetic energy for fighting, fleeing, mating, hunting, maintaining dominance and protecting turf. According to Schechner, 'crisis – the sudden and unstinting spending of kinetic energy – is the link among performance, hunting, ritual, and play' (1988, p. 97).

Being young normally means that you have a lot of kinetic energy to spend, made up of dreams, fantasies and instinctual drives all surging ahead, building for the future. Schechner (1988) suggested this currency needs 'to be spent in behaviour that is not only harmless but fun. Decisively, play allows kinetic potential to be maintained not by being stored but by being spent' (1988, p. 97). He expands on the link to our ancestors, suggesting that play is in fact a form of hunting, and that hunting is a kind of play. 'This kind of playing is strategic, future-and-crisis-oriented, violent and/or combative; it has winners and losers, leaders and followers; it employs costumes and/or disguises; it has a beginning, middle, and end; and its underlying themes are fertility, prowess, and animism/totemism' (1988, pp. 99–100). Note that this description could be equally applied to sports. Also note his characterisation of a trinity relating to the beginning, the middle and the end of a hunt. This trinity is a reality of life that will feature regularly in this book.

Finding your senses

A Buddhist monk once tried to shock and encourage me at the same time by shouting 'clarity, David, clarity!' This is a familiar refrain and it remains a challenge for the athlete, raising levels of urgency and focus while not raising anxiety. Performers can experience a state of mind of being caught in a vortex of self-conscious fear. To stay out of this experience, one generally has to be able to 'be in one's body', which is not a very Western thing to aim for. Among many of the young people that need clinical attention, this is evident. The computer age appears to be reducing the way many people use their senses, especially the young. It is not a bad exercise for young athletes to list their senses, then relate how they experience each one on a match day. In my experience, this is something most have never been asked to do before. Why not?

Earlier, we discussed the impact of 'cultural anamnesis', discovering something we already know. The development of 'dialectical behaviour therapy' by Marsha Linehan in the 1980s was the first widely used clinical model that attempted to teach skills related to 'being in your body'. Eastern cultures are more acclimatised than the West to the idea of settling the mind, and regularly practise these principles from an early age. Western children in today's schools are comparatively impoverished, with little on the syllabus reflecting this subject as any kind of priority. Dweck clearly demonstrated that your fortunes can depend on the culture you inhabit. Perhaps mind calming and settling are essential skills that are perceived as religious expressions and therefore are off the syllabus. Like many life skills and experiences, their benefit is difficult to measure or weigh. Therefore, they can become sidelined by budget-conscious schools who need to count the costs. Oscar Wilde (1854–1900) famously wrote in his *Picture of Dorian Gray*, 'Nowadays people know the price of everything and the value of nothing.'

Renowned jungian analyst and author Robert Johnson (1987), in his book *Ecstasy: Understanding the Psychology of Joy*, investigated the mythological figure of Dionysus, who was once widely celebrated in ancient Greece as a source of creativity and fertile expression. However, Johnson charted the rise of a more removed, Apollonian tradition in the Roman culture compared to Greece. The Romans, he suggested, replaced ancient Dionysus with Bacchus, more associated by them with drunkenness and materialism. This was not the creative free sprit in motion, it was the same spirit that mistakenly describes three-day drug binges as 'playing hard'. He follows on with the theme; 'When Western society chose to follow the erratic footsteps of the degraded Bacchus instead of the joyful dance of

Dionysus, it began to confuse materialism with sensation. As a result we citizens in the late twentieth century can truly be said to have lost our senses, or at least to have lost contact with them' (1987, p. 22).

George Leonard is an experienced martial artist who incorporated Eastern philosophies into his own work, *The Ultimate Athlete* (2001). He also suggests there remains a lacuna in the West which has become a cultural shortfall we have to compensate for in other ways. He suggested that there was a 'mind-body-spirit' split in modern Western culture, which he called 'a major error in Western thought' (2001, p. 290). Perhaps the split is not uniquely a Western problem, especially of late. Reports from China are suggesting that they too are discovering a generation of computer addicts and compulsive gamers. Cleverly, online games can give you a feeling of competence in a short time. Life on life's terms is far more difficult and, for some young people, better off avoided. Leonard wrote his comments before smartphones and the Internet had the level of influence they do today. Rising anxiety levels in the young, suicide and drug overdoses at epidemic levels suggest that something is missing or has been lost – perhaps even replaced?

Earlier I described hearing athletes lament how they wished they could approach the game in the same way they did when they were children. They recall a comparative age of innocence. That has since been set aside by the loaded implications and politics of being on a team and being 'forced to deliver'. But if we follow the model we have established here of a connection to hunting, we can expect that there may also have been a heavy pressure and responsibility for our ancestors. The great hunters, like the great players of today, will have made a big kill when folk at home needed it the most. Conventional archetypal identities such as the 'hero' thus emerged relating to our need to create and hold figures within a community who found a way to get the job done and 'bring home the bacon'.

Sport at a high level does become more influenced by psychological qualities and abilities beyond a player's technical capacities. Sadly, a natural desire for a young person to play often now translates to 'partying'. Today more than ever addiction and abuse can become dangerous. I don't mean normal drinking or partying, I mean the serious consequences of intoxication and fatal overdoses. Addiction is always dangerous. Requiring a dopamine rush can be a dangerous thing if you are addicted to opiates, crystal meth or heroin. Dopamine receptors do not care whether the supply came from a Wimbledon-winning serve down the sideline or the crack dealer on the corner of the street.

As alluded to earlier, it is a common if not ubiquitous experience during drug intoxication, prayer and play that perceptions of time change. Time becomes fluid, shifts and is not a consistent experience. Satellites that power navigation and clocks on earth have to be adjusted for this reason. A Western view of time is linear, with the length of time representing the size of the gap between. Eastern time reflects more an emphasis of things that happen at the same time, representing a closer approximation of Jung's ideas regarding synchronicity. We can all account for bizarre and strange coincidences happening in our lives when seemingly impossible chances came together. Our perception of time appears to be conditioned, and an open mind here would be a value worth holding. If we are to achieve excellence we must strive for new understandings that test us, and time is one of them.

Suspension of any kind implies a kind of buoyancy; it has a 'bounce' and is an expression of fluidity and freedom. Play can therefore be difficult for individuals who suffer from self-consciousness or anxiety. I have heard it said that 'imagination requires a risk' and this risk represents another challenge. Becoming agitated by surrounding conditions or entities releases too much norepenipherine, which constricts the freedom required for creativity. This, remember, is the fear-inducing neurotransmitter that sometimes (at the worst of times) calls our attention to the outside world and not the inner. Kairos disappears and leaves the scene. Actors lose their lines and soccer players lose their touch. We have all seen nervous singers or actors who can sometimes make an audience nervous too. Our energies are transmitted and received all at once, mixed together in the public setting of the theatre or a stadium. One of the attractive prospects of attending a live performance is the experience of all being connected at the same time. There is a risk and that is the very stuff of life.

The American George Carlin (1937–2008) was a well-known live performer and comedian who had a funny but germane rant about 'playing with a stick'. Carlin derided the modern 'play date', complaining about how play had been sectioned off and neutered by the over-management of 'helicopter parents' or commercial enterprises. The Apollonian trait of over-management and separating vital activities had begun. He moaned to his audience, beseeching them: whatever happened to the notion of telling children to 'go into the empty yard and play with a stick?' He touched on an important issue that play in essence lives a spontaneous, quixotic life and defies being structured. Today, all the gaps in life can be conveniently filled by staring into an object like a smartphone. Just watch a group of any people in public or at home in the industrialised world and at any moment they will be looking into to their smartphones.

Robert Johnson earlier referred to Dionysus, the spontaneous and creative god in the Greek world who was the son of Zeus, and a central figure of sport that we shall explore in the next chapter. Earlier, we also quoted Nietzsche, who was fascinated by the relationship between these two archetypes, Apollo and Dionysus. His most successful book, *Thus Spoke Zarathustra* (1891), is related to this diametrically opposed set of relationships. The gods Apollo and Dionysus were brothers, so they were, indeed, related! The next chapter will explain how and why this relationship is also essential for a performer.

Does the music play us?

Jessica Benjamin, in *Recognition and Destruction* (1990), writes about the relationship of play to the early relational needs of children. She agrees that it constitutes a vital stepping stone on the way to a successful relational life, but adds another perspective: 'I would agree that this space constitutes an advance in recognition of the other, but I think the earlier interaction can be considered an antecedent, in the form of concrete affective sharing. Certainly, from the standpoint of the mother whose infant returns her smile, affective sharing is already the beginning of reciprocal recognition' (p. 188). Children enter a state of reverie for the maternal which then morphs into other familiar behaviours as we grow older.

In the first chapter we explored our deeper relationship to inner animals, so what do we have here? Is this an inner animal or an inner child? There wasn't always a delineation between these two forms; this is a modern interpretation. They both share the same qualities. Whenever we play we become immersed in what *is*. During the Axial Age, the Buddha Gotama Siddhartha had an insight relating to a blissful experience he had as a child, which came to represent the 'first level', or *Jhana*. This was a spiritual principle so simple that a child could comprehend it. This spiritual disposition is so central to human experience that it may represent a previous incarnation and state, but one that was more normal for our ancestors. Why is this the case?

Andrew Cooper suggests that a sporting performance 'is anything but instinctual, the idea crops up too frequently to deny that there is something about it that makes it feel that way. That something is immersion. What feels like instinct is the absence of fear, doubt, worry and unnecessary self deliberation that result from self consciousness' (1998, p. 45). Is the liberation of this consciousness a simple task? We psychotherapists know that of course it is not, and here is the opportunity that depth sport psychology has for internal sports injuries that only immersion can cure.

English pioneering analyst and clinician Donald Winnicott wrote the book *Playing and Reality* (1971) accentuating the vital function play has for interpersonal relationships and other experiences that are a natural part of life. Along with his contemporary Martin Buber (1878–1965), he was concerned with interpersonal relationships as the focus of investigation. Both developed and expanded the earlier psychological traditions that initially focused solely on the individual – referring to the traditional one-to-one psychotherapeutic relationship of patients being sat in a chair. Their emphasis related to the relational plane, and how we are all immersed in countless interactions as adults. Buber called this space the 'dialogical space', an 'in-between' space that is crucial for the development of a healthy relational psyche. This later became referred to as the *I-Thou* space, where we must become immersed, recognising that we are all challenged to relate to this world with our 'whole being'.

During a meditation, if we think about the act too much we are liable to degrade our connection to the experience. Much of my past career was as a professional actor, mainly in the theatre. Sometimes it was a frightening experience – the audiences were so large – but somehow I managed to hold on and let enough of myself go to be able to enter the role, and 'play'. I suspect the quality of the culture gave me the strength to overcome my nerves and join (although I learned my lines before anyone else). The legendary English comedian Spike Milligan (1918–2002) once said 'the cliche is the handrail of the crippled mind'; for the actor, the lines are the handrail, which is why some of the most nervous players can be the greatest performers in sports.

Danish bestselling author and scientist Tor Norrentranders explores this duality and the battle with oneself in his book *The User Illusion* (1991). He echoes Buber and Winnicott, describing the struggle as between the more egotistical *I* and the perennial being within us all, *Me*. Speaking of the actor type of agoniste, he says:

> Theatre involves setting the *Me* free so it can unfold. If the *I* does not set the *Me* free, we get a performance riddled with vetoes. The consciousness wants to control and monitor all of the time. As a result, the performance is uneven and lacks credibility, because no emotion appears credible if it is controlled and hampered by the consciousness. But the problem lies in giving *Me* this freedom. It requires trust on the part of the *I*. A trust that only comes through practice.
>
> *(1991, p. 264)*

As an actor for many years, I also want to reiterate that the climate, the culture one works within, can also affect one's capacity to trust the *I* over the *Me*.

My personal experience testifies that this capacity and skill can be consciously created and realised. Norrentranders mentions the 'monitor', which Freud referred to as the 'super ego'. This is an internal voice that can be overcome, but there are rules and conditions. This is not a new idea, and is the reason why the Greeks consciously held the space for the ephebes, the adolescents who would one day, like Alexander, maybe conquer the world. But our athletes are the lucky ones who need never kill. Whatever the purpose, the implications of nurturing and safety always apply for cultures of true learning and growth. The reason we can say this relates to the inevitable vulnerability exposed during play. After all, can we play in the presence of danger? One would imagine not. Creative cultures thrive on atmospheres where there is a preponderance of freedom and a kind of trust in the air.

Some sports cultures, especially after a series of defeats, can be vulnerable to losing the playful quality that becomes subsumed or corroded. Many team sport cultures reflect the individuals that run them, and this can be for good reason. The coaches and managers are the arbiters and sometimes awkward moments or feelings are a reflection of honest differences being shared. This is also reflected in the psychotherapeutic relationship, necessity at times for a 'frank' exchange. But for children and youth cultures this is a different issue, something we will explore Chapter 7 relating to youth sport. However, sports academies are also full of children, and we have to be able to nurture and hold the space for growth. A characteristic spirit of estrangement, exclusivity and isolation characterise the 'talent cultures' that Dweck (2006) warned against earlier.

For play to freely exist it needs a kind of oxygen, which in our case might relate to trust and confidence. Social cooperative relationships between comparative strangers are a form of achievement, for a young adult at least. Trusting relationships are more than just a term, they have to be nurtured. As stated at the beginning of this book, the etymology of confidence is 'confide', and normally to confide in someone is an act of trust. Early hunters will indeed have been in many situations where they had to trust each other. In the 2017/2018 Premier League competition, those managers with the 'softer' people skills are those that are getting hired. As we saw in the last chapter, you can be confident such huge financial concerns do not routinely elevate the 'soft skills' as a priority unless there is a simple rationale that this approach is most effective. Just like a Shaman's role in the past, the managers are the conductor and and cantor in one.

This idea of play as a reversion of some kind is at the heart of our discussion and what perhaps gives it its universality. Without its expression, we can see the human spirit either fails to develop, suffers or dies. We clinicians all know from bitter experience that for some individuals trauma can be a fatal experience, never to be recovered from. Consequently, play represents a vital domain that we can easily suggest as a component of emotional recovery. Many individuals we know suffer from depressive conditions that immobilise the psyche and defy movement. A true emotional recovery will reflect what you are doing, not just what you are thinking. Certainly, play can take a role. Clinicians would do well to enquire about how the client plays, what music they listen to and so on. Can we, like Plato, learn something about someone just by knowing the music they listen to?

Music remains a universal medium that most humans enjoy, and like play it seems to give pleasure as well as hold a place for our pain and loss. The study of music is revealing important insights that are relevant to any performer – sports or otherwise. Likewise, we can mistakenly underestimate play as just a joyful, happy-sounding dance. This afternoon I walked past a children's park. If I hadn't known it was children playing in a park, I might have thought there was a shocking and violent crime unfolding. Like music, play holds a space for us to fill in with our fears, longings and celebrations. Something else is being learned in play, in this case how to scream and be terrified. Only the context of the situation stopped me being terrified. Music shares this capacity to become a vessel for different kinds of deeply felt human emotions.

Music is another experience that joins sport and drama, in that it involves play and performance. As with play, music represents another form of expression where there is often an invitation to join. Musicians 'play' their instruments, just like the actors play their roles in a performance. Music is another spiritual realm, in that we join with it and suspend ourselves in an altered state we can snap out of. These ancient recreations and shared expressions have survived and constitute a vital part of human culture today. Outdoor music festivals such as Glastonbury near Stonehenge in England and other similar concerts are thriving popular events, even in this computer age of remoteness and isolation.

It's delightful to think that since the earliest times human beings partied – and, we can assume, with music too. More on that later, but we know good musicians understand prosody: how to create sounds that are melodious, attractive and even seductive. The 'prosody' of a sound means the tone in which it is delivered. The pitch of a sound is known to have a deep unconscious affect on the psyche, as for babies it is an elementary language and initial bond to the mother before being born. If we are lucky as a baby, we normally first experience prosody from our mothers when we hear a lullaby. The lullaby represents an important early emotional regulator for the young, providing an anchor for the undifferentiated self of the baby. It is a maternal call to return to the dream, the formless world from where the baby came.

Some dream states can be tough to 'snap' out of. My experience suggests much of chemical addiction emanates from this soothing call later recreated by drugs and alcohol. *Morphia* is a cardinal and seductive goddess of the underworld. The lullaby is also like the Shaman in that it represents an incantation, not to hunt but, in the case of the baby, to calm and send to sleep. Later on in life, that lullaby will change its form of delivery and set one dancing or into a trance through headphones. We remain 'captivated' or seduced by music as we grow older and, as with play, we allow ourselves time immersed in another mental space and dimension where listening is the method of being in touch. We suspend ourselves again and are at the same time moved.

Since the time of the Shaman, it has been natural to expect a child to join in either community activities and gatherings. It is also natural to assume they want to be involved in synchronised activities in a communal setting. We cannot know what happened when peoples gathered together, but we have cause to believe there was joyful dancing, music and ecstatic unions. Dance is another form and expression that takes us into 'our bodies', and into another interior world. As mentioned earlier, hunting communities were small groups or bands of 20–35. They had an instinctual need to meet up with different tribes and perhaps to swap dances. We know that some sites such as Stonehenge had the alternate purpose of becoming venues where people could get together, swap stories and, of course, much more.

Communal shared activities will have helped to create new uniform neurological pathways, group behaviours and identifications through entrainment and 'modelling'. Modelling happens when we consciously or unconsciously copy others, adopting their traits, mannerisms and behaviours. Remembering that numanism can also represent that which is 'greater than thou' while being a member participating in a group, communal activities were opportunities to merge, synergistically fostering a feeling of group identification. One of my earliest clients said his greatest ever life experience was at a 'rave' dance; he felt more complete in that time than ever before or since. Today we can still see forms of religious practice involving passionate singing and clapping. These soulful expressions may be the nearest we now come to a human experience that goes back as far as we can imagine.

'Entrainment' is a term used to describe how humans can synchronise with each other often on an unconscious level. Perhaps we all unconsciously experience this when we tap our feet to music. Consultant psychiatrist and clinician Iain McGilchrist reiterates the importance of music to early communities: 'In more traditionally structured societies, performance of music played both an integral, and an integrated role not only in celebration, religious festivals, and other rituals, but also in daily work and recreation; and it is above all a shared performance, not just something we listen to passively' (2009, p. 104). Ethnomusicology is the study of music as played by our ancestors, representing a more in-depth investigation of this subject and the relationship it had to early communities.

Joseph Jordania is an Australian–Georgian ethnomusicologist who has studied these issues in depth. He is currently professor of ethnomusicology at Melbourne University, Australia. In 2011, he published *Why Do People Sing?* His research suggests the human capacity to be entranced was an instinctual development aimed at inspiring what he calls 'the specific altered state of consciousness, battle trance' (2011, p. 2). By raising dopamine levels, humans felt less fear and were able to take more pain. Individuals became entrained, united in a collective identity which he suggests helped us face the predators from the beginnings of human time. I would also suggest that what he calls the 'battle trance' state is also a 'hunter trance'. Dancing and singing were present after a hunt, for sure, but we can also imagine they were a vital part of hunt preparation.

Remarkably, new research is suggesting music has a primal core human function that goes deeper than first thought. Primary in this field is Steven Mithen, who wrote the book *The Singing Neanderthals*, explaining the early power of music. His research indicates that music may be older than words and verbal language itself. Iain McGilchrist (2009) adds a fascinating connection to this idea for us; 'But if it should turn out that music leads to language, rather than language to music, it helps us understand for the first time the otherwise baffling historical fact that poetry evolved *before* prose' (p. 105). We know that the Greeks had a system of storytellers travelling Greece telling the best versions of Homer and Hesiod. The *Vedas* of the Buddhas Pali texts were the same.

We can imagine that some great Greek storytellers could captivate a town using a rich prosody and all the tricks of entrainment. At the very beginning of his book *Playing and Reality*, Winnicott writes that 'a phenomenon that is universal, like the one I am considering in this book, cannot in fact be outside the range of those whose concern is the magic of imaginative and creative living' (1971, p. xi). This magical imagination and spirit was once the claim and domain of the Shaman. It was their job to translate, to lead and inspire minds with captivating engagement. If we are fortunate we get a good clinician, coach, teacher, priest, musician or soccer manager to do the same.

Nevertheless, we live in an age where for many or most that voice will be a computer. Stuart Brown, Donald Winnicott, Martin Buber and Tor Norrentranders all appear to suggest the same thing: in order to play we need to learn how to trust a part of ourselves. It is a critical reality for every actor, musician, poet, hunter and athlete. It is, of course, easier said than done. However, there appears to be little attention given to this subject ('trusting ourselves') in this way for the athlete or many children in school. I have known many soccer players who have gone on to successful careers who were at one time convinced that, for some reason, they were finished and had no chance for success. They were young, defeated and without hope. It follows then that the sport psychologist, coach or mentor must hold the place of hope for an athlete when all seems lost. As Odysseus showed, the hero's journey often encounters times when all seems lost, but one can't always count on a young person knowing or believing that these challenges can be overcome.

Guy Clayton is an award-winning British analyst and author who adds to the chorus above regarding this relationship of inner trust, adding a nuanced contribution for our cause;

> As we saw in our brief discussion on creativity, the ability to relax some of these neural constraints − to *stop* doing the inhibitory trick − is essential of fresh patterns, links and ideas to be discovered. The mature brain learns more by finding new connections between what it already knows and by the earnest acquisition of new information; to do that, you need reverie just as much as you need reason.
>
> *(p. 306)*

Here he uses a vital word we explored earlier in the book; a 'reverie' is another kind of suspension, a stepping-back from life as if children once again, observers experiencing 'awe'. As discussed earlier, the capacity to experience a state of reverie was a development that helped make us unique and therefore provided a keystone for our future growth.

The American physicist and philosopher Richard Feynman (1918–1988) suggested 'Nature uses only the longest threads to weave her patterns, so that each small piece of her fabric reveals the organisation of the entire tapestry' (1965, p. 34). If so, play has a crucial role as a primary colour and part of our developmental tapestry. Without it there is a hole in the psyche that cannot be easily filled. The missing thread extends throughout life so the implications and urgency for children to play freely appear vital. Play is a thread made of the Agon, the Alea, mimicry and the whirlpool, Ilinx. Each of them are required by life, reflections of inevitable demands that life will place on us all at some point. They are central strands going deep into our psyche.

Earlier we mentioned the Minotaur, one of the earliest Greek myths. Thanks to Arachne and her thread, Jason had a way of returning to the world. Play is a form of preparation, a psychic building block that relates and sustains other aspects of later life − not just hunting or sports. We love to do it as children or adults and it retains a spiritual quality. It is one of a group of activities that appear to relate to our deeper past as a species, characterised by the consistent feature that the quality of time changes as we access our unconscious realms. It can be developed, lost or rediscovered. All of my experience as a psychotherapist and sport psychologist in England showed me that we can learn to live again when we learn to play again.

Principles important for play

safety

reverie and awe

suspension

transformation

fluidity

buoyancy

freedom

trust

types of play

Agon: competition

Alea: chance

mimicry: disguise

Ilinx: extremity

What comes after play? A capacity to play alone will not take an athlete to success, but it is a necessary platform. We can now move onto the middle of this book, the meat and the prize, the next requirement for the athlete who wants to get better, the real soul of the competitor. Danger lies ahead.

If you want to win, the author of the following is the man to have at your side. He was a great writer so let him conclude this section from his famous speech in 1942. In the words of Winston Churchill, 'Now is not the end. It is not even the beginning of the end. But it is perhaps the end of the beginning.'

References

Benjamin, J. (1995). 'Recognition and Destruction: An Outline of Intersubjectivity', in *Like Subjects, Love Objects: Essays on Recognition and Sexual Difference*. New Haven, CT: Yale University Press.

Binswanger, L. (1960). *Melancholia and Mania: Phenomenological Studies*. Pfullingen: Neske.

Bohr, N. (1954). As quoted by Edward Teller, in 'Dr Teller's Magnificent Obsession', Robert Coughlan, *Life* magazine, 6 September 1954, p. 62.

Brown, S. (2007). 'Animals at Play'. YouTube. https://m.youtube.com/watch?v=iHj82ot Ci7U (retrieved 1 December 2017).

Caillois, R. (2001). *Man, Play and Games (Les jeux et les hommes)* (M. Barash, trans.). Chicago, IL: University of Illinois Press (original work published 1958).

Churchill, W. (1942). 'Now is Not the Beginning', Mansion House speech, London.

Claxton, G. (2005). *The Wayward Mind: An Intimate History of the Unconscious*. London: Abacus.

Cooper, A. (1998). *Playing in the Zone: Exploring the Spiritual Dimensions of Sports*. Boston, MA: Shambhala.

Dweck, C. (2006). *Mindset: The New Psychology of Success*. New York: Ballantine.

Feynman, R. (1965). *The Character of Physical Law*. Boston, MA: MIT Press, Modern Library.

Huizinga, J. (1955). *Homo ludens: A Study of the Play Elements in Culture*. Boston, MA: Beacon Press.

Johnson, R.A. (1987). *Ecstasy: Understanding the Psychology of Joy*. San Francisco, CA: Harper.

Jordania, J. (2011). *Why Do People Sing? Music in Human Evolution*. Tbilisi: LOGOS Publishing Programme.

Jung, C.G. (1990). *The Collected Works of C. G. Jung*, Vol. 17. Princeton, NJ: Princeton University Press (original work published 1951).

Keats, J. (1817). Letter to George and Tom Keats, 22 December.

Kornfield, J. (2001). *After the Ecstasy then the Laundry*. New York: Bantam.

Leonard, G. (2001). *The Ultimate Athlete*. Berkeley, CA: North Atlantic Books.

McGilchrist, I. (2012). *The Master and his Emissary: The Divided Brain in the Making of the Western World*. New Haven, CT and London: Yale University Press.

Mithen, S. (2005). *The Singing Neanderthals: The Origins of Music, Language, Mind, and Body*. Cambridge, MA: Harvard University Press.

Nietzsche, F. (1982). Prologue to 'Thus Spoke Zarathustra', in *The Portable Nietzsche* (Kauffman, W., trans., 1954). London: Penguin.

Norretranders, T. (1991). *The User Illusion: Cutting Consciousness Down to Size*. New York: Penguin Books.

Rogers, C. (1961). *On Becoming a Person: A Therapist's View of Psychotherapy*. London: Constable.

Schechner, R. (1988). *Performance Theory*. New York: Routledge.

Schechner, R. (1993). *The Future of Ritual: Writings on Culture and Performance*. New York: Routledge.

Sutton-Smith, B. (1997). *The Ambiguity of Play*. Cambridge, MA: Harvard University Press.

The Scotsman (2018). '25 of Spike Milligan's Wittiest Jokes and One Liners', April 16. Online. www.scotsman.com/read-this/25-of-spike-milligans-wittiest-jokes-and-one-liners/ (retrieved 29 June 2018).

Virgil (1997). *Aeneid*, Book 6 (J. Dryden, trans.). London: Penguin.

Wilde, O. (1988). *The Picture of Dorian Gray* (J. Bristow, ed.). Oxford: Oxford World Classics.

Winnicott, D.W. (1971). *Playing and Reality*. London: Penguin.

The middle: performance and dealing with the opposition

5

DEALING WITH THE OPPOSITION

The Shadow force of competitive edge

If you engage the Shadow forces of the psyche, man or woman, you can expect the unexpected. I hope by now themes are emerging for you, dear reader; how time changes when we enter the realm of the unconscious through play, spirituality, sports and sexuality. The power of play as a medium of peaceful and healthy expression. The hazards of sporting cultures as well as their promise and potentiality. All that in a world today that can be as dangerous as it ever was, but also pleasurable. This is about another experience that bends time – it is a spirit, it can play, and it likes to play.

What is it that makes a great athlete, a great actor or a great anybody? Nobody really knows for sure, or there would books and apps guaranteeing greatness. It has been said that in Hollywood there are three golden rules for success – the trouble is, no one knows what they are. Many have tried (sport psychology certainly has tried), but the single idea or revelation that beats all of the others hasn't arrived yet. The magic formula for guaranteed sporting greatness (or any greatness) remains elusive. This chapter is about an elusive subject, an 'X factor'. Those that have it are the kind of athlete or performer that people will pay to see.

One of Jung's central theoretical models was the archetype of the human 'Shadow'. This *terra incognito* may be the best place of all to discover the soul of the athlete.

Great actors and musicians also possess an 'X factor'. We all occasionally need some kind of 'factor', especially if we have to battle with something. Even the most diehard pacifists must sometimes fight against something, even if it is just a cold. A part of your physiology will always fight to stay alive even when the will to live has been lost. This middle section is about the fight and dealing with opponents, for men and for women. It can be an agonising process. It is essential for every successful agoniste. The Shadow appears to be a useful candidate to have by one's side in a fight, a compelling force and reality within us that appears to have a long track record of sometimes dark and evil crimes. Living out of sight, our dark side can erupt dramatically like a volcano. This force can also make for true sporting greatness.

In his book *The Vocation of Man* (1799), Johann Gottlieb Fichte offers this advice:

> I must, however, remind my reader that the "I" who speaks in the book is not the author himself, but it is his earnest wish that the reader should himself assume this character, and that he should not rest contented with a mere historical apprehension of what is here said, but really and truly, during reading, hold converse with himself, deliberate, draw conclusions, and form resolutions, like his representative in the book, and, by his own labour and reflection, developed out of his own soul, and build up within himself, that mode of thought the mere picture of which is laid before him in the work.

This is a quixotic subject and if it is done right, you shall have to hold onto your hat!

I have discovered that if you speak to the Shadow, it speaks back. Sometimes it speaks to us all. The 2006 Football World Cup Final, against Italy, was French captain Zinedine Zidane's final match. Having put his team ahead with an audacious goal, the Italian team valiantly fought back and the game was drawn. International football's presiding body FIFA must have been thrilled it was all going so well. Any great athlete knows how to deliver at the right moment, and the stage was set. Zidane had to seize the prize, score a goal and break Italian hearts. At the perfect moment he so nearly succeeded, but for a marvellous save from the Italian goalkeeper Gianluigi Buffon. Many soccer fans recollect that Zidane then headbutted the Italian defender Marco Materazzi and had to leave the pitch in disgrace. That was his end and – worse – France went on to lose the match.

The world had witnessed Zidane's bewildering, self-destructive act of violence. While there have been many speculations as to why he did what he did, none have come from the Jungian world. The Shadow is a force to be taken seriously. In the Jungian frame, the counterpoint of the Shadow is the archetypal force of the Anima. This represents our inner fixer and healer, our nurturing spirit that leads us toward inner harmony and peace. This is a teleological archetype, in that it is nature's force of the inner feminine. Earlier chapters described the ancient power of the feminine in hunter societies; the mother was the supreme creative supreme deity.

Lesson one appears to be that the Shadow may defy the rules of convention at the worst of moments, like a visiting relative who shows up drunk and makes a scene. Mental hospitals used to be full of such people and cases. If the Shadow was only a negative force, we would do well to keep it hidden. However, there are grey areas in life, and the Shadow may be better described as residing in a location more grey than black and white.

At the time of writing this section it is Halloween in Los Angeles. The festival blends with the ancient Mexican tradition of the 'Day of the Dead' and sees many adults dressing up. Anyone can instantly become a skeleton, a gothic ghost, a serial killer. All ages and kinds of people dress up to represent ghastly, macabre visions of gore and horror, and we are all expected to participate and suspend our fears to join with the dead.

As it is with children playing in the park, it is only by suspending our literal sense that we give permission for Halloween to be fun and not disturbing. Mexican tradition suggests it is wise to give the dead gifts, so that they stay where they are. This is nothing new, of course; from pagans to pantheists some acknowledgement of the Shadow is represented in many rituals and holidays. Historically, the Greeks and Romans held festivals honouring the underworld and 'Saturnalia'. Before that, there was the Celtic festival of 'Samhain', at the end of October, when the divide between the living and the dead was relaxed. This was a time for Celtic farmers to bring cattle down from the pastures and kill them for winter. For our Animist ancestors it was all a kind of death, the move from light onto darkness and winter. As mentioned earlier, even the purpose and design of Stonehenge related to this theme.

Modern Halloween has many 'add-ons', such as pumpkins and candy consumption. In the US, children are a key feature of Halloween. Some still dress up and visit local houses at night (with their parents) for 'trick-or-treating'. It is a perfect time of the year to catch a shimmer of this elusive Shadow reaching out from somewhere deep in our souls.

It seems like the stage is set, and these are disturbing times for real. As I write this, my watch buzzes to alert me: 'New York terrorist mass murder atrocity unfolding'. What everyone represents in costume in Los Angeles is happening for real right now over in New York. A few days after writing, a terrible mass shooting at a church in Texas. This time the perpetrator massacred children and the congregation with relish. All this not long after America's worst mass shooting in Las Vegas.

Mass murder was not a regular occurrence during the America of the sixties or seventies, but it is now. In 2018, America is also experiencing an epidemic of homelessness. Yet, the stock market has been rising for a year. Many homeless appear to be mentally ill or suffering from addiction and are living the consequences. They now resemble the wealthier Halloween folk dressing up for fun. There are considerable tensions at the moment. This is a stage in the process of degeneration ancient alchemists would have called '*solutzio*'. Yesterday, I passed a man in the park who was unconscious in the bushes, with both his feet stuck up in the air; it was indeed a dissolute tableau. Some streets are lined entirely by homeless in tents or under plastic bags. Like a tectonic plate in motion, 'society' is changing and tensions and divisions are everywhere.

This can be true for an individual or a culture, the 'collective', but this chapter relates more to the personal Shadow than the collective. The manipulation of the collective Shadow was what happened in Nazi Germany in the 1930s. Shadow is the name given to this archetype because it is generally out of sight; perhaps we prefer it out of sight. As with emotions, the Shadow cannot be measured, but evidence of its presence is everywhere, especially if you know what you're looking for.

Is there anything positive to be gained by it? The link with the Shadow archetype and creativity has been explored by Stephen A. Diamond (1999) in his book *Anger, Madness, and the Daimonic: The Psychological Genesis of Violence, Evil and Creativity*. He suggests that the Shadow forces operating within us 'are acting upon us all of the time—and we, in turn, are interacting with them—whether we are aware of this fact or not' (1999, p. 105). The idea that we each have a dark side, or that we are in the presence of forces flowing inside, is, of course, not a new one. As early as the fifth century BC, the Zoroastrian religion recognised that we have a dark side that could be useful and hold meaning if we sought to understand it. We are still at a time in our evolution when these powers can destroy us if they remain ignored and misunderstood. In *Apology*, Plato quotes Socrates as saying at his trial, 'the unexamined life is not worth living'. What does all this mean in our sporting world?

When I was a trainee therapist I heard a lecturer say that 'a negative system was alive' within a client. It was a slightly uncomfortable image for me. I had never heard a description of our interior mind put quite that way. Indeed, I have heard it said that one is 'seduced by a mood', which alludes to some kind of compliance with something. Jung noted how a step forward in life often involved an inner bargain; 'if we do this, we will be able to do this'. Goals, desires, strivings and what we long for are all kinds of missions – some that we may never complete. They are all callings that we might not hear, or be able to hear, sometimes at our peril. Renowned Jungian scholar Robert Johnson (1991) has written an aptly titled book called *Owning your Own Shadow*. Especially applicable in the case of Zinedine Zidane, he warns that if we do not own our own Shadow, 'we are suddenly subject to explosions that have the power to overturn the product we have worked so hard to create' (1991, p. 49).

In general, the Shadow has a bad reputation. This uncontrolled presence in the psyche presents itself as a liability, not to be trusted. As Andrew Samuels wrote,

> In 1945 Jung gave a most direct and clear-cut definition of the Shadow: 'the thing a person has no wish to be.' In this simple statement is subsumed the many-sided and repeated references to the Shadow as the negative side of the personality, the sum of all unpleasant qualities one wants to hide, the inferior, the worthless and primitive side of man's nature, the other person in one, one's own dark side.
>
> *(1986a, p. 139)*

If the 'other person' described here is the sum of all our 'unpleasant and worthless qualities', then what do we do with them?

Freud believed that we automatically repress unwanted (but also wanted) desires and impulses. We send them down to an internal refuse bin called the 'unconscious'.

One of the main differences between Jung and Freud was over this issue. Jung did not see a bin – he saw other things. Jung believed the unconscious was an ineffable dimension, a largely unexplored and unknown place. He suggested our unconscious interior was more like an enormous universe housing distinct archetypal identities that want to reveal themselves; also crucial here, it houses identities we can enter into dialogue with if we want, and if we know how. More than that, rather than 'if only' or 'maybe', more assertive mindsets are required. Shakespeare's Richard III gives Hastings some bad news when Hastings has the temerity to even use the word 'if': '"If?" Thou protector of this damned strumpet, thou talks to me of "ifs"? Thou art a traitor – off with his head. Now by Saint Paul I swear I will not dine until I see the same' (*Richard III*, Act 3, Scene 4).

The Shadow acts assertively on occasions and knows what it wants. Shakespeare's Richard III was a perfect Shadow figure, full of menace and power. The Greek form of stage drama was resurrected by the booming society in Elizabethan London in the early 1600s. The rich language we see used by Shakespeare evolved from a densely populated and rich cultural melting pot on the brink of the Renaissance age. Skilful playwrights like Marlowe and Shakespeare created dramas that could hold all of the intrusive thoughts, the love, laughs, darkness and mystery of their world. Shakespeare's is a voice that time has not diminished. As with Dickens, his influence has increased thanks to a globally connected age. Some things do not die out. The real King Richard III is another such example; he was discovered under a carpark in Leicester, England, under the letter 'R', largely due to the work of one woman, Philippa Langley. She had a premonition and followed her intuition through.

This event defies rational understanding, and is a timely reminder that we are in the presence of powerful events and motions that defy rational explanations. Langley described her experience as she neared Richard III's grave, at the time completely undiscovered and unknown.

> I found myself drawn to this wall and, as I walked towards it, I was aware of the strange sensation. My heart was pounding and my mouth was dry – it was a feeling of raw excitement tinged with fear. As I got near the wall I had to stop, I felt so odd. I had goose-bumps, so much so that even in the sunshine I felt cold to my bones. And I knew in my innermost being that Richard's body lay here. Moreover I was certain that I was standing right on top of his grave.
>
> *(Langley and Jones, 2013, p. 4)*

Richard III is a remarkable character and was at the time Britain's only undiscovered monarch. She was sensitive to some kind of energetic source, like a Geiger counter. Current science cannot understand or explain this.

'Star Wars' is one of the greatest box office films of all time (20th Century Fox, dir. George Lucas). The main character, Darth Vader, is another force that lives on. In 2017, in the latest incarnation of the franchise, 'Star Wars: the Last Jedi',

Darth Vader is the Shadow figure, dressed all in black, with a black and white army. Jungian depth psychology can claim an unusual relationship with this phenomenonal film; seminal Jungian analyst and author Joseph Campbell played an important role in its production, helping George Lucas identify and locate the archetypes he wanted to convey. Campbell's book *The Hero with a Thousand Faces* has been a classic text for scriptwriters and Jungian scholars ever since. These are ancient archetypal themes, St George and the Dragon being one, only this time with lasers and spacecraft, human themes of duality we are all born into. Diamond's suggestion that forces are acting all of the time may indicate that they have been with us for all time.

Like day and night, black and white, we live in a world of many opposites. These forces we can acknowledge or deny, or they may be hidden, but regardless, they are there. By 1917, Freud had good cause to believe his theory – that we were only two competing drives, sex and aggression – was right. By that time, many millions of young men had been killed senselessly in the fields of France. It is also by no means disrespectful to suggest that during such a bleak time people must have wanted to have a lot of sex as well. This is a legacy for the nascent school of psychoanalysis and psychology in that the earliest pillars of the community were introduced to a bewildering scale of of killing and carnage, unique to that time. It does seem that evil forces were at work when so many millions of innocent people died so horrifically; World War I was a dark time of suffering and cruelty worldwide.

The Rolling Stones song 'Sympathy for the Devil' refers to the devil, Lucifer, as in need of restraint. Is that what our Shadow is, a kind of devil? In her book *Shadow and Evil in Fairy Tales*, Marie-Louise von Franz explored the the Shadow in depth, illuminating how the archetype is represented in common mythology and folk tales.

> In Jungian psychology, we generally define the Shadow as the personification of certain aspects of the unconscious personality, which could be added to the ego complex, but which, for various reasons, are not. We may therefore say that the Shadow is the dark, un-lived, and repressed side of the ego complex, but this is only partly true.
>
> *(1974, p. 3)*

In order to get a better impression our research may have to search in the dark for a while.

Factors such as experience cannot yet be taught by an app or with a theory alone. In 'doing' we have to meet our less-formed, less-clever side in order to develop, learn and make progress. It is a paradox, and one for the athlete not to repress or avoid. The old task, to 'know thyself', remains an imperative and the way forward. It was imprinted on top the Parthenon, and is as true now as it was then. What may also be the same for many sportspeople is the lack of a figure to explain and help one understand this motto.

Shadows disappear when we shine light on them. Here, again, I must confess that one could write volumes on the Shadow. Nevertheless, in this case, we shall make a little go a long way. Whatever your mission, dear reader, my best tip for you is that you can expect hidden benefits and significant steps forward in life from the least likely of places. It is axiomatic to suggest that professional athletes are likely to be found, statistically speaking, at the edge of the 'bell end curve'. That means that the distinguishing features of excellence for a public performer will often be less obvious and even obscure. This, then, is a good place to look for our athletes soul. Not many search here, but our science of depth psychology can try and look in the less-likely places.

Jung personally upset Freud over a number of matters. Freud could not forgive Jung for (as he saw it) jeopardising his nascent science of psychoanalysis with Eastern spiritual or religious interest, and his less-empirical perspectives. Lord only knows what Freud would have made of this mentoring by Jung:

> Anyone who wants to know the human psyche will learn next to nothing from experimental psychology. He would be better advised to abandon exact science, put away his scholar's gown, bid farewell to his study, and wander with human heart through the world. There, in the horrors of prisons, lunatic asylums and hospitals, in drab suburban pubs, in brothels and gambling-halls, in the salons of the elegant, the Stock Exchanges, socialist meetings, churches, revivalist gatherings and ecstatic sects, through love and hate, through the experience of passion in every form in his own body, he would reap richer stores of knowledge than text-books a foot thick could give him, and he will know how to doctor the sick with a real knowledge of the human soul.
>
> *(Jung, 1916)*

University Admission departments of course do not tend to share the above when you join the university clinical programme. My university motto is 'Animae Collindae', which translates from Latin as 'tend to the soul of the world'. So perhaps the first place to look for the Shadow is in everyday life! A friend of mine who is a perfect gentleman shared with me recently his concern regarding his occasional impulses: he no longer felt compassion for some people and wanted to strike out at random objects. He was bothered by the impulse and thought he was going mad. We all have to manage, it seems, a more primitive, subterranean voice within us that cares not for social convention. Freud called the internal manager of this voice the 'superego'. For Freud, this represented the repressive mechanism in our psyche giving us impulse controls necessary to live in society. If the superego fails, you might go to prison or the mental ward, or – worse – be consigned to a slow death on the streets in the city.

Jung was different and saw other things than the wastebin Freud imagined. He heard voices, saw identities, universal archetypal forms seeking to emerge and be realised through us. Each had their accompanying potentials and desires, some good, and some not good. For an athlete who wants to make progress there will remain the ethical 'deal'. This means a devotion to the sporting gods and a capacity to practise restraint. Devotion to any calling means a case of sacrifice (or investment, if you prefer). Some criminals can be so devoted to crime that they sacrifice normal things as a result. Devotion doesn't always mean to something good. However, I have not known an academy player make it to professional grade level without being a 'devotee'. Character is normally revealed by what someone can resist, rather than what they cannot restrain themselves over. The Shadow can test these capacities, and perhaps it should.

So what does the Shadow want or not want? 'The Devil finds work for idle hands to do' is an old proverb which most of us may recognise as having some kind of collective archetypal truth. In the future societies of the West, there may be very little labour to actually do. In which case, considering the above proverb, we might have some trouble. The collective Shadow can be inflamed and seduced by poverty or oppression, as Hitler so well understood. His dramatic oratorical outbursts of indignation seduced a nation. Von Franz suggested that 'in some aspects, the Shadow can also consist of collective factors that stem from a source outside the individual's personal life' (1964, p. 174). In terms of the inner life of individuals, most people appear more emotionally alive when they have some positive direction or path to follow, something that holds meaning inside. Individuals or even societies with no path, no life structure, can fall into the bad-strife kind of life that Hesiod described for a number of reasons.

Conviction is another term for imprisonment, and commitment is what happens when you get sectioned under the Mental Health Act. As with the inner animal relationships described earlier, we are in the midst of a significant force within us that need not logically make sense, be widely appreciated or understood. Jungian psychological approaches are deeper and generally more comfortable dealing with the idea of 'forces'. They do exist in the world, externally and internally. Many of them are greater than we can control. Many victims of internal devastations such as addiction will testify an important principle, often bitterly learned: when you experience a sensation that feels good, it does not mean that good things are happening. Conversely, when bad things happen, they can be a precursor to personal growth, and to very good things happening as a result.

As I type this in December 2017, my university in California Pacifica is close to being burned down in one of the biggest fires in California's history. California's plains remind us that we are still subject to nature's forces. What is on the surface is not what is necessarily beneath an experience. Last year, California received much-needed rain and the drought was relieved. A lot of rich grasslands grew as a result, the same ones that are rich fodder for flames and are catching fire now. But out of this we can be in awe of the great heroism of the firefighters and volunteers. They give their all. The spirit of living with your heart and working together and helping each other was part of the message of all the Axial Age thinkers.

Some politicians intuitively know how to exploit our needs for togetherness and unity with seductive incantations. Adolf Hitler valued and appreciated core virtues such as loyalty, yet it didn't prevent him from being pathologically evil. Jung wrote, 'Unless he stands firmly on his own feet, the so-called objective values profit him nothing, since they then only serve as a substitute for character and so helped to suppress his individuality' (1957, p. 67).

We cannot hope to find the soul of the athlete by describing the core ethical values and virtues in themselves, nor the negative ones. The Shadow force often has other imperatives. It can reside in groups, in the worst cases being the kind of mobs that Hitler recruited. Proteus was the Greek God of transformation and morphing into other things. It is the canon of the sociopath and social chameleon. Individuality in the West is an important priority and also a recognised human goal in Jungian psychology. The term Jung used was 'individuation'. To fully comprehend this term, it is helpful to remember that at the heart of the word remains the mathematical idea of indivisibility, and is the Jungian goal of separating oneself from a dependency on the collective. This means, for example, not just 'going along' with something because someone else thinks it is good idea, but having your own. Just like gold, individuation is its own thing, not an amalgamation that can be divided.

The Shadow is an archetype that will devour itself and/or others, as demonstrated by Hitler and Stalin. The ubiquitous presence of the Shadow in fairytales indicates the centrality of this archetype from an early age and throughout our lives. Freud wrote about children but didn't really work with any. Melanie Klein was the first psychologist to truly work with babies and young souls. Klein noticed how babies get so angry they have a need to project outwards the pain they feel inside. This can create further tensions that might need to be released and relieved by directing them into others. Stalin (Conquest, 1991, p. 10) and Hitler (Diver, 2005) both had fathers who beat them, cultivating a buried rage they would eventually project onto the world.

Klein wrote about this subject and how negative impulses become dis- and re-located.

> And if the conscience and morality within us are not the representatives of our love, they become vehicles of our hate; if they are deluded, they dupe us in turn. They may then, for example, mislead us into the complacent search for badness, partly indeed as a defence against self deception. But since we find evil more readily in others than ourselves, this is no cure for self deception. All these dangerous and difficulties tend to turn us away from the problems of goodness within, for fear of disillusionment, and the helplessness and insecurity that then threaten us.
>
> *(1964, p. 51)*

This means we have to find a way to integrate our natural forces – good and bad – and must somehow face and meet our inner problems without becoming like Icarus in the myth, too high or too low, against his father's warnings. We began our last chapter with the original academic, Plato, and his often attributed statement about the soul that gets revealed by play. Here we can give him a more certain citation. Here he describes his sense of the inner character of Eros, the cherubic archer who sits and chooses lovers from afar. Eros is the stereotypical embodiment of the playful erotic spirit of falling in love. Plato describes his view of the sweet cherub; 'First, he (Eros) is always poor, nor is he delicate and lovely as many imagine him, but harsh and squalid, barefoot and homeless, sleeping on the naked earth, in the streets and doorways beneath the open sky, and like his mother (Penia) he is always in want' (Symposium 203c.) It is not the sweet cherub after all, but a poor hungry wretch.

Meet your inferior relative

Someone often left in the shade when the origins of depth psychology are considered is Austrian-Hungarian pioneer Alfred Adler. Jung, Freud and Adler were regarded as the three earliest depth psychologists at the turn of the twentieth century. Cardinal Jungian author James Hillman cites him as a part of the 'triumvirate who originated the field' (1983, p. 95). Adler made his best-known contribution in the recognition of how birth order influences personality – quite a revolution at the time. These were the very first psychoanalysts in the world who studied and developed models of the unconscious as a science and also a source of medical healing. Jung was effusive about Adler; 'no one who is interested in "psychoanalysis" and who wants to get anything like an adequate survey of the whole field of modern psychiatry should fail to study the writings of (Alfred) Adler. He will find them extremely stimulating' (Jung, 1930).

At the turn of the last century, deeper understandings relating to sickness in the mind were evolving and entering into mainstream medical science fields. Adler didn't use the term Shadow, but like Plato he didn't offer a flattering perspective on the soul either. In 1917, Adler published a work called *A Study of Organ Inferiority and its Psychical Compensation: A Contribution to Clinical Medicine.* The term Adler gave to his theory was 'organ inferiority'. He suggested that we are naturally inclined to feel and operate from a position of literal inferiority. What we do about that fearful position is compensate with our longings, ambitions and designs. Creativity is one of the most positive ways we can do so. All of the 'triumvirate' agreed creativity was a very healthy way to sublimate and deal with our neurotic troubles. Adler supported his theories with many examples of famous people who had compensated for some kind of physical inferiority with great achievements.

Adler believed inferiority was a central component of the human condition, not a secondary part of our reality. To him this was an all-encompassing influence upon us. He said: 'The inferior organ constantly endeavours to make a very special demand upon the interest and the imagination' (1917, p. 11). Adler was also the first to talk about deep-seated 'feelings' and longings, and how they push and pull us. Considering our earlier chapters, it is not difficult to imagine how our ancestors required perceptions that were tilted towards the negative in order to survive. 'Curiosity killed the cat' goes the saying, and many a human will have discovered a twig breaking to be a big lion whose eyes then lighted upon them. It may have been better to keep clear and come back to eat another day. This must have been an ancient truth for all beings attached to self preservation.

In the bull-and-bear markets of the business world ancient mythological and archetypal figures are currently big business. Even in the computer age non-digital characters and archetypal presences remain. The book and film series *The Lord of the Rings* by J.R.R. Tolkien has gone on to have global success, beyond even the author's imagination. Along with other such as the *Harry Potter* series, its success illustrates how mythological characters and themes of old still hold a deep appeal. The names of the characters may change, but their essence and archetypal identities remain consistent. One of the central characters in *The Lord of the Rings* is Gollum, who covets his 'precious' in a Shadow world. Earlier, we described the animal helper Toto in *The Wizard of Oz*. After Dorothy finishes her ordeal, she discovers that the scary wizard behind the angry voice is just a tiny little man. Adler didn't suggest that we are all Gollum deep down, but he did suggest we must strive to not become so.

In 1990, American author and writer on masculine psychology Robert Bly published *Iron John*, his depth-psychological interpretations of a Brothers Grimm fairy tale by the same name. The story, he says, predates Christianity by 'a thousand years or so' (1990, p. 8) A royal child steals a key from his mother to unlock a large, hairy imprisoned man imprisoned in his father's castle, 'Iron John', who has possession of a 'golden ball'. For the boy, stealing the key is highly significant as it is an emblem for the boy separating from the mother, something she would not initially encourage. I can testify that the world at large really functions like this. Iron John befriends the boy and takes him away from the castle on his back, on a journey of self-discovery and manhood.

Iron John is a Shadow kind of figure, with rusty hair, rags and an earthy aura. At the same time he is portrayed as a trustworthy and positive influence for the boy. Bly suggests 'The Wild Man is not opposed to civilisation; but he's not completely contained by it either. The ethical superstructure of popular Christianity does not support the Wild Man, though there is some suggestion Christ did. At the beginning of his ministry, a hairy John, after all, baptised him' (1990, p. 8). Our inner guides and healers might not in reality look like what we might expect. A man I knew who had over 30 years of sobriety from alcohol said of his experience as a member of Alcoholics Anonymous that 'It was the sinners that got me well, not the saints'. Our teachers may come in many forms and guises.

Adler also recognised that our past as a species was vulnerable and exposed compared to now. We had few of the material protections and powers we take for granted today. As a result of our inferior position he suggested humans, therefore, had to 'strive for superiority'. This is not so much superiority in the material-world sense, although that can be included. He meant superiority more in terms of an interior, energetic desire to rise above our primitive inferior side and navigate our lives better. Adler believed that 'The realisation of somatic inferiority by the individual becomes a permanent impelling force for the development of the psyche'

(1917, p. 1). This means that transcendence over our complexes will start with the complexes themselves, and our relationship to them. Many addicts lose their lives trying to get high, after all.

Inferiority might seem on the surface a lousy place for a public performer to start from. Surely athletes have to be confident, and want to be positive, captured by bright dreams and visions of glory! However, evidence and experience suggest that we can only achieve or realise ourselves as the result of a relationship with our inferior, less-formed side. We can convert our vulnerabilities and tensions into strength, as the Greeks showed with the Olympics.

Klein recounts her interaction with an opera singer striving for superiority: 'In addition to the material, sexual and inquisitive satisfaction is her voice brings her, the *superiority* of her voice over others has become her chosen way of feeling secure, and is her insurance against the fear she of evil in herself leading to helpless isolation and the sense of death' (1964, p. 37). Adler's 'inferior' voice can have a powerful protector role, an archetypal force that gives her some status to compensate for the fear of having none. It seems like a good deal.

Perhaps it would be fitting here to share my own experience as a young theatre actor in England. All of a sudden, I was surrounded by actors at the top of their field. Scary! I was fearful and nervous from the beginning. The stage and spotlight partly terrified me, and partly inspired me. I had a passion to be an actor (and probably more than to act), so I committed to learning my lines inside-out and back to front. As a way to defend against my inner complexes, I can testify this was a very effective strategy. Learning lines is like learning technique for a sportsman. Eventually, because of my fears, paradoxically I developed a professional reputation as disciplined and trustworthy. The word 'disciple' relates to devotion and an intention to give all to the cause.

Everything so far suggests we can aspire for the heights and the gold medal, but this success can will only evolve in relationship with our inferior voice. Particularly if we want to create great things, we must remember an old clinical truth that 'negative systems resist change'. Inner lack of discipline or deficiencies can exist for many reasons. Clinical experience often reveals that they, in fact, have distinct reasons for being in place, in spite of what we feel about them. It was said that the Buddha Gotama Siddhartha recognised he could not entirely get rid of the inner voice of doubt, the devil the Buddhists call 'Mara'.

In the last chapter on play, we cited Jung as suggesting that another permanent impelling force and identity also searches for wholeness – the child. Like Jung (but less like Freud), Adler prescribed self-dialogue and a bolder connection to our inner nature as a way to feel more whole. Rather than repressing or denying the Shadow forces, the Buddha welcomed the Shadow in, and literally offered Mara a cup of tea. The Western Christian tradition has generally encouraged people to 'cast the devil out' and become 'pure'. Other traditions such as the Jewish faith, Buddhism and the Muslim faith appear to suggest other approaches.

It is true that we must stumble through the dark in life sometimes, although not necessarily alone. In *Living with the Devil*, Stephen Batchelor suggests 'the devil is a way of talking about that which blocks ones path in life, frustrates one's aspirations, makes one feel stuck, hemmed in, obstructed . . . The Greek *diabolos* means "one who throws something across the path"' (2005, p. 17). It is often said that the highest level sport consists of immensely psychological processes, and an athlete knows how not to let the negatives get in the way of their performance or expression, and battle ahead.

In *What Sport Tells Us About Life*, Ed Smith (2009) covers the subject of self-doubt for a professional athlete.

> Anxiety is one of the obstacles. Worrying was one of the obstacles. Thinking too far ahead of yourself is one of the obstacles. Not playing in the now is one of the obstacles. Failing to focus simply on and only on the job in hand is one of the obstacles. Getting sport out of proportion is one of the obstacles. Believing your life and your struggle to be disproportionately important is one of the obstacles. Dreading failure is one of the obstacles. Now you are thinking like a player again. That is usually the beginning of a return to form.
>
> *(2009, p. 24)*

As a matter of urgency, it seems athletes are presented with so many challenges to the psyche and spirit. Most spiritual traditions seek to dull this inner questioning mind that can never settle.

It is our choice how we do this, but the challenge remains for us all. The good news appears to be that we can make profitable use of this Shadow power. We just have to use our imagination. In *Living with the Devil*, Batchelor suggests, 'Without the devil to obstruct it, one could not create a path. The path is kept open by overcoming the hindrances that prevent freedom of movement along it. If Mara did not get in the way, there would be nothing to give us the purchase we need to prepare ourselves out of a crisis' (2004, p. 122).

Stephen Batchelor is not referring to sport here, but again, it seems special benefits are on offer if we apply this idea to sport. The Shadow here appears to give us an important capacity – one we can channel into our performances – the capacity to deal with a crisis and live naturally in our element within a crisis. Sport is one big crisis. This is why the necessary quality of urgency is so often needed in a team. The lack of the Shadow is obvious. Professional sports clubs tend to prefer athletes who can respond to a crisis. It is a performer's meat and drink. Watching a skilled athlete transcend chaos is to witness a kind of ancient poetry in motion. The Shadow may get the most publicity when it does bad things, but what about a positive side? Is there one?

The positive path for our Shadow worker

Are we narrowing in on the identity of the Shadow? Maybe, but a bit like UFO seekers today, we don't have a craft or anything physical yet, just snapshots. So no, not really, not just yet. This is a quixotic element, still not yet in the open for us to see.

Happily, Jungian depth methodologies have a rich palate of approaches to this problem and ask questions in different ways.

What if this Shadow dance partner just wants to step on our feet? Is this Shadow Darth Vader? Richard III? Whitman, all the other mass killers since then? If so, then thanks very much for the offer but we will pass. Hillman makes the point directly; 'how can we discern whether these images are evil tempters or guardians? How do we know whether they mean well with us or would possess us?' (1983, p. 75). What exactly are we looking to encourage or develop here?

In clinical settings, I have noticed, that people often respond better when I have shown a positive approach or some appreciation. I see the Shadow energy but I don't see a devil in sports. Let us look with a more therapeutic eye at this wilder side we all carry around – or underneath, as Freud might have preferred. Hillman reminds us of an ancient truth; 'We find Gods amid our obstinate "demonic" psychic problems, if we look with a critically imagining eye' (1983, p. 77). Let's do exactly that and examine this troublesome part of us we cannot completely get rid of. So far, we have compiled the picture of a dark raven – a negative force, a primitive animal devil with an inferred idea by the author that there are fringe creative sporting benefits to be had.

Perhaps, in order to be who we are, we as a species have learned a dubious kind of denial, an ability to view ourselves as separate and 'above' the animal kingdom even when of course we remain a part of it ourselves. We hear people castigate those they hate, labelling them 'animals', as if no longer animals themselves. It appears to be the same for most of us with our Shadow. Working with this element is a challenge and mission every athlete has to accept. The visiting 'in-law', the relative who is just out of prison and who drinks too much. We have to find work for this shady uncle! The good news is that here is your secret Shadow weapon, one that also presents us with an opportunity to grow as a person.

Diamond cites Jung's perspectives on this matter: 'For Jung, the "Shadow" should never be mistaken and dismissed as merely evil or "daemonic", it has positive potentialities too' (1999, p. 96). Look how important sport is for people; try to walk on the court during a Los Angeles Lakers basketball game and see what happens. Elite professional sports are an important theatre of awe, intertwined with painful and intense personal battles played out before us. Like drama and music, followers develop an interest in the personality of the athlete and 'support' him or her. Modern 'stars' and 'legends' are the modern kind of pantheon now growing all of the time. Gods in Greek culture did not have to answer for their consequences. Modern stars are also forgiven their foibles, inside a sports team and out. Zidane is one such example; this is the logos of sport. Would great hunters of the past be forgiven?

Shared expressions held special meaning for Adler and Jung. They both appreciated that communal experiences resonate from deeply within the soul and are also vital human expressions. They recognised that powerful possibilities for personal transformation take place on these occasions. Earlier, we mentioned how the shared experience of music held profound meaning for humans and was likely to have predated verbal language. Shared experiences do appear to recreate ancient human patterns and behaviours, providing a platform for all kinds of rituals, ecstasies and reveries. This naturally must include sports arenas and teams. Adler called this ideal for humans the 'Gemeinschaftsgefühl', which is translated as a form of 'community feeling'. Even today the supporters of a professional club generally represent the lifeblood embodied within the community. It is a positive expression of the collective that has real effects on a community.

This is an authentic picture. This is why the 'dark side' is given a special place in so many religions – because it is regarded as the real you! And, therefore, closer to God. For an athlete this means a kind of faith, giving one's best when things do not work out, continuing to fight, to strike and find drive when you feel like it the least and are at your worst. Joseph Campbell famously said that 'where you stumble, there you will find gold' (1988). We have to meet ourselves at this time of stumbling. New discoveries can propel a life forward while we are under duress. If we have the right support, that is. The ancient alchemists sought to discover how the properties of the physical, external world could represent this recognised internal passage of transformation. How to make gold out of base metals is one aspiration of psychotherapy – at least bronze, if not gold (just not lead). Athletes don't necessarily need psychotherapy, but they do need skills to be able to transform their anxieties and negative systems within, and transcend them.

A drama lecturer once suggested during a rehearsal that 'we wouldn't be doing this if we weren't all a bit mad'. As he said it, a part deep inside of me was thrilled and had to gleefully agree; like a naughty schoolboy I felt I had arrived at a class I truly wanted to be in. It was a romantic idea, one that might naturally appeal to the 'angry young man' that I was. The Shadow can be an ambitious, rebellious spirit within that doesn't mind being called a 'bit mad'. After the session I told the director that indeed 'I am definitely a bit mad'. He laughed, slightly uncomfortably, I noticed! When embodied, the Shadow drives forward, tending not to seek introspection or self-analysis. Perhaps restrained by a life underground, the Shadow specialises in explosions of passion. In soccer, I have witnessed bursts of intensity and magic that propel a game and a career forward.

The greatest engine ever made – that used for the Apollo moon missions – still needed a spark to get it going. Apollo is a great choice of name for the epitome of science. Anger is not so calculated, but it can be one kind of alchemical spark that ignites athletes or teams into positive actions. In teams it can become an irresistible force and catalyst for change. It is a broad emotion and a form of passion. I once had to present a psychology session in a small soccer changing room because of a mix-up. I was annoyed as I couldn't use images I had carefully prepared for the session. I only had a small dry-wipe board and, as they say in America, 'I was pissed'. I thought it would be a disaster, but no. After the session I was conscious of how well it had gone. I had expressed myself assertively and with clarity and drive. The session had what I seek – energy and life. If we don't have that chemical spark, we might as well be studying Sudoku. Material shortfalls had not cost the quality of the session; in fact, the change of location helped realise it.

A capacity to express anger appropriately can be the hallmark of emotional strength and professional team sports. I have seen much good come from the use of appropriate expressions of anger. Personally, until psychology and sports came later in life I had no real grasp of the idea that anger could be positive. After all, the vicar was supposed to be a paradigm and was always so peaceful looking. My father was a war veteran, and internalised anger sometimes frightened me. I remain compassionate, but Hitler had that effect on a lot of people back then. I am grateful he never vented his Shadow on me. Nevertheless, I had always connected anger with fear and was uncomfortable around the expression of it. Sports environments should never discourage the expression of emotion; it is something to be trusted in, and not the reverse.

Ever since the soccer changing room incident I always embrace the unexpected when working in a sports club – and make a point of it. Someone walking in on a class, something breaking, going wrong, I love it – it is sporting life. Dealing with it well is the reward you get for attaining a capacity to be present and respond well to uncertainty. I mentioned earlier how emotional anger was characterised by a lack of calculation. As a result, increased wishes to measure coaching in the future will perhaps seek to discourage the expression of emotions in coaching relationships, which would be a mistake. Emotions are something that an increasingly left-brain-dominant culture may want to do without in many subtle ways. It would be a mistake and you can bet clubs will have to find a way around it.

Much of the social good in terms of civil rights in the past was created by people who had enough and said the dangerous word: 'no'. The genius of Martin Luther King helped develop a nation with his rejection of modern, subtle forms of racism and slavery. His passion and conviction made him a captivating orator and great leader of people. The Shadow need not be inspired by bad causes. It is an act of assertion, an act of making change in the world. In army circles there is a term for this type of person; it is recognised as a quality called 'healthy dissent'.

This is the quality of not just 'taking it', but being able to question things and desiring to make a change. But it is a fine balance; disruptive elements in a group feel very different. Anger of course can result in bad things happening, but bad intentions are not at the heart of this force. Rage is the truly negative emotion. That is when we become 'psychotic' and don't know what we are doing. It is not good for sports as we are no longer self-contained. In my experience people get angry in professional sports and anger is sometimes a critical emotion for change, but only when restrained.

Gold is serious business. The Californian Klondike gold rush in 1896 was an amazing social experiment. In the tradition of Hesiod, America for the first time invited anyone to just 'go out there and get it!' One can never imagine this condition in a territory owned by a king. Today it is difficult to see how it could ever be repeated. Those times illustrated how this prize of gold generated intense slow-burning fires of passion and endurance. Men and women underwent many privations and ordeals of misery, suffering and danger. This was not of course a public demonstration of heroism or self sacrifice. Greed is the other quality inspired by gold. As we know in the Klondike and every other gold rush, the vast majority lost out.

King Midas is the best-known Greek myth relating to the lust for gold, which ended in misery. By one account he turned his daughter into gold by mistake and eventually starved to death. For all the beauty of gold, it has a dark side, so this seems a promising world to locate the Shadow. Gold is everywhere in sports. Soccer fans know the World Cup trophy is golden, depicting the goddess of victory, Nike. Each year soccer players compete for the FIFA *Ballon d'Or*, or golden ball. Gold has become in recent years a euphemism for sexual delight. Gold cannot be reduced as a material reduced into anything else, so for alchemists it symbolises the source and form of the universe itself. In the Jungian world we call this the *prima materia*, something Socrates and Plato both sought to understand.

Originally the ultimate Olympic prize and award were just laurels. The influence of commerce soon meant that athletes were paid huge sums, but this was not always the case. The reward was not gold, but the lure for the Shadow worked. Something else proved to be enough to satisfy the drive of the Shadow. 'Kleos', the Greek concept of sporting fame, arose. Gold was the prize and it seems it was enough. The Shadow is more than just gold. In his book *Inner Gold*, Robert Johnson describes the less-obvious positive aspect of our Shadow. This is not often explored in psychology so, in the way of this book, we shall seek to do exactly that. Few have written more about the Shadow than Robert Johnson.

Johnson suggests most of us project this positive Shadow quality outwards rather than for ourselves. Unlike the Kleinian anguish and pain, this is a positive projection, heaping adoration on the recipient. Sports athletes are significant commercial assets. Agents and shirt sponsors are happy for them to be known as 'stars' and 'legends'. Sports stars are by their nature always coming and going. However, we still bestow 'deification' in the same way we did in Greece. Heroes and heroines are portrayed in light as if they were religious symbols with haloes. As Johnson points out, 'The first inkling of this is when the others person appears to be luminous, that he (or she) glows in the dark' (2008, p. 4). The soccer player David Beckham eventually became known by the name 'golden balls'. We should not forget Jung's earlier reference to 'Helios' and how the common person is raised up into golden light. Our ancestors believed the Sun was our maker, and they were right.

We all have to learn how to operate within a psychic framework and if we slip, like Zidane, we may lose. But as a process gets more developed, in a game or career, those challenges can intensify. They do not get easier. I let young players know that they have a problem to tackle. The more successful they become, the more there will be reasons for anxiety. They get it. To some extent this can explain the logos, the reason, why Zidane did what he did. Tensions rise as we reach a climax; the edge becomes a finer balance and anyone can fall from there.

Zinadine Zidane is a great man with intelligence and a capacity to be a figure of huge respect and authority. He was also a great player who, with his charisma and skills, spread much joy for so many. His World Cup headbutt did not define him.

Recently, he resigned at a kind of pinnacle –after winning his third Champions League title, as the manager of the great soccer team Real Madrid.

There is also a big lesson to be learned here for any athlete. Hillman writes:

> With every increase of the spirit's heat, there needs to be a corresponding increase of the soul's capacity to contain it, to amplify within its inner sacral space. This space, this colourful and intricate carpet of the soul, its bordures and silks, is the vessel of the anima-nurturer, weaver, reflector. The *conjunctio*, here, is that contained spirit, this spirited, inspired containment.
>
> *(1983, p. 81)*

It is the *conjunctio* that must follow the *solutzio* stage of the alchemical process. This is the joining together of a soul, not a fractured representation.

An actress friend once told me she used to drink uncontrollably, and that for a time it was only acting professionally that kept her sober and happy. She said she had a 'feral' side to her character that she called 'kitty'. She said: 'If I don't work [as an actress], she scratches at my door a bit, and sometimes at me too, unfortunately.' For all of the world she described her inner daemon, 'kitty', as if it were a separate side of her that could physically attack and harm her. Jung declared that his inner guide Philemon had told him: 'thoughts are like animals in the forest' (1961, p. 183).

We cannot perhaps escape these thoughts or impulses but it seems we can ignore, repress or rationalise them away, like many do. But if you have digested the work thus far, you will know there is another more romantic alternative. Athletes can call on daemons, our animals inside. If we ask, they can become our workers and defenders. The Quakers (or Friends) have a rich tradition of having scientists, poets and artists in their ranks. One of the best poets I know of, Stanford Searl, writes this opening for his poem *Point Guard*:

> I loved being point guard
> for the Black River Presidents,
> our Vermont high school basketball team
> of slow white guys,
> because it helped me
> to be someone else.
> That other self
> played with some fury,
> passionate about tracking down loose balls,
> obsessed with defence and the team.
>
> *(Searl, 2016, p. 49)*

One of my few significant intuitions in life suggested 'if you call on your ancestors they will come to help you.' The Shadow can work for us; it wants fury, passion and obsession, as described in the poem above. If unemployed or ignored it may work against us. I was fortunate to play villains, which in theatre are often the most involved and interesting parts to play. Once, during a rehearsal, I overdid the anger and was going a bit mad. The unimpressed director chided me paternally with 'Drama is a controlled form, dear boy'. It was a lesson I had to learn. It is the containing boundaries that enable the magic of competition or play to exist.

These are the Apollonian traditions in a Dionysian world, another illustration of how the two gods must work together. As we saw in the last chapter, play happens within a frame and container. It is the sports and performance world that gives an athlete permission to let their 'dog off the lead', as I have told many soccer players in England. You cannot make bread without flour and water, and it appears you cannot harness the Shadow without conviction and commitment. Perhaps we can be romantic and say the Shadow is the yeast that makes the bread rise.

You can often see the lack of it in sports. But this is a passion, something of the heart is here, the same heart the great philosophers all called for in the Axial Age, the beginning phase of the evolution of consciousness. I understand that when I write 'give it your all', I know that means different things to different people, but we can clarify something here for our context of sport. James Hillman writes of a philosophy for living, but its relevance to sport is evident: 'authenticity is *in* the illusion, playing it, seeing through it from within as we play it, like an actor who sees through his mask can only see in this way' (1983, p. 39). It is a paradox that some of the most commanding public performers are not the most secure or confident people off-stage. As we described earlier, competitors can be compelled to technical excellence because of many fears and failings. But here he also mentions something else, a quality of suspension. The same suspension and essential component of play is here what enables the Shadow to do its work.

A university lecturer made the class laugh when she compelled us to 'celebrate your weirdness!'. This was such a funny idea and at the same time very wise. Much humour can be based on revealing the absurdities of life, faults and misunderstandings. The Greek word 'pathos' is also used to describe a form of humour. In particular, this is when the 'protagonist' suffers for foolishness or misfortune. It is also the root of 'pathological', when a human medial condition will result in suffering if help is not given. The Shadow and humour are related, a point made neatly by the longevity of the term 'gallows humour'. Hermes was the god that travelled between the underworld and the overworld. Comedy is another vehicle or container where we can see that dynamic in motion. Comics that achieve fame are often controversial and, like the court jester of medieval England, they tread a fine line; they have edge. Comedy is a performance and a shared experience. Like in sport, those with an edge are the ones we pay to see.

This edge is indeed a fine line. The god Kairos is the god of opportunity, the moment at which you can dodge as a performer, or take on. It is especially germane in sport. As depicted earlier, we see Kairos holding a set of scales in one hand, walking on a fine line. A good comic or actor knows all about this fine line. Good comics create tension; they have the power to make people shriek. The margin between comedy and terror is blurred on occasions. When a person 'goes too far' in life, bad things almost always seem to happen.

For an athlete a bad tackle might mean getting sent off the field for misconduct and getting a three-match ban. For someone in public, tackling someone like that might mean a spell in jail and the end of their dreams. Any athlete must build a kind of engine, one in their mind that can be a container for their passions, one that can house sparks, explosions and expressions of fire all housed within the frame of an athlete's body. An engine is a good metaphor because without the 'controlled form, dear boy', we aren't much different from the powerful racing car engines that always blow a gasket.

I was a child who underwent a baptism of trauma. It was my dreams, fantasies and ambitions that sustained me from entering a deep depression that I might never have climbed out of. Adler would appreciate that it was feelings of inferiority and pain that spawned any great ambitions on my part. When I was 19 years old, thanks to my wise older sister I gained employment as a stage crew member at the Chichester Festival Theatre in England. There I watched the greatest actors in the world go through their motions and I was inspired to 'make it'. My Shadow side, like the actress and her 'kitty', had located a spiritual home where it was prepared to be patient and follow a dream. Here, my Shadow could be expressed and directed instead of devouring me in self-directed anger.

I was very hungry for success and captivated by the prospect of being an actor. Being in the place felt like a kind of personal victory. To me it was a kind of school that was not at all like school. At the same time, I was a frightened and anxious orphaned child desperate to 'make it'; it all meant so much. When the Shadow is employed, it is prepared to be patient.

I have to repeat that: When the Shadow is employed, it is prepared to be patient.

When anyone sets themselves a goal in life they also commit to a journey, aiming for a destination. In acting rehearsals we would often begin by seeking out a character's 'super-objective'. This asks the question 'what does this person really want from life?' We can say for an athlete that the answer will be: the best time, the best team, the best you can be – 'striving for superiority', as Adler put it. Melanie Klein sheds light on why it was natural for me to be so ambitious, and yet so afraid.

> Whether or not constitutional differences exist in the strength of the acquisitive impulse in individuals, there can be no doubt that accentuation of the desire to take in, as a defence against disintegration within, is an important factor wherever greed is at all marked. The connection of greed and acquisitiveness with security is in any case evident.
>
> *(1964, p. 26)*

Call it greed if you will, but we can always demand more in sport. Adler would approve.

Research studies on trauma by sport psychologists in England recently produced some unexpected results. Collins and MacNamara (2012) discovered a correlation between past trauma and achievement. Their research indicated those athletes with traumatic experiences in their lives were more likely to succeed in sport. The reasons for this are not conclusive, but the study indicated that a difficult beginning in life does not mean a bad ending, especially if an athlete is able to integrate themself into a *supra family* (Burston, 2015). That means a set of individuals who recreate a family containing uncles and aunts, and parental and maternal figures in the guise of coaches and managers. Again, we see culture and structure play a huge role in the chances of anyone making it. Isolation, loneliness and a lack of direction is a danger for any animal or human.

Considering the above we can assume that early humans will have required some kind of mental protection against trauma – a mental shut-off valve if you will, but, unlike the ostrich, one that can respond and react. We all know life can bestow great pain upon the innocent and most vulnerable, even at the worst of times. That nature is not bound by fairness is an honest assessment. As the human psyche evolved through history we can imagine that the capacity to feel bonds of love and attachment also grew. The rough part of the deal is that as a result this must also correlate to our capacity to feel loss. Humans who cared always had to reconcile themselves with grief and loss, sometimes suspending painful emotions in order to carry on regardless.

For us to have survived as we have, it means we must have, in enough numbers, found a way to endure the emotional pain that happens in the world, a way essential for any agonistes, a way to pick ourselves up and carry on despite fear, pain and loss. We need something to live for. Consciousness itself was perhaps the response to this vulnerability. Even so, it meant the same then as it does today. It means a capacity to go back out and hunt another day, despite the empty plains, to plow the field regardless, even if last year's work was a waste of time because the crop failed. The Shadow knows how to be in the drama of the ever-moving world of sport, where the logos is chaos in motion. Nietzsche suggested, 'One must still have chaos in oneself to be able to give birth to a dancing star' (1982, p. 129).

Zeus energy

The Olympics were dedicated to the number-one Greek god, Zeus. Zeus was the archetypal supergod; we shall cover the supermother in the next chapter. The Greeks had a respect for the Shadow, male and female. We can be sure nothing much about the psyche got past them. They called the sort of energy needed to be an elite anybody 'Zeus energy'. 'The Greeks understood and praised positive male energy that has accepted authority. They called it Zeus energy, which encompasses intelligence, robust health, compassionate decisiveness, good will, generous leadership. Zeus energy is male authority accepted for the sake of the community' (Bly, 1990, p. 22). Speaking about the great spiritual figure Mahatma Ghandi, Jawaharlal Nehru, the first prime minister of India, stated: 'A leader or a man of action in a crisis almost always acts subconsciously and then thinks of the reasons for his action' (Nehru, 1981, p. 506).

Now, in the computerised twenty-first century, the role and place for this 'male authority' appears in danger of becoming redundant. The world of men is changing in the West. There are not so many jobs as there were, and those that remain have been changing. Computers are doing more and more of the work and there may be unpredictable implications set in motion. Like some endangered species, our energetic Shadow might have less and less space to roam. The Shadow exists as part of a relationship, and like all relationships this might decay or manifest if not tended to. Unfortunately, it may even turn nasty. The Shadow is a force that, if ignored, will turn inwards, amplifying the inner daemon of doubt, 'Mara'. We see constricted animals in zoos or cages exhibit stereotypical repetitive behaviours and patterns when they run out of space. Some psychiatric conditions also display these patterns, as we can see in modern illnesses such as OCD and anxiety disorders.

It's not new to suggest that we need to exercise in order to sublimate negative energy. If we can afford it, a lot of us expend our energy at gymnasiums, as was once the case in Greece. Nowadays they are not the houses of philosophical enquiry they once were, but that is changing; many athletes could benefit from philosophical or psycho-educational development in gyms. Socrates recommended internal enquiry as an essential, and a sense of humour too, no doubt. Let's suspend ourselves and imagine, what would a modern Socrates say? In 1982, Italy played Brazil in what has often been labelled the 'second-greatest game of all time'. Brazil has a rich soccer reputation as the Dionysian, Samba-playing dancing soccer elite of the world; Pele, a universal golden figure who helped establish this place, is much appreciated as Brazil's football ambassador.

However, in this 1982 contest, it was another legendary Brazilian, Socrates, who played a leading role. Socrates was a famous player as well as being a long-haired medical doctor, smoker, drinker and political radical who bravely spoke out publicly against his own military government. He was an archetypal Dionysian figure, like his hero Che Guevara. He was a great man and also a great philosopher. Brazil lost the match, and afterwards he said:

> To win is not the most important thing; football is an art and should be about showing creativity. If Vincent van Gogh and Edgar Degas had known the level of recognition they were going to have, they would not have done the same. You have to enjoy doing the art and not think 'will I win?'
>
> *(Socrates, 1982)*

His point about painting is well made for our purposes here. Self-conscious art is different from the free-flowing brush Van Gogh and Degas used. What came from their minds was an intuitive, free expression that may have been made a less-honest expression by anticipation of what might happen in the future. Steve Jobs, the founder of Apple, echoed all of our Axial Age philosophers when he made this plea to a group of students in Stanford: 'Your time is limited, so don't waste it living someone else's life. Don't be trapped by dogma – which is living with the results of other people's thinking. Don't let the noise of others' opinions drown out your own inner voice. And most important, have the courage to follow your heart and intuition' (Jobs, 2005).

Van Gogh was a tragic figure in his personal life, largely obscure, in poverty and misery, just like Plato's Eros. He was known to be emotionally troubled and often had to seek treatment. He was also passionate about his art. His character embodied the two tricky brothers: conviction and commitment. If we were looking at the Shadow with a judicial lens, then perhaps this might suggest a verdict of 'not guilty'. I can see that perhaps it was his Shadow that kept him alive to the world. It sustained him, propelled him long enough to paint for us the pictures he did. His passion for art may have kept him alive and may not have been any kind of negative force. He had a reason to live, and for that he was wealthy when compared to some.

Renowned cultural historian Gary Cross exposes some of the emotional and developmental consequences of this new age of instant gratification.

> It is an active force that has packaged and packed up pleasure into a thrill culture that the displaces refinement and sociotemporal ties. That thrill culture seems to defy all definitions of maturation and makes it very difficult to embrace a more thoughtful and responsible way of being. It has challenged the 'reality principle' of the ordered life promoted in Freud's notion of 'civilisation'.
>
> *(2008, p. 255)*

Written ten years ago, in this book represents important knowledge. All great competitors will see a cultural slide as an opportunity to profit. My advice to any athlete now would be this: if we are in an age where the capacity to concentrate is diminishing, then redouble your efforts at becoming strong, as this is your advantage. Make a study of difference by understanding what is the same.

The Shadow is not a guarantee of success but it appears to be a vital component of drive, happenings and sport passion. All the ingredients of the Shadow combine together, especially if we are conscious of this element and, like a good relative, stay in touch. Donald Kalshed refers to an Inuit carving of a man who looks like he is winking. 'So through the inward-looking eye of our Inuit sculpture we encounter the ineffable – the mysteries of the soul and spirit, intimations of the infinite and the eternal. This world is often potentiated by early trauma and so a complete story of trauma must include its perspectives' (2013, p. 8).

Both of the Socrates certainly were in touch with their Shadow forces. They were both swarthier types, and less bothered about their 'image'. Those Greeks who only valued surface beauty detested the hunchbacked Socrates for that reason alone. They were both 'people's men', connected to community issues and welfare. They were also both comparatively unrestrained figures, especially compared to today's honed and health-conscious athletes and scientists. Both Socrates had what actors sometimes call the 'force of personality'. It is when confidence meets character and commitment that we can enjoy a marvellous soccer player, personality or actor. They had another factor; both would have been good men to have in your corner in a fight. As we know, the life of an agoniste represents a kind of battle, inside and out. It is said that a soccer player must be a 'soldier and an artist.' The greatest of them all, Sir Winston Churchill, was a painter and soldier.

Zeus threw thunderbolts and was a source of energy and action. He was a symbol of anger, at times made mistakes and was a passionate lover. Zeus didn't have to answer for his mistakes, so he did not need restraint. He was not a predator devil and nor is the Shadow. However, the Shadow still needs some restraint; it is not Zeus. Character is what makes us all individual. James Hillman adds a crucial point for us: 'Dionysian consciousness understands the conflicts in our stories through dramatic tensions and not through conceptual opposites, we are composed of agonies not polarities' (1983, p. 40). That means we are never going to be black and white – that is the robot. We all possess our different small internal struggles that nature invites us over a lifetime to realise. And there Hillman uses that 'agony' word again.

For the rest of society it may be a struggle to realise any dream. We all carry our individual struggles. But for an athlete, the Shadow is an instinctual energetic archetypal force that lives through us, giving us every sign that we must encourage the expression of our 'agony' through sport and performance. We can all see its effects, faults and limitations as well as the positives if we look deep enough. The sporting world replicates and even relieves us with a human pattern we have come to express in sports. It is a kind of photographer's negative we can hold up to the light. We cannot see much of this Shadow, but when it is expressed it is always compelling to watch. Whether we shriek with horror, awe or joy, we speak with our unconscious, which is why the hold is what it is. I was in a restaurant today and a glass broke and everyone looked. This is perhaps why Zidane's headbutt was the cover image for *What Sport Teaches Us About Life* (Smith, 2009).

Sport is like life indeed. Our final image takes us back to our past, more mundane and primitive priorities, described earlier. Life is struggling amongst other struggling animals and plants, all striving to survive a wild world. This is a human instinct and archetype that seeks to be expressed. It has become submerged in our deeper senses and as a result it always appears to be pushing up for air. There is, we know, the unbridled side of the Shadow, the less restrained kind that gets in so much trouble. Do not expect heroism from it, it needs to be managed and supervised, trained by ethics and restrained if necessary! That is, if you are a disciple of sport. Human beings in the modern West are not accustomed to seeing themselves as inferior or primitive. Harari reminds us how the instinct of co-operation has been late coming for human evolution; we are still beginners. Look at all the wars in the world.

Post-match interview and analysis

So let us have a talk with the Shadow – if we are brave enough to ask it questions and not worry if it looks silly or not, in the spirit of the Shadow! In *Wisdom for the Soul*, John Naisbitt suggests that 'Intuition becomes increasingly valuable in the new information society precisely because there is so much data' (Naisbitt, 2006, p. 419). The intention here is to help this Shadow form express and reveal itself to us. Let us at this time remind ourselves of some of the characteristics we can discern.

1. Characteristics of the Shadow

    It is not all bad.

    It is often hidden or denied.

    It can be seen at Halloween and in public performances.

    It can exist within an individual as well as a group.

    There is an inferiority complex in the Shadow.

    It sees targets and goals and is hungry like Eros.

    It does not care for conventional rules or expectations.

    Unleashed in sports, it flows, is expressive and creative in the moment.

    It requires a price to be paid, and the individual might be that price.

    It has assertive capacities and moves forward.

    It can be projected onto an individual, group or even nation.

    It is a creative force, if only because it defies systems.

    It lives in every gender.

    It likes sex and aggression and crisis.

    It can be romantic; a dream can inspire it.

    It knows how to be in crisis.

    It will be patient if there is a defined target and hope of achieving it.

It is my belief that performers can call on this daemon and it will respond. By entering into a dialogue with it the Shadow identity twinkles, reciprocates and in turn does its magical work. Our creative side is a dormant sleeping friend for so many, and so often never called for. The Shadow responds; pleased, it will in turn inspire the curious to enter its libidinal chasms and create, play, give music and score great goals. In terms of sport, this is our secret weapon and winner, if we can understand, pay heed to and recruit it.

2. How do we inspire our sporting Shadow?

> **Call on it**. Like a Kundalini snake, it is coiled within until you tell it what you need.
>
> **Find it a prize**. Set it a target worth achieving (in a day, a match, a season, a year and so on).
>
> **Use anger**. Direct and channel it to assertiveness at these times. However, if unrestrained anger becomes rage.
>
> **Use paranoia**. Paint a bleak picture, a vision that will come true if you do not mobilise! This is a very productive way to initiate drive, assertion and force.
>
> **Have a point to prove**. A personal point can be useful; these can be the best, but remember that resentment is drinking poison and expecting someone else to die of it.
>
> **Keep it fed well**. Don't waste energy on trivial pursuits or the underworld of drugs and nightclubs.
>
> **Teach it**. The Shadow learns restraint throughout life; you need to teach it, speak to it and encourage it toward temperament.

3. What does the Shadow feel like? The embodiment of the Shadow

Drive.	Fire.
Passion.	Clashes.
Hunger.	Sparks.
Aggression.	Venom.
Assertion.	Finishing.
Movement.	Zest.
Stealth.	

Finishing off the Shadow

Sport psychology is a lonely profession on occasions. After a heavy defeat and a poor performance in an important competition it feels like an unusually lonely spot – for example, when someone from the visiting team asks, 'so what do you do then?' In a world where winning is so important, I have felt physically sick, nauseous at times, in defeat. My Shadow side feels, sees it as a kind of death. At times in a career you can feel that it is all over and you are finished. But, they say, that is the hero's journey. It is not just a game. In professional clubs, someone's job and mortgage are on the line.

Whatever it is, we have to live with it. So far, we have seen that the Shadow force constellates play, sex, love, all of the ecstasies and otherworldly experiences where the experience of time disappears. Like play, it is an ancient paradigm, greater than ourselves, living in our unconscious. To some extent, therefore, it transcends time. As we found with play and prayer, both activities engage the unconscious levels of the mind and thereby change the perception of time. The Shadow is a 'soldier artist' who thrives on dopamine, the acquiring neurotransmitter, and can live assertively in chaos.

The Shadow is to some extent a slave of the context it is born into. At times of war departing soldiers can be hailed a heroes, but soundly jeered as they return if the war turns out to be bad, as some GIs discovered when returning from Vietnam. Life is not fair and the Shadow does not make it so. Either way, it is greater than circumstance. Van Gogh lived out of the public limelight, tormented and obscure, in pain and alone. In 1990, his 'Portrait of Dr. Gachet' sold for $82,500,000, and he remains one of the greatest artists of all time. The Shadow does not mean cash and prizes. Nature has not left us its legacy in buildings, armies or even hospitals. However, nature has left us a residue, so to speak. Our past experiences as a species have somehow remained, encoded within us. Nature has bestowed upon us intellect and logos, but left its trust in the Shadow.

It is not a redundant force any more than food in a freezer is redundant. Shadow energy remains an active part of day-to-day life. What gets you up in the morning? If you shrug your shoulders at that then maybe you need space for your Shadow to thaw and roam a little. Our focus here is the Shadow in sport but, naturally, it has a role in day-to-day life – or *can* do, if we are in relation with it.

If all hell breaks loose, our rational perspectives and analytical observations may lose some currency on earth. Thoughtful and reflective capacities might even be liabilities. Ask the residents who went through the 1994 Northridge earthquake in California. Life can turn on a sixpence. As I write, my university is close to being burned down by fire. And now as I edit soon after, much of Malibu near here has been consumed by fire. For all of our medicines, policemen, therapies, hospitals and science we humans might one day be reduced to an Adlerian 'inferior organ' again, anxiously scrabbling for something safe to drink. Parents can get really mean with others when it comes to protecting or just feeding their children. The Shadow is capable of bad acts but that does not define this force. If the next Tsunami hits, or the nuclear button is pressed, those that remain may re-discover why nature bestowed its trust in our Shadow.

It was the great Greek genius to realise this instinctual force and give it new life in the frame of competitive performance. Races could replace battles, and it was discovered that the Shadow likes that too. Perhaps we are not as aggressive as Freud was led to believe. The Shadow is one of Jung's archetypal identities that he discerned from the depths of his intuitive processes. Ego strength is the engine we build in order to contain these forces. Relationships and experiences have always made the difference and the growth of e-sport will not change that. We are emotional animals, not computers, and our world is a field of physical activity and motion.

In Jungian psychology, the Shadow is masculine. For women, there is another Jungian archetypal identity, the Animus. Considering Hillman's reminder above, we must be cautious in assuming that it is an opposite of the Shadow. We can say here that it is not. So in order to keep our balance, it is now to women's sports and the Animus that we must turn.

References

Adler, A. (1917). *The Neurotic Constitution* (B. Glueck and J.E. Lind, trans.). New York: Moffat Yard.

Adler, A. (1930). 'Individual Psychology', in *Psychologies of 1930*, C. Murchison (ed.) (pp. 395–405). Worcester, MA: Clark University Press.

Batchelor, S. (2005). *Living with the Devil: A Meditation on Good and Evil*. New York: Riverhead.

Bly, I. (1990). *Iron John, A Book about Men*. Reading, MA: Addison-Wesley Books.

Burston, D.H. (2015). *Psychological, Archetypal and Phenomenological Perspectives on Soccer*. London and New York: Routledge.

Campbell, J. (1988). *The Power of Myth* (B.S. Flowers, ed.). New York: Doubleday.

Collins, D. and MacNamara, A. (2012). 'The Rocky Road to the Top. Why Talent Needs Trauma'. *Sports Medicine* 42(11): 907–914.

Conquest, R. (1991). *Stalin: Breaker of Nations*. New York and London: Penguin Books.

Cross, G. (2008). *Men to Boys: The Making of Modern Immaturity*. New York: Columbia University Press.

Diamond, S. (1999). *Anger, Madness, and the Daimonic: The Psychological Genesis of Violence, Evil and Creativity*. Albany, NY: State University of New York Press.

Diver, K. (2005). 'Journal Reveals Hitler's Dysfunctional Family', *The Guardian*, 4 August. Online. www.theguardian.com/world/2005/aug/04/research.secondworldwar (retrieved 2 July 2018).

Fichte, J. (1799). *The Vocation of Man* (Die Bestimmung des Menschen) (W. Smith, trans., 1848). London: John Chapman.

Hillman, J. (1983). *Healing Fiction*. Woodstock, CT: Spring.

Jobs, S. (2005). 'Text of Steve Jobs' Commencement address (2005)', *Stanford News*, 14 June 2005.

Johnson, R.A. (1991). *Owning Your Own Shadow*. San Francisco, CA: Harper.

Johnson, R.A. (2008). *Inner Gold: Understanding Psychological Projection*. Kihei, HI: Koa.

Jung C.G. (1957). *The Undiscovered Self*. New York: Mentor.

Jung, C.G. (1961). *Memories, Dreams, Reflections* (R. and C. Winston, trans.). New York: Random House.

Kalshed, D. (2013). *Trauma and the Soul: A Psycho-Spiritual Approach to Human Development and its Interruption*. London and New York: Routledge.

Klein, M. (1964). *Love, Hate and Reparation*. London and New York: The Norton Library Press.

Langley, P. and Jones, M. (2013). *The Search for Richard III: The King's Grave*. London: Murray.

Naisbitt, J. (2006). Chapter in *Wisdom for the Soul: Five Millennia of Prescriptions for Spiritual Healing*, Larry Chang (ed.). Washington, DC: Gnosophia Publishers.

Nehru, J. (1981). *Jawaharlal Nehru: An Anthology* (S. Gopal, ed.). Oxford: Oxford University Press.

Nietzsche, F. (1982). Prologue to 'Thus Spoke Zarathustra', in *The Portable Nietzsche* (Kauffman, W., trans., 1954). London: Penguin.

Plato (1899). *Apology* (S.T.G. Stock, ed.), 3rd edn. Oxford: Clarendon Press.

Samuels, A. (1986). *A Critical Dictionary of Jungian Analysis*. London: Routledge.

Searl, S. (2016). *Homage to the Lady with Dirty Feet and Other Vermont Poems*. Kanona, NY: Foot Hills Publishing.

Smith, E. (2009). *What Sport Teaches Us About Life*. London: Penguin.

Socrates Brasileiro (blog) (2014). '30 Great Quotes by Socrates'. Online. http://socratesbrasil eiro.blogspot.com/2014/03/30-quotes-by-socrates-give-my-goals-to.html (retrieved 15 January 2018).

von Franz, M.L. (1974). *Shadow and Evil in Fairy Tales*. Boston, MA: Shambhala.

6

WOMEN'S SPORT

Creating *epoche*

As I write this chapter, mother nature has taken another turn. Evidence of the fires I described in the last chapter still remain, although they are out. The blackened canyons are grim reminders in Los Angeles of the nightmarish experience that surrounded so many communities in California. My university and community was in a lot of peril. Strange experiences and sights have since come to light; I have heard accounts of bears and mountain lions on the roadside with burned paws, moaning in pain.

It is not just the grass that was consumed; the roots in the soil also died. And now, bewildering news – after a spell of heavy rain a mudslide has so far killed 21 in Montecito, close to Santa Barbara. Mother nature sounds like a nice, nurturing kind of spirit. Our ancestors dealt with the truth. Santa Barbara is a community that will not be feeling positive awe for a while. Mother nature can be awful – or is it father nature? Who knows what is what anymore?

This chapter is about women in sport. I have had the good fortune to work with a few women's teams, and this is my respectful tribute to them all. In 2018, women's sport cultures are finding new levels of attention, finance and, more importantly perhaps, respect. In November 2018, one of the largest sporting bodies in the world, the US Professional Golfers Association elected its first female president, Suzy Whaley. She is a paradigm of Artemis, and openly dedicated to inclusivity and equality. Quickly on the heels of that optimistic statement is a sad reflection: this new attention is mostly in the West, and even then is not a concerted effort. Further, these new heights have come from a fairly low bottom.

Evidence suggests that women played as much sport as the men of any era allowed, and much of the last century was a man-made wilderness for women athletes and performers. However, out of that bleak reality is emerging a much brighter picture regarding women and their right to enjoy sports. We can also reveal something new here in our search for the soul of the athlete. This chapter concerns performance psychology for women, and contains useful information for the male athlete.

As far as I know, my PhD dissertation was the first, to study the way sportsmen and women think about their sport by comparing them directly. The study had a phenomenological methodology, which meant that the focus of the enquiry was the inner experiences of young men and women who play football as a career. Identical sets of questions were asked to each about their game on and off the sports field. They were then compared using the carefully constructed methodology of Amedeo Giorgi, a great phenomenologist. The study revealed distinct differences in the way the sexes process and feel about their sport. This chapter will explore those findings and what they can mean for a woman athlete.

In order to create as much objectivity as possible, I have taken steps to minimise my influence. This approach is how we create *epoche*. Phenomenology as a research methodology must be as forensic as possible, in order to minimise contamination of the results. That means that as a male I have to be conscious and conscientious about any subtle influences that I might have over the argument. Women who play sports like football often get coaching input solely from masculine sources, many of which may be of great value. One way we can try to minimise male influence in this chapter is to only reference women authors.

My first ever session with a women's team gave me a dilemma. I could surely not have described the virtues of the male Greek gods; it would be so obviously sexist and erroneous. What about the female gods of Greece, what could they say about sports? Jungian psychology is rich with women's deities and figures to choose from, and not just the Greeks. We shall explore women in history who have demonstrated a personal power that can captivate nations and move mountains. Women are ordinary mortals too, of course, and have to, like Icarus, keep their feet on the ground. Depth-psychological approaches incorporate and distinguish 'feminine psychology' as a relevant and vital source of knowledge, which is all too obscure for many young people I meet today. We are not all the same; nature has a good reason for wanting us to be different. Later, we shall share an example of a Jungian approach to feminine psychology in the 'four trials of Psyche' myth.

Earlier chapters in this book described how influence and communal authority shifted for the sexes as humans began to gather in towns and cities. Women's rights declined and became delineated within paternalistic systems of government dependent on armies and soldiers. Nevertheless, history provides us with evidence that collective farming did not herald the end of women leaders. Women such as Cleopatra (69–30 BC) and Boudicca (33–61 AD) demonstrated that early cultures could be and were led by women. In the case of Britain, Boudicca was the last woman queen until Henry VIII's daughter, Queen Elizabeth I (1533–1603), was crowned in 1559.

In 1588, Elizabeth made an important speech at Tilbury docks near London. Queen Elizabeth obviously had personal qualities that any good athlete should aspire to. The speech was delivered at a critical time, when Britain faced imminent invasion by the Spanish Armada. It was one of the great speeches in history, and in it she even mentioned sport. Only Winston Churchill later rivalled her capacity to inspire a nation into conviction and commitment during a war of survival. To set the scene: many people will have been seeing and hearing her for the first time. Dockyards are muddy, messy places and her sparkling royal retinue must have made quite an impression. William Shakespeare was 28 years old at this time and would certainly have recognised Elizabeth's command of language. Records suggest she had immense bearing and dignity as a queen, with a real capacity to inspire and connect to ordinary people – and there were plenty of ordinary people there that day.

Halfway through her speech, she changed her tack and began to more closely qualify her presence:

> And therefore I am come amongst you at this time, not as for my recreation or sport, but being resolved, in the midst and heat of the battle, to live or die amongst you all; to lay down, for my God, and for my kingdom, and for my people, my honour and my blood, even the dust.
>
> *(Marcus et al., 2002, p. 325)*

Elizabeth sets a tone of humility which for the men must have had a great appeal, even promising to join them.

> I know I have the body of a weak and feeble woman; but I have the heart of a King, and of a king of England, too; and think foul scorn that Parma or Spain, or any prince of Europe, should dare to invade the borders of my realms: to which, rather than any dishonour should grow by me, I myself will take up arms; I myself will be your general, judge and rewarder of every one of your virtues in the field.

Queen Elizabeth was here a blend of Nike, Psyche and Artemis in one, making the right speech at the right time.

Margaret Thatcher (1925–2013) became Great Britain's first female prime minister in 1979. Thatcher was a controversial leader who grew up in a greengrocer's shop during the war. Victorian Britain was the society that gave birth to the stereotypical, genteel vision and ideal of the woman most comfortable at home. It is curious, perhaps, that all of the women described so far share the same fate – to lead a country into war, in Margaret Thatcher's case when Britain tragically clashed with Argentina in the Falklands War in 1982. While some of those geopolitical issues are yet to be settled, the two nations once again compete peacefully in sports.

The cardinal French feminist author Simone de Beauvoir (1908–1986) may be an unusual choice to cite in a book about sport, but I hope you are accustomed to the idea that unusual sources may have the most to tell us. She certainly had plenty of soul, suggesting that 'Self-knowledge is no guarantee of happiness, but it is on the side of happiness and can supply the courage to fight for it' (1968, p. 203). Considering her character, Simone de Beauvoir would also have been a great player to have on your team in a tight spot. In traditional psychology much has been written about the nurturing side of the female soul, the Anima, but here we shall look at its counterpoint, the Animus.

Men and women share an Anima, but in Jungian psychology the Animus is the name women have for their own Shadow. Susan Rowland provides a definition:

> The animus is the archetype of the masculinity in the unconscious of a woman. Like the anima, this does not lock Jungian theory into perpetual gender opposition since the unconscious contains androgynous archetypes. Nothing can be securely known or fixed in the unconscious. So masculinity is rather one of a series of types 'otherness' for the psyche of a woman.
>
> *(2017, p. 172)*

This is a reminder of Hillman's important distinction relating to the limitations of dualism. We all have our individual struggles and agonies to play out on different planes and ages, all as a consequence of the biological and cultural realities our 'selves' are born into.

In the Jungian journal *Psychological Perspectives* (vol. 3, 2017), Jungian analyst Diane Eller-Boyko is in dialogue with Fran Grace in a chapter called 'Longing for the feminine; reflections on love, sexual orientation, individuation, and the soul'. A title like that looks a promising place for us to search for the soul of the woman and the athlete. Diane has over 40 years of experience in the mental health field and here discusses her sense of feminine individuation: 'for me individuation is a lifelong process that has taken me on a journey to become a "woman unto myself". Now, I want to give something back'. Grace shares her own perspective: 'Self discovery is never for oneself alone, as Jung emphasised. The transformed person returns to society to make a contribution forged out of her or his singular existence' (Eller-Boyko, 2017, p. 290). Teams are a society, and those who can work for the service of others tend to do well in competitive sports.

This is an important time for women's sport globally, and I want to help that if I can. It matters on many levels; as we shall see, some countries in the West are now actively creating and developing more professional opportunities for women. Some countries, of course, do not even recognise women's access to sport as a serious issue. I recently read the following quote, which I think apposite for what lies ahead. Written in wartorn England in 1917, a young author offers this advice: 'life ought to be a struggle of desire towards adventures whose nobility will fertilise the soul and lead to the conception of new, glorious things' (West, 2005, p. 21).

A question: do you have any sense as to the gender of the author? That passage was written by Dame Rebecca West DBE (1892–1983), once an eminent English author, journalist and critic. Initially this passage reads to me like the sentiments of a colonial patriarch, especially considering the date. 'Struggle', 'desire', 'adventures', 'nobility', 'glorious things'; it all sounds like the language of 'Muscular Christianity' endorsed by the culture of the British empire needing its 'strong arm' to keep the rule of law.

Rebecca West wrote about these kinds of passions at a time when women didn't even have the vote. She was a woman of her time, excluded from many things that mattered. In the emerging cultural landscape this was never going to last long, but women like her needed to approach life with sometimes fierce determination and courage. Political and social reforms in England were in large part because of women who were committed to fairness and had the conviction to see it through. As a consequence, many ended up in prisons or lunatic asylums. Suffragettes began a long struggle for emancipation and equality; most of the personal suffering was on the micro scale – countless tragedies we will never know of. Some were more public; in 1916, Emily Dickinson was trampled to death at Epsom racecourse when she stepped into the path of the king's horse.

As World War I's new industrialised form of human catastrophe continued, inevitably women were required to fill the gap left by the absent men. Many were keen to, and were drafted into factories making munitions in poisonous and hazardous conditions. All over the country women in factories were getting together and working in teams under pressure. One of those groups in the north of England was in Preston, Lancashire, a county with a world famous football culture, home to the famous Manchester United FC. One group of factory women formed a soccer team called 'Dick Kerr's Ladies' in 1917, named after their particular factory, and they kept the name after the war. A women's team was no problem; the spirit of the time was 'go right ahead'. The government endorsed sport for fitness reasons and women's soccer was encouraged. But the biggest issue for women at that time was not sports emancipation – it was the right to vote.

The Animus, the fighting spirit of women, was needed elsewhere and women like Emily Pankhurst had led as a captain from the front. Back in 1903, she formed the Women's Social and Political Union (WSPU), with the slogan 'deeds not words'. By the end of the war they were an established thorn in the lion's paw. Pankhurst took on the embedded male patriarchy in London, which used prisons and police to repress protestors, often brutally. Soon real pressures began to tell on David Lloyd George's wartime government (1863–1945), which tried to contain the issue. His was the most powerful government in the world, but without women workers it was finished. In 1918, the Representation of the People Act granted votes to males over 21 and women over 30 who qualified as property owners. Women were allowed to vote on equal terms with men for the first time in 1928. Tragically, Emily Pankhurst died just a few weeks before the passing of the Representation of the People (Equal Franchise) Act, on 14 June 1928.

As with Simone de Beauvoir and Queen Elizabeth, Emily Pankhurst would have been a great leader on any team. She had courage, conviction, commitment and the other crucial factor, restraint. She knew when to make her move. She was intelligent and organised, and chose her battles and her friends wisely. Emily Pankhurst visited America in 1913, seven years before full US emancipation in 1920 with the 19th Amendment to the US Constitution. While she was in Hertford, Connecticut she told an assembled group of supporters; 'Women are very slow to rouse, but once they are aroused, once they are determined, nothing on earth and nothing in heaven will make a woman give way; it is impossible' (Pankhurst, 1913). Perhaps those men that resisted emancipation knew that women do have their own voice, their own logos. If we approached the psychology of women's sport as if they have the same logos as men, we would be making a big mistake. Remember, when we ignore the unconscious we create the conditions of epistemological violence.

Irene Claremont de Castillejo (1885–1967) was one of the most prominent and pioneering female authors to write about the psychology of women. A student of Jung, she was one of the first Jungian psychotherapists in London to focus solely on women's issues. Her classic book *Knowing Women* was published after her death in 1973. Castillejo was interested in the implications of postwar cultural emancipations for women and what had subsequently transpired. For the Animus, she used the term Shadow, perhaps complimenting Susan Rowland's point regarding the androgynous nature of these archetypal forces.

Earlier, I wrote about the use of emotions in sport and how vital they are as a primary condition. It is no different for women; Castillejo echoes Pankhurst's conviction to the power and potentiality of the feminine soul; 'It may sometimes be wisdom to use one's Shadow deliberately. Anger is a Shadow quality in our well behaved society, but consciously directed it can move mountains' (Castillejo, 1974, p. 40). We have seen how women have achieved vast strides forward based on their mobilised anger, crucially directed towards a cause. In sport and life, anger is best converted and channeled in a direction or a cause. Castillejo points out; 'Jesus Christ vented his anger on the moneylenders in the temple. He knew what he was doing. We also need to know what we are doing, as it is only when our Shadow comes up unbeknown that it causes mischief' (1974, p. 41). Women who succumb to the sinister, undifferentiated Shadow are as vulnerable as men.

Psychosis is normally the clinical term for when we 'don't know what we are doing'. I was fortunate once to play a theatre role in Japan in *Medea*, the classic play by Euripides. At the beginning of the play Jason informs Medea that he is happy with her and their two children, but needs to marry another woman. As his new bride-to-be is a royal connection, Jason hopes Medea will be a sport about it and see the positives. She does not, and, driven mad with rage, she kills the two children. 'Hell hath no fury like a woman scorned' goes the saying, which does not underestimate the power of women for those traditional male attributes – violent assault and aggression. British Victorian society laid the foundations for culturally appropriate visions of women who could only be capable of genteel, 'lady-like' actions.

Susan Sing PhD, a member of the US World Cup rowing team, knows what it is like to win and lose. A competitor of the highest order, she has written an insightful book for our purposes called *The Spirituality of Sport*, wherein she speaks of the soul of women conditioned to win.

They find no ultimate peace in the means, only the outcome is their goal. Great athletes – and perhaps here I should distinguish that I am referring to coaches and athletes alike in that term – learn to lose and learn through losing because any time two teams compete on a field of play, someone wins, someone loses. I don't think any self-respecting athlete can let go of a loss easily – a loss haunts all of us, but the ability to overcome adversity and loss without losing oneself in innumerable ways, is the soul of the true competitor.

(2004, p. 55)

First, however, we must feel that loss, or – evidence suggests – we do not grow in the same way.

Castillejo goes on to say, 'We need at times to use our Shadow, but never to be its victims' (1974, p. 41). The best soccer player I ever saw live was a man called Ledley King. Tennis star Billie Jean King was likely the best women player many ever saw. She remains today an iconic example of the power of determination and action for women's rights. She carries all the same regal traits of the great women we have discussed so far, and was able to move mountains through sport.

In her glittering career, she won 39 Grand Slam titles, 12 of them in singles competitions, 16 in women's doubles and 11 in mixed doubles. She won a record 20 championship titles at Wimbledon. But perhaps her finest achievement was the founding of the Women's Professional Association in 1973, and the Women's Sport Foundation in 1974. In 1973, she famously beat Bobby Briggs in the 'battle of the sexes' competition. This was not just a game; it was a symbol of the times that helped change the attitudes of an entire society towards women in sport.

Castillejo and de Beauvoir encourage women to obtain self-knowledge as a tool and defence against victimhood. Emancipation and liberation are a way to arm oneself against destructive Medea-like rage, a phenomenon known as the 'Uroborus'. I have worked with clinical cases with women who have levels of rage, as poisonous to them as rage is for men. Many women are sinned against and can never escape the victim stage, maybe for entirely understandable reasons, but it is the case. Rage creates victims. The good news for sportswomen is that sport is a venue where the expression of the Animus can make someone feel whole again.

The effect of the Animus turned inward is the same for women as men. Castillejo warns women;

I cannot close this one without speaking of women's direst and most destructive Shadow. The witch is chiefly women's responsibility. All women who have not totally lost power with the unconscious are in touch with power ... dark shadows, once conscious, can to some extent at least be curbed from causing mischief, and their dynamism can be redirected.

(1974, p. 42)

Psychologist Sian Beilock suggests self belief and leadership potential are qualities that can be determined. In her book *Choke: What the Secrets of the Brain Reveal about Getting it Right When You Have To* (2010), Beilock refers to important research relating to women's self-belief in their own capacities to lead and succeed. She cites how Nilanjana Dasgupta (2004) interviewed US female first-year college students about leadership and gender roles. She discovered their belief in their own capacities, over those of the men, were most influenced by one factor. She found that 'attitudes about their own sex potential for leadership in the first year of college – regardless of which school they attended – was completely driven by the number of female faculty the students had. When female students are exposed to female faculty their attitudes about women change' (p. 170). Considering the levels available for female coaches in sport, this surely represents a disadvantage from the start.

In a subsequent piece of research (2017), Dasgupta and Tara Dennehey then studied a group of female engineering students, finding that, 'Notably, grades were not associated with year 1 retention. The benefits of mentoring endured beyond the intervention, for year 2 of college is the time of greatest attrition from science, technology, engineering, and mathematics (known as S.T.E.M.) majors'. It appears that as examination pressure increased for second-year students, the men were able to benefit from mentorship in a way the women could not, at the very time women needed women mentors the most. The reasons for the low numbers of women in the corporate world is for another book. The sports world is our world here, and in this case women – so what is happening?

The research suggests that female leaders and coaches are badly needed. Getting them, however, maybe a harder task. In terms of statistical sources, we have a good source in UEFA, the Union of European Football Associations, one of the governing bodies of the world game, of which the Football Association of England is a member. In 2017, UEFA, published a report including statistics relating to women's participation in soccer, including coaching. They found that in the 'majority of the national associations coaching staff are employed on a part time-basis'. They also stated that '80% of women's football coaches are male. Of the 221 women's national teams . . . 107 male coaches and 64 female coaches' (UEFA, 2017, p. 21).

Comparing recent years is also revealing; in 2016, the UEFA report *Women in Football* indicated a rise in female qualified coaches to its highest level; '17,550+, a 31% rise' (UEFA, 2016). This meant that during one year more than 5,000 female coaches had taken up new professional roles since the 2015/2016 season (UEFA, 2016). For some reason this has now slowed down substantially. In their 2017 report, there were only 1,921, towards a total number of 19,474 in Europe. Even if cultural attitudes in some places are shifting, it does not mean that the cultural realities of being a woman are shifting. Being a male sports professional is more likely to be a simpler task in life. Unlike women, who become mothers, men need not physically give labour or be committed to intensive time and nursing with a young baby. If a woman is a mother, she may not be able to attend training for years. Even after schooling starts for children, the demands on women's time is different than on men. This may provide a subtle and very real explanation for deficits beyond simple male prejudice. To their credit, the FA and Professional Footballers' Association (PFA), based in Manchester and the older such organization in the world, are on the right track.

This issue is being tackled by the governing bodies of sport. A BBC Radio 5 Live programme in 2017 discussed this issue in an edition of their magazine show 'Sports Specials'. They refereed to recent revelations by the Football Association of England that in December 2017 they were 'struggling to find a replacement' for the vacant senior women's team manager. The England soccer manager is probably the pinnacle point of any coaching or managerial career, so the shortage of suitable candidates was puzzling.

The Head of Women's Football, Baroness Sue Campbell, told the BBC programme that:

> I don't think we have failed people, if you look in most sports you would find familiar patterns of women possibly coaching at the bottom end but not making it through the system. And we've got to think very differently about the way how we offer courses how we make them accessible, people have got lots of demands on their time.
>
> *(BBC 5 Live, 2017)*

They eventually hired a man, ex-player Phil Neville. Again, their decision was hampered by a lack of candidates suitable for the role.

I must share a conflict of interest. I have worked with the Football Association for many years and intend to continue to do so, as I care passionately about the development of psychology for young people in sports. I know from personal experience that the FA cares as well. Indeed, since 1998 the organisation has always supported my work. When I was beginning with my ideas of connecting actors and football players, the head of the psychology department at the FA, Dr Andy Cale, regularly met with me at the old FA Headquarters in Soho Square. He was encouraging and most generous and would give me an hour of his time. I am very grateful to all of those people who put their faith in me or gave me their time freely at club and national levels.

I have since met several times with Dan Ashworth, the Head of Development at the FA. He cares about people, and his staff are progressive and inclusive, and they listen. Positive cultural change has happened on all fronts, but soccer is so prominent now it is liable perhaps, like a referee, to be consistently viewed negatively or as having acted too slowly. Culture is moving fast and organisations have to keep up, which is a new kind of reality for the age. Our cultural institutions may not be able to keep up with social changes; even the laws are struggling to reflect the world of the internees. These organisations are under much scrutiny but are now undoubtedly forces for good in the world. The PFA 'Kick it out' campaign was revolutionary and undoubtedly helped create social change for good around racism and, to some extent, homophobia. The Football Association has a creative syllabus it now teaches to coaches at every level at St Georges's Park.

The England senior men's team is very conspicuous in world football, and represents the pinnacle of the English game. In 1966, England won the World Cup with a side captained by Bobby Moore OBE. He was of the wold's great defenders and an epitome of ethical leadership and humility. People like Booby Moore had come out of a war culture, supreme athletes housed in the psyche of elite members of the World War II Commandos. Currently at its zenith and still climbing, the Premier League is the most competitive soccer league in the world. Yet the men's national team never reached its potential after 1966 – although that has now changed. The 2018 World Cup was a success for the new, younger England, managed by the young, inclusive and ethical manager Gareth Southgate. In November 2018 this young side consecutively beat Spain and Croatia to reach the semi finals of the inaugural UEFA nations league cup in 2019. But before this, the women's team already showed that something important was happening within the culture of English football.

This chapter is written partly as a result of inspiration from the England women's soccer team, commonly known by their nickname 'the Lionesses'. It is the lioness that does the hunting in the wild, and in the case of England the women have psychologically been better performers. In June 2015, the England women's team were not given much of a chance. Winners of competitions in soccer are not always obvious at the beginning; psychology plays a vast part in the outcome, as well as luck. Tournament psychology is different; teams can gain or lose momentum, an issue often determined by the collective culture. In June 2015, the England women's team began to win and progress through the competition stages. As they progressed and beat their opponents, they attracted a lot of attention in England from a nation hungry for success.

As I write, the men's team is playing for third place in World Cup 2018, something the women's before them managed in 2015. The women's team effectively rewrote the rulebooks of women's soccer in England. Of special interest to me was how easily they captivated so much attention. Very few people were unaware of the progress of 'the Lionesses' in England, showing how women and sport have the power to capture a nation just as the men can. In our current global climate success by any international team is conspicuous and, depending on the sport, virtually assured of a following. To what degree women's sport get carried along with the current financial media plume is yet to be seen. When I worked with female and male soccer players in the United States, it was their heartfelt and honest conviction and commitment (inspired by the US men's soccer coach Bob Ammann) that inspired within me a deep respect and determination to do the same for them.

Determination is an infectious trait within and outside of soccer. The inspirational effects are not gender-specific. On Sunday, 23 November 2014, 55,000 tickets were sold for a match between the England senior women against Germany. Sales had been capped at 55,000 because of planned tube engineering works that day. Eventually, that meant 10,000 of those spectators were unable to make it to the game. The previous friendly played there by the senior men's team was versus Norway, with the lower attendance of 40,181 (Keegan, 2014). It is not likely that engineering works would have been planned for a men's game, but regardless – the decision adversely affected the event. It was not the first time.

Few soccer fans know that during World War I in Britain, women's football flourished and was greater than the men's game. Earlier we mentioned how because of their experience in the munitions factories, women had become great team players. Soccer is a natural team game. Scotland had won their first international matches against England because the public school ethic of Muscular Christianity was no match for the Scotsmen, who worked in factories together. They developed the game as a team effort, working together. It was the same for the women, and soon a rich tradition of women's soccer teams began to emerge and develop out of and beyond the war. On Christmas Day in 1917, two women's teams played in Preston, watched by 10,000 spectators. On Boxing Day in 1920, Dick Kerr's Ladies played St Helen's Ladies before 53,000 spectators at Goodison Park in Everton, home of the men's team, with many more locked outside (Simpkin, 2014).

Something was going wrong here for the men at the Football Association. On 5 December 1921, they banned women from using FA-sanctioned grounds, which meant those with stadiums. Unlike during wartime, women playing was now deemed inappropriate, especially because of its popularity. They stated that:

> Complaints having been made as to football being played by women, the council feel impelled to express the strong opinion that the game is quite unsuitable for females and ought not to be encouraged – the council request clubs belonging to the association to refuse the use of their grounds for such matches.
>
> (The Times, 1921)

This meant that the women's game was not to be developed, and declined until in 1971. After a long time in the wilderness, the Women's Football Association was formed in 1969, followed by a lifting of the ban in 1971. Ironically this was done by the Football Association to help save the women's game.

At that time the great Bille Jean King was a pioneering and positive influence on social justice and inclusivity in sport and society. She was openly a lesbian and with her courage helped many others face prejudice and shame – the great disabler of young people.

Lily Parr, the woman history could not forget

This chapter would not be complete without mentioning another heroine like Billie Jean King, who was also a queen of the stage. Lily Parr, on the cover of this book, was raised in Preston, Lancashire, home of the Dick Kerr ladies. Biographers suggest it was her brothers who taught her to play, something often the case for women, as my previous research has shown. Most of them related soccer to family experiences when younger. She had a lithe frame which was also strong, so she was able to compete with the boys her age and older at rugby and football as she grew up.

Dick Kerr's ladies became a major going concern, and soon they were forging new territory for women and sport.

> As one of the earliest known women's association football teams in England, they were pioneers – the first women's team to wear shorts, tour the continent and the United States of America, and represent England at the first official international women's football association game – which raised an estimated one million pounds at today's valuation for post-war charities.
>
> *(Nande, 2017)*

Like the Brazilian soccer star Socrates, Lily Parr had a large appetite, and she smoked Woodbine cigarettes – one time even requesting to be paid in them (Arnot, 2011). Parr worked in factory at the same time that she became a famous woman in her own right. In Jean Williams' excellent book, *A Game for Rough Girls? A History of Women's Football in Britain*, she describes Parr's actions in a match versus Stoke Ladies: '[Parr] scores goals from extraordinary angles with a left foot cross drive, which nearly breaks the net' (Williams, 2003, p. 51). Lily Parr was like Billie Jean King – a leader and a woman who did things better than the men.

Lily Parr was a child prodigy, making her senior debut in front of 10,000 spectators when she was 14 years of age. Nande also describes Parr's then-teammate Joan Whaley: 'She was the only person I knew who could lift a dead ball, the old heavy leather ball, from the left wing over to me on the right and nearly knock me out with the force of the shot' (Nande, 2017). Nande also tells of how 'Her male contemporary, Scotland international Bobby Walker, calls her the "best natural timer of a football" he's ever seen'. The article speaks about her contribution to the wider feminine issues of her day just as many of the women mentioned did before her.

In our case it is of interest perhaps that after the ban she retired and became a mental nurse at the Whittingham Mental Hospital in Preston, England. Lily Parr was a significant woman in her community who connected and cared for the men and women in her own life. In the sporting pantheon Lily Parr was never given the public recognition she deserved. She broke the rules, or rather conventions, of her age, and by doing so pioneered a path for those to come later – and also paid the price.

She knew how to live, and had integrated her Animus into her identity, eventually becoming a healer. She was a sublime performer who is certainly now beginning to find her place in the pantheon. If only we could see her today. Sport and culture evolve throughout history, but not necessarily at the same time. Today things are improving for women, but it has certainly been a low bottom. But in times of darkness, one can often see the brighter stars – all the better, perhaps. In our case there are common themes can we discern from these great women and players.

Many heroic women have stories that remain untold, their gifts undeveloped or suppressed in the culture of their time. In her informed and passionate article, Nande finally laments:

But how many will know about one Lily Parr from St. Helens who had the world in the palm of her hand? Her dream might have come true, but it's up to us to keep it going for her, and for every aspiring woman footballer to come. It's up to us to remember her. Isn't that the least we can do for the first woman superstar of the beautiful game?

(Nande, 2017)

When we look beneath the surface, we can see there are other masters, often those in a man's world, that can surpass them all. Lily Parr threw a javelin, perhaps not knowing the ancient lineage she was replicating.

The archetypal lineage of the female archers

As Lily Parr was dominating the football world in England, a contemporary of hers, Annie Oakley, was also at the height of her powers, although at a much later age. Football is a young person's game; Annie Oakley was in her sixties, but in her prime. Like Lily, she was a child prodigy, and has a revealing story to tell relating to the psychology of top-grade sports women.

Annie Oakley (1860–1926) was born Phoebe Ann Mosey, and is a woman who has mostly been kept in the shade, in this case perhaps because of her prominent identity as the woman who could do fantastic sharpshooting tricks. It was not her fault that she grew up in an age where you earned far more as an entertainer than as an athlete. She was not from the middle class, where sport was the privileged pastime for the cultural elite. Like Lily Parr, Annie Oakley was not from a privileged background, but rather the earthier world of the Ohio working classes. She is rarely mentioned in sport psychology; I could not find a reference connecting the two. Her skill and precision would have won her many gold medals – she was incomparable. What is remarkable about Annie Oakley is that her success makes no sense. The United States was a country forged by the gun and Annie Oakley was better than the all the men with a gun. How can that be possible?

Depth sport psychology does have a lens we can use which connects Annie and Lily and all great sports women to universal archetypal identities. Annie was born in 1860 in a small town called Willowdell in Darke County, Ohio. She was the sixth of nine children and must have suffered emotionally when young, as her father died of pneumonia when she was six, after being exposed all night in a blizzard. Her mother eventually remarried, but also died in tragic circumstances. We know Annie did not have much of a formal education, although her parents were Quakers. The Quaker tradition was a new way of worship inspired by the Englishman George Fox in 1650s England. Quakers are traditionally known as pacifists, who worship in silence. They consequently develop powers of focus, and also make fine hunters.

The fellowship of Quakerism is still practised today and can lay claim to having produced many great figures in society with a rich tradition of social change and emancipation in areas such as prison reform and education. In the 1700s, Quaker whaling teams were the best on the east coastal ports of the young Unites States, partly because they were so inclusive as a tradition and had no colour bars. Quakers believe that God is to be found in everyone and they encourage equanimity, a practice and ethos similar to Buddhism. Internal reflection and a kind of meditative practice called 'waiting on the Lord' is prescribed. Annie was safe at home, but outside things were less certain for the poor in wild America. She grew up in poverty and hunting was for many people the only way to get a good nutritious meal.

Biographies suggest that when she was ten she was 'bound out' to a local family for some kind of domestic apprenticeship. They neglected her and treated her cruelly, one time locking her out of the house in the snow with no shoes. Remembering how her father died, this must have been a traumatic experience for her. We do not know exactly what happened to her at this time. In her own autobiography she did not refer to this family by name. She eventually would refer to them as 'wolves' (Riley, 1994, p. 7). Annie eventually returned home aged around 12, and began to hunt again for food for the family. Biographies suggest Annie would then sell her game to local vendors and hoteliers. She was evidently another prodigy, becoming so successful she paid off her mother's mortgage when she was 15 (Riley, 1994, p. 7).

At that time in the US, many men carried and used guns. In 1875, a sharpshooter called Frank E. Butler came to town, challenging all comers. Substantial sums of money were involved in side bets. This was no small matter for the town and as we have described these events created a lot of opportunities for vendors to sell food and drink. Annie stepped out of the wilds into the hotel lobby, volunteering as a contestant. 'The last opponent Butler expected was a five-foot-tall 15-year-old girl named Annie' (PBS, n.d.). Annie never lost – so she beat him, and the rest is history. Butler was obviously impressed; the two formed a working relationship as travelling sharpshooters. They eventually married in June 1882 and performed together until she died in 1926. Frank was devoted to her and there are reports he did not eat again after she died, passing away 18 days later (Shirl, 1992, pp. 243–4).

In 1904, newspaper publisher William Hearst published an article falsely accusing Oakley of cocaine smuggling. The report arose because a woman arrested in Chicago for the charge claimed her name was Annie Oakley. The real one spent six years going from state to state challenging each newspaper that published the article defaming her good name. She was interested for wider social concerns, and did not hesitate to become involved in the deeper issues and needs alive in the young US nation. Few appreciate or recognise the depth of her involvement in causes that helped women become educated and achieve independence. At one point she wrote to President McKinley offering her support for the army and 100 sharpshooting women if the country went to war against Spain (Isenberg, pp. 175–6).

Oakley was involved with women's lives; they mattered to her. As a woman of her age, she encouraged other women to be taught shooting as a means of independence as well as self-protection. Annie Oakley would have been a bad opponent to have against you, but as a citizen she made her presence known. After a lifetime in entertainment Annie will have earned a fortune, but records show that she did not leave much money. Various records show that her dedication to charities and young women's causes meant she left very little. Her early trauma did not make her a victim of life but in many ways she became a champion, initially feeding her family and then sharing her gifts with others and becoming a kind of twentieth-century Western deity.

Annie Oakley continued shooting into her old age and is perhaps the most famous example of the archetype of the female archer. The last section spoke of Lily Parr's football powers in crossing a ball with force and precision. Both women were at the same time dominating traditional male occupations – football and shooting. The world was turning on its head and these incredible women emerged for us to still marvel at today. So where are the modern Lily Parrs and Annie Oakleys?

An archetypal presence has to be something we can all see elsewhere. It is a form or pattern we can identify. Annie Oakley is not the only young female hot-shot to have been. In 2015, Shyanne Roberts was aged ten when she 'beat out adult women to place second in the Women's Division of the New Jersey Ruger Rimfire Challenge' (Zdanowicz, 2015). Kimberly Rhode is another example of note – perhaps the most successful women's shooter ever and triple Olympic title holder. She won her first world championship when she was 13, in the double trap competition.

What do these children show us? Child prodigies, of course, are nothing new – male and female. Wolfgang Mozart (1756–1791) was six years old when he performed an exhibition concert before the the court of Prince-elector Maximilian III of Bavaria in Germany. He was tutored by his father but he soon could do 'more than he was taught' (Solomon, 1995, pp. 39–40). Earlier we described how it was possible that music might have been a form expression that predated language. The way child prodigies so easily reproduce and naturally replicate skills is a curious manifestation that deserves more research. It appears as if some past inherited capacity is being accessed lived through the person, irrespective of age. Women archers hold rifles today, but then, of course, it will have been the bow and arrow.

We cannot know exactly the role of female archers pre-history, but the Greeks certainly had their own archer deities. The Greek god Apollo held a bow and arrow, representing his precision and skill. It is less-known that his sister, Artemis, also carried a bow and arrow. This is a vital female archetypal presence we can still see everywhere around us, if we look. Artemis is the Greek goddess of the hunt, forests, hills and the moon. Homer described her; 'Artemis of the wildland, mistress of animals' (1896, p. 470). As much of this book has so far related, this connection with animals denotes the 'inner animal' we must retain and be in relationship to. Artemis was not just a hunter; she was connected to women's issues and was thought to be the goddess of midwifery, as some sources suggest she helped give birth to Apollo. Lily Parr, Annie Oakley and Billie Jean King were all intimately related to women's issues and Artemis was likewise much more than what she could do.

Later in Roman times, she became the goddess Diana, and many myths relate her presence. Annie Oakley had hunting in her system from when she was young, Callimachus records how Artemis collected the things she needed to hunt when a child (Callimachus, 1921). Artemis is a noble deity. Like Annie Oakley, you would not call her a cocaine dealer and get away with it. These deities must be respected and not ignored. As with Apollo and Dionysus, being the offspring of Zeus gives Artemis a central place in the personal world of the internal psyche. She had 'Zeus energy' alright. One myth involving her illustrates this point nicely and indicates the depth of the powers we take on for our good or for our peril. The following was the first mythological story I ever told a women's team.

The hounds of Acteon

Acteon was a great hunter. The myth regarding him has variations, but the essential themes are as follows. Acteon loved to have big parties at his mansion and was also a dedicated hunter. He had popular gatherings, was not a bad man at all, and enjoyed respect and honour. Over the course of a couple of days he lavished his guests with good food, wine and hunting. Acteon's hounds were renowned as the best ever dog team. Sources mention that they all had different identities and different jobs; please note that, dear team players. Together, they worked in unison and were a marvel in themselves – but they were all different.

There was a curious Shadow side to his success and popularity. People still attended his gatherings but in time things began to change. Acteon had become so skilled, so successful with his team that there weren't many animals left to hunt. Herds began to thin out, and soon there were days when nothing was caught at all. Acteon could see that his dogs were getting frustrated and started to worry about the situation. He decided to go out into the forest without his dogs to see if he could discover what was going on. Acteon was determined; he stayed out for days travelling, looking for a new herd or at least some tracks to follow. He found nothing and was miserable about it. On his return, he approached a pool and heard a young woman laugh in the distance.

He kept a low profile and saw women bathing, and then a few more. A couple of women were washing the back of an older woman – who also very attractive, he thought. Quietly, he crept up for a closer look, not believing his good fortune. As he crawled up to the edge of the bushes, he saw the older woman more clearly. A tiny twig broke as he leaned over, and Artemis caught sight of him. Well, Acteon thought, this was hugely embarrassing, but he was the Lord of the manor, and besides, he well knew how to charm them. Great idea – he thought – he could invite them all over for a party. He stood up, and Artemis stared at him with icy diamond eyes that looked fit to kill. Just for a moment, Acteon may have realised what a terrible mistake he had made. Artemis instantly turned him into a stag.

Acteon, aware of his predicament, immediately went wild with panic and anger. No more parties, no more fun; encroaching on Artemis was a life-ending idea. He knew his hounds would be wondering about him, and he missed them. By now his dogs were missing him too, and being loyal, of course, they had come looking for him. Not finding Acteon, they happened upon his new incarnation, mercilessly pulling him to shreds and devouring him.

It is worth recounting that there is another myth reciting the same theme. A young Cretan hunter called Siproites stumbles across Artemis bathing and she turns him into a girl. Artemis is a queen, a hunter in her own right, and not a woman good at doing such things. She must not be violated; normal patriarchal climates are not strong enough to save transgressors. Some sources suggest that Artemis is a goddess of the pre-Greek era (Rose, 1959, p. 112).

It is not recorded if the Greeks had any influence over it, but Nordic mythology has its own hunter-archer queen. Nordic mythology has a rich tradition, which was studied by Jung and others locating the universal archetypal identities and figures. In Norse mythology, Skaði (also known as 'Skadi') is major deity, often seen on skis, armed with a bow or a spear. She was said to have married the god Odin, again suggesting the centrality of her character to the Nordic psyche. Her love of archery was apparently a trait she inherited from her father Thiazi, who was killed by the gods. In return the gods granted her gifts and favours. Skadi is a universal Nordic legend that fits so neatly into this repeated archetype of the woman archer.

At the same time on other side of the world, twelfth-century Japan may not have been a likely place to find a superlative female Samurai warrior, but there was one. Her name was Tomoe Gozen (1157–1247), but she needed to be nurtured, like all prodigies. Her father was a well-known Samurai, and from an early age she studied combat. By the age of 21, she was a fully fledged warrior and unique in Japan, specialising in bow and sword. Her lover was Minamoto no Yoshinaka, an important royal figure who supported and nurtured her, taking the brave step to make her a captain.

Before two Samurai armies clashed on the battlefield, their top two warriors would fight it out, one to one, in front of the watching soldiers. At the battle of Awazu in 1184, Yoshinaka gave Gozen the honour and, clad in armour, her opponent had no idea who she was. She defeated the Samurai warrior Honda no Moroshige, beheading him. Before Honda died, she revealed to him and everyone watching that she was a woman. This will have caused severe shock and distress to her opponents. Samurai warriors were not accustomed to shrieking – but we can imagine that some did.

Her eventual death at 90 years of age gives a clue as to her skills as a warrior. In 2018 we can see that archetypal identities may not be acknowledged or have any meaning attached to them in order for them to exist. *The Lord of the Rings, The Hobbit* and the *Harry Potter* series all testify that we recognise consistent mythological archetypes who are ancient, alive and well. Much like the global media that spawns them, they are expanding outwards and into the world. They are everywhere; here I have listed the female archers in pop culture of modern times, starting with a classic text much-respected today.

Emma Woodhouse, *Emma*, Jane Austen (1815).

Susan Pevensie, *The Chronicles of Narnia*, C.S. Lewis (1950).

Abigail Whistler, 'Blade: Trinity', David Goyer (director, 2004).

Neytiri, 'Avatar', James Cameron (director, 2009).

Hanna, 'Hanna', Joe Wright (director, 2011).

Katniss Everdeen, 'The Hunger Games' series, Gary Ross (director, 2012); Francis Lawrence (director, 2013–2015).

Princess Merida, 'Brave', Mark Andrews, Brenda Chapman, Steve Purcell (directors, 2012).

Perhaps it is because we live paradoxically in a computer age that these films have found a recent popularity amongst all ages. Recent films in 2016–2018 about Winston Churchill may also be speaking to a similar unfulfilled need for public figures with character whom we can trust.

We can see that Artemis is a deity connected to the earth. She hunts in the forests, where she is queen of animals, an Earth mother – which is why she took such exception to Acteon. Artemis is connected with reproduction and care for mothers. Acteon had inflicted damage on the wildlife by over-hunting, and he paid the price. Artemis is often depicted as bathing, connected to and tending to her body. Her body and mind are one. It is for this reason that she can fire arrows with great precision. In the case of Lily Parr, hers were initially capacities to cross a ball; later, her energies went into the care of patients in hospital. Care is a kind of focus, and I would say the world was lucky to have Lily Parr, for she knew the exclusion and disappointment of a society not ready for her. Annie Oakley also knew rejection and pain as a child, but with her Olympian capacities, she gave all she had to charities and women's causes.

Before we meet Psyche, let us be rigorous and boil down some of the characteristics we can identify in Artemis.

Artemis: a profile

Equipped with bow and arrows (symbolising precision and focus).

Honest and true (leading to accuracy).

Connected to women and women's issues.

Endowed with an inner animal (she is alive and lives in motion, as the queen of animals).

Uses her senses; is a hunter (discovers Acteon).

Can beat men at their own game.

Was hunted as a child.

The four trials of Psyche

We will first go through the story of Psyche, and afterwards examine its meanings for athletes. If you are an athlete, male or female, perhaps you will anticipate these meanings as the story unfolds.

The story of Psyche is a universal archetypal myth, very helpful as a model especially for the young female. For all her good fortunes, Psyche had troubles. Aphrodite had a big problem with sweet, young, lovely Psyche, and was determined to make her suffer; ageing, Aphrodite became jealous (envy is wishing for something that another possesses; jealousy is wishing that the other did not possess it either).

Aphrodite's greatest nightmare was happening before her eyes – a rival to her beauty – and she wasn't going to relinquish her place in the pantheon easily. She frankly and openly disdained this young pretender (who so many were attracted to). Aphrodite's scorn was too much for Psyche, and she became very anxious – exactly what happens when adults overdo psychological punishment of the young. Tearfully, she ran to Demeter, the goddess of the seasons, complaining bitterly and asking her advice.

Demeter was very wise. Her daughter Persephone had once been kidnapped by Hades. Demeter was the kind of woman that even Hades had to listen to. Demeter thought of Persephone and her plight, and instantly empathised with Psyche, advising a solution but warning of its risks. She suggested that Psyche approach Aphrodite again, be humble and respectful, and ask her for acceptance – and only that. Demeter cautioned Psyche that Aphrodite would initially refuse, but that she must persist, and that Aphrodite would then present her with four trials. Demeter cautioned Psyche that each would seem impossible, and warned her that she would even feel suicidal and want to give up hope (hope, remember, is crucial, because despair is what happens when we lose hope). Demeter encouraged Psyche to carry on regardless and not to give up, as help would be close at hand.

Psyche dutifully arranged a time to visit Aphrodite (through one of her assistants, naturally – remember what happened to Acteon, who just appeared in front of Aphrodite). Psyche knew the dangers, but she trusted Demeter. She took a deep breath, gulped and presented herself to Aphrodite. Following Demeter's advice, she carefully shared her reverence the elder goddess. In Los Angeles today, she would say 'I've seen all of your films! I follow you on Facebook and Twitter, and I "like" everything you post'. Aphrodite was not impressed; she had millions of followers. When I was a writer in Los Angeles, I once had a meeting with a well-known producer. Outside, before entering, his assistant categorically told me: 'nothing you have ever done will impress him'. Aphrodite was not impressed either, but she had to give it to Psyche – she had sung all of the right notes. She would give Psyche a chance.

Aphrodite led Psyche into a large barn. In the middle of the floor lay a huge pile of different kinds of grains, all in a large mound. Aphrodite told her:

> Your task is this: here is some wheat, barley, oats and corn, all mixed together. I want you to separate them all by morning. Only that young lady, only that, nothing arduous. Put them into four neat little piles, only four. Then, I will come back. And we shall see what you can do, and what I am supposed to be approving of.

Psyche gave her a polite smile and a quick bow as she agreed; 'I will do my best'. Aphrodite disdainfully stared at her for another moment, spun on her heels and left. As she did so, Psyche considered the pile, a growing sense of dread rising from deep within her. What on earth had she gotten herself into? She felt like a fool. What was she thinking!? She expected eternal humiliation. Alternatively, if she made a stand and attempted to take on Aphrodite, she would end up as chopped liver.

Like Artemis, Aphrodite was a mature deity and a substantial woman in her own right. Psyche was slight; she couldn't take that much. After all, her parents were only mortals. She had another frightening idea. Maybe Demeter had made a mistake, thought she was stronger than Psyche was – maybe it was all a misunderstanding. She collapsed to the floor and sobbed.

As she lay there, she became aware of a tickling sensation on her nose. It was an ant. She wiped her eyes and then saw another, and another. As she looked at them, she followed their trail, and as she did, the black line grew thicker and wider; there were thousands, maybe more. A flood of ants was coming up from underneath the wall in the corner. Unaware of what was happening Psyche became instantly afraid. They were heading for her. Then she had some relief; she saw they were in fact heading for the grain pile. She witnessed a wonderful sight. One by one, each ant lifted up a grain and began hauling it away on its back. What's more, each kind of grain was going off in a different direction, to all corners of the room. Psyche was dazed and confused but also becoming brighter by the minute, inspired by the realisation that this could actually work out, thanks to the ants!

After a couple of hours, the miraculous labour was complete. There were so many ants she didn't know who to thank, so she thanked them all. Relieved and a little giddy, Psyche settled down, still amazed by what just happened. She did it, they did it, whoever did it, it was done. She relaxed and waited until morning for Aphrodite's return. Psyche even got a chance to sleep a little. At dawn, light flooded into the space as the doors burst open. A surprised and slightly jilted Aphrodite surveyed the scene. And there was Psyche sleeping comfortably, surrounded by four perfect piles of oats, barley, wheat and corn. As soon as she realised Aphrodite was there, Psyche jumped to her feet and courteously wished her a good morning. Aphrodite was surprised but had to be decent about it; after all, somehow the young girl had done it. She led Psyche out into the courtyard and handed her a glass. It was an empty glass. Psyche was puzzled – was Aphrodite going to fill it?

Aphrodite told her: 'You must fill this glass with the water that flows through the river Styx. Fill it for me, then return it, that's all, and you will have passed. It is as simple as that'. Psyche bowed and turned, nearly dropping the glass as she went.

The Styx is the river that flows from the overworld into the underworld. Coins have been discovered in the mouths of people in many ancient burial tombs, placed there to pay Charon the ferryman to take the individual to the other side of the river. Psyche merely had to get the water from the overworld part of the river, but nonetheless she was horrified. She knew that the Styx was guarded real estate – no one helps themselves to Styx water, especially those with mortal parents. In Los Angeles this would mean CCTV cameras two miles out and ferocious dogs waiting, patiently hoping, praying that an invader enters their space. There was no CCTV watching over the Styx, but many ferocious animals lived nearby.

As Psyche approached the river, she could hear their sounds. Signs read, 'Why are you here? Please go back'. She knew she had to press on. One sign said, 'River Styx and eternity, one mile'. Another said, 'Turn back, while the going is good'. She was frightened, and she hadn't even seen the monsters yet – but they sounded awful. As she moved further towards the river, her feet stopped working. She sat under a tree in the warm late-morning sunshine. Psyche did not know how to go any further. She nearly dropped the glass. She told herself that she could call it a day and leave gracefully, but she had to accept the challenge.

She sat bewildered, not sure whether to scream out or cry. She would not succeed; she would be devoured horribly before she got near. Maybe that would be best, she thought. At that moment, she looked up as the sun flickered above her head, like a kind of strobe light going on and off. Psyche was helplessly confused for a moment, before realising what was happening. It was a bird above her, flapping its wings and coming closer. This bird had been sent by Eros, who was watching everything from above – but of course Psyche didn't know that. Eros was in love with her, and he had sent some help.

Zeus had an eagle, and Eros asked if he could borrow it for this special task; the majestic bird gradually came down to meet her. With grace, this powerful beast descended, blowing all of the leaves from the tree. Delicately its talons took the glass from Psyche's hand and it flew up and away towards the river. As if a helicopter had just been there, Psyche was stunned. In less than a minute the eagle was back again, and with divine power and dexterity the glass was gently lowered and presented to her. Then, in a flash, the awesome bird was gone. Psyche called out her thanks but it was too late; there was only an empty blue sky. She peered into the slightly green water, which fizzed a little and seemed to move around inside the glass – all very odd, but that did not matter one bit. She was free; she had not been eaten by a monster after all.

Aphrodite was now definitely becoming a little suspicious. This time Aphrodite, presented with her glass full of Styx water, had to acknowledge some kind of respect. But she also was a little concerned; Psyche was a tough customer who might need something a bit tougher to do. 'Fetch me some Golden wool from the island of the rams', she told Psyche. She didn't use the word 'killer' to describe the rams, but that would have been a more appropriate way of putting it. She didn't mention it because everyone knew it. Many brave men had died trying to steal their wool. Like guard dogs, the rams spent their days hopefully watching our for anyone who fancied their chances. Nobody had ever bought the rams' golden wool because none had been acquired to be sold. Individually, the rams were formidable; together, they were invincible. What was Psyche to do?

As she sat by the banks of the river, she gazed at the river bed and that familiar feeling returned. She didn't have a clue what to do. She should have called it a day and she would have had some stories to tell; perhaps this last task was impossible. Then she heard the reeds in the river speak to her. She heard the soft tones of a woman whispering to her a message. 'Take a boat and cross the river by night while the rams are sleeping. Take a small branch with you, and scrape at the bushes where the rams scratch their backs. Wait until it is the coolest point of the evening and then you will be safe . . .'

Psyche did exactly that. She slept for part of the evening by the river bank, and then set off at night when it was most calm. Gently, quietly and carefully she rowed her way across the stream. Gingerly, she stepped out on the bank and didn't have far to go before she saw shimmering strands in the moonlight. She used her branch as instructed, collecting the fine golden threads, enough for a handful. Her hands were small, but it was enough for Aphrodite. Three tasks down, one to go.

Aphrodite was now more than suspicious; she was furious. 'How did you accomplish this?' she demanded of Psyche, who firmly reminded her 'that requirement was not part of your challenge'. 'Never ask a magician her tricks' is an old adage. Aphrodite could see that Psyche was growing in confidence; she was being helped by someone, or something. If she found out who it was, there would be trouble. As time had gone on the challenges had been more difficult, and this time Aphrodite would seal her fate. Aphrodite told her:

> I see you have something about you. If you do this, you will certainly have my approval. I think you are little vain, and a little beyond yourself, young lady – and this might prove my point. Go to visit with my old friend, Persephone. Fetch for me a jar of her ointment; that would be lovely. Only that, only that.

Psyche knew something we all know. If one ventured to the underworld where Persephone lived, one would not come back. Only Demeter had managed that, but Psyche was no goddess like Demeter. Anyway, Psyche had mortal parents; she was not cut out for that coming-back-from-the-dead business. Demeter only got her daughter back in the overworld for six months of the year, which is why we have the seasons we do. Psyche realised that she would have to live an eternity in the underworld, and this was the worst punishment of all. Some could live there, but she knew she could not. This time it was the end; Aphrodite had set her a challenge she knew she could not achieve.

Psyche quickly forgot the lessons of the past and became desperate. Like a 'dead girl walking', she felt that old feeling stronger than ever before. She couldn't go on and this time, and as emotions welled up inside her, she felt that her feet were moving her to a destination, and quickly. She couldn't do it. She ran up to the top of the Tower of Knowledge, the highest place in the land. She would rather take her own life and at least be in charge of that. Out of breath and crying, she reached the top, still wailing, a complete mess. She collapsed onto the stone floor. She realised this time she was going to end it all and throw herself off the tower, for real.

After all, Psyche thought to herself, she was not Ajax – she was just a girl, not any kind of warrior. Anyway, she was destined for so many better things, she thought, but she must have upset the gods for this to happen. She would kill herself; she knew no other way; it was better than what Aphrodite had planned for her. Eros was watching, distraught – he was freaking out, as they say – he could see that Psyche was serious. Remembering Plato's idea of him, he perhaps thought that he could he not go on without Psyche, the one he loved.

As Psyche took a deep breath to pull herself up from the floor, the building shook – just enough to have her lose her balance and fall back on the floor. The cold stone turned warm to her touch, soft even. The tower was an auspicious palace. Like the original library in Alexander that burned down in 391 AD, it contained every book, all of the accumulated knowledge of the Western world. At that moment the building began to shake.

A woman's voice began to speak to her. In her anxious state, Psyche felt much relieved that someone was there; she was in such a state that she knew she couldn't trust herself. The voice said the following.

> You must do what you must do. Go down the pathless pathway. Do not stop and help anyone, however much you are tempted. Keep on your path. Take two coins for Charon; he will take you to the underworld. Take two barleycorn cakes; feed one to the devil's dog, Cerberus – one on the way in, and one on the way out. Do not dine with Persephone; just eat bread and water. Never open the jar, for what is inside will kill you. You will return safely, if you do these things and only these things.

Caution readers! We are back to 'if', again and we know that can be trouble. Psyche took heed; this was her chance and she had a lifeline back to the overworld. Every time she was told that things would be fine, they had been. Inspired and refreshed, she plucked up some courage and began to walk down the pathless pathway. She carried on and on, wherever it went, reassured and following instructions beautifully. As time went on, she saw a man coming towards her carrying a bundle of sticks. She saw he was blind and was stumbling along; he was dropping them as he went.

She remembered her instructions and this time she carried on, even though she felt bad about the man. Then came a similar situation, with a man on a mule. He was bumping into things and moaning. Psyche remembered the advice to carry on and help no one, but she didn't like it. Psyche really was a good person and would help others all day long if she could. The pathless pathway was the route around the monsters, and after a morning she reached the river safely. There, the nice old ferryman Charon was waiting, always smiling and knowing where to go. She paid him one of her coins and they left the shore. After some time, things went dark and the river changed its speed. Soon after, she arrived, and the boat glided towards the torchlit jetty.

It was very quiet, a fairly barren kind of wilderness. Psyche stepped off and followed the only path. It looked like it was well-used and she became aware of another sound. At a kind of passageway and entrance, a large ferocious and violent dog was straining at its chains, trying to attack her. Psyche did have courage, and she also knew how to keep a safe distance. She showed Cerberus the barleycake and noticed she was getting somewhere. Cerberus softened his act and Psyche slowly approached. Cerberus became curious about the little morcel in her hands. Cerberus was not necessarily loyal as a dog. He didn't love his owner in the same way overworld dogs do. And, anyway, Psyche had a barleycake. Hades had never given him barleycakes, after all, he thought. He beckoned with his head – toss it over and you can go on your way.

Psyche did, and then skirted around, walking gingerly up to a stone hallway cut into the earth. As she turned the corner there was a welcoming sight, for once. Persephone was there, dressed in her royal red robes, looking amazing. She knew Psyche was coming, of course, and had been waiting. As Psyche approached, she held out her arms to greet her. 'You have done so well to get here! Are you alright? Come in, thank you so much for coming!' One important and subtle distinction here, please note; Persephone herself was not a bad woman. She had been captured but not captivated by the devil. She welcomed Psyche, who in no time felt like a weight was lifted off her shoulders. 'You must come and eat something'. Psyche gracefully thanked her and, saying she was on a 'Paleo diet', requested her bread and water. Persephone gladly obliged. After a pleasant time and conversation together, the two parted as friends.

Psyche had enjoyed a nice visit, and with her jar of ointment happily made her way back, no longer scared of anything. Cerberus was pleased to see her, hoping she had another cake for him. Psyche didn't disappoint and he wagged his tail for her – a special honour from Cerberus. She gave her second barleycake to the dog, her coin the Charon, and before she knew it her feet were back on the pathless pathway. As Psyche neared home, she reflected that she had finally done something in her life. Perhaps now she could have faith in herself. Why? She should even be grateful to Aphrodite after all, she thought. Oh, and then she thought, yes, she could deliver the jar to Aphrodite. Psyche told herself, 'the look on her face will be priceless!' What was in the jar, anyway?

Perhaps it would not do any harm to see what was inside. Perhaps it was all part of the plan? That she could get something that Aphrodite couldn't? Besides, everything had worked out well – a little peek wouldn't matter. She thought to herself, 'what woman ever in history with mortal parents ever had this kind of thing in her hands? Fame at last!' She felt a tingle as she clasped the ointment, studied it a moment and then, of course, she opened it. That was Psyche's big mistake – and in a flash it was all over. Psyche's spirit and life left her as she fell to the dust.

Eros, according to Plato, was a homeless wretch – and now he was a devastated one. Zeus took pity and at the last minute granted Eros a favour. Eros fired an arrow that rescued Psyche, bringing her back at the last possible moment. Psyche had received a second chance, and Aphrodite left her alone after that, giving her credit and growing old more gracefully. Aphrodite realised that if she had friends as powerful as these, she must accede and be gracious about it.

What does that all mean for women in sport?

Psyche continually fought with herself throughout the trials. She had had to struggle with her Animus, which, when completely frustrated, turned inward, giving rise to her suicidal ideations. We cannot blame Psyche for this, as she was young. She was truly dealing with forces and challenges we would all find difficult to manage. Each time she was presented with something that seemed beyond, her she gave up. She forgot that there were forces out there to help her, as kinds of clues revealed though interactions with nature.

Each trial has its own meaning, of course, and we shall go through each of them in order.

1. Separating the grains

    Ants are the tiny workers who saved Psyche here. This trial implies the need for organisation. Especially in the twenty-first century, life is very complex. My car alone has thousands of objects that can fail and require attention. Each kind of grain had to be separated and put in its proper place. Today as a psychotherapist I am going to be in trouble if I don't keep an organised calendar. You can be as right-brained as you like, but we all need an element of organisation in our lives. Do the little things, the small details! You need to have an organised approach to life, as a kind of foundation. If you are coming late to training, it is a sign you are not organised enough. If you are an adult and someone takes care of all of your life issues, then you might be suffering as a result. The mind needs some kind of organising principles and capacities. One tip; if you see some rubbish, pick it up. You may think it has nothing to do with your future, but I think it has everything to do with your future. An organised approach is a discipline that every professional needs.

2. The glass of water from the Styx

    Life is fragile. Psyche was given a glass to hold, which could break at any time; there was a need to keep it safe. The bird came from above. Birds can see the bigger picture which is why their image was loved by the Egyptians and has remained so ever since. If you are young, you might like to engage in 'horseplay' with your friends. Your body is your temple. You must be careful as many athletes hurt their chances by damaging themselves off the track in unrelated situations. Do not get lost in the smaller pictures. When the Animus is upset, it tends to present the immediate issues in life as the bigger picture, when they are not. Knowing when to see the bigger picture is a skill.

3. The island of the rams

Psyche had to listen to the reeds in the river, who were her counsel. Reeds in a river imply the emotional flexibility necessary for Psyche. Muhammad Ali once won a great fight against George Foreman by flowing like the reeds, rolling with the punches and always springing back. Psyche went about her task at night when it was cooler, avoiding a confrontation with the rams directly. Psyche was not a fighter. She could never take on the killer rams head-on and win. She was not made of this stuff. Most athletes need to be fighters on the field – but not off it. If you are in opposition with a killer-ram-type person, act when things are cool. If you want to achieve anything, life will go against you at some point. You will need the emotional flexibility that the reeds embody so naturally. This means seeing the bigger picture, bending with the feelings and not being brittle. 'Going with the flow' relates to this, of course. Take the hits that life throws at you but bend and roll; you will bounce back. Choose your battles wisely.

4. Returning from the underworld

Psyche's counsel this time came from the tower that held all human knowledge. Knowledge is the responsibility of education and a crucial aspect of what makes humans so special on Earth. Psyche had to have faith in order to go down the pathless pathway. In order to do so she needed a belief in someone and something outside of herself, something we will visit later with Mickey Mouse. She had to look after her own mission and not be a 'people pleaser' or some kind of saviour, as she had her own mission to complete. Clinically speaking, you can see new clients diverting themselves from their own issues by 'caring' about the issues of others and bypassing their own.

Psyche was told not to dine with Persephone. The Greeks thought that if you dine with the devil, as Persephone unwittingly did, you never entirely come back to who you were before. By dining with Persephone, Psyche would be 'identifying' with her. Without this advice alone, note, she would have shared the same fate. Many young people overdo things and damage themselves internally or physically and life changes as a result. But Psyche was lucky, she had a mission to direct herself toward. She knew she had to return to the overworld in order to complete it. Finally, she could not overcome temptation. She could not differentiate, or resist, her Animus, the shadow part of us that grabs out for things and doesn't think of the consequences. Psyche had gained confidence, and at the most important moment of all, her mind began to wander. Perhaps she was just too young to be an Ajax, as she said herself. However, Eros was the soul that completed her and this appears as an important message in feminine psychology.

Women may or may not have external, physical romantic relationships in the world, but inner relationships are a different priority. These are the crucial ones to integrate and mediate for a healthy psyche. Psyche could not go on without Eros, meaning she had to incorporate that side of her into her own psyche in order to progress. Eros is a romantic expression, a dreamer-lover and a believer in miracles. Our athlete must also have these qualities, or find them somewhere if she can. And remembering that Eros is a Platonic pauper means we can have our inferiorities; they are a natural part of us. Emotional strength for an athlete incorporates and integrates those realities.

This does not mean that a woman has to have a man to rescue her, at all – this must be understood. That is the choice of the woman. She does, however, need her own Eros, especially if she is to be in the creative world.

What does this mean for the athlete?

You need knowledge: intelligence.

You must walk the pathless pathway: faith.

When you are on a mission, do not get diverted: focus.

Do not dine with the devil: conviction.

Become good in the final stages: resilience.

Integrate, get to know and trust your inner Eros: communication.

Do not look back on the field of play, be here, now: presence.

The young, which means most in elite sports, need knowledge in order to progress. They don't always get it. Life is increasingly complicated, the young need information and this is just one kind. That should not mean all mentors and models are either only male or only concerned with quantifiable sources of learning. Not in sport and performance worlds. An important kind of knowledge is represented here. Without life skills the mind may not be strong enough to overcome temptation, or have enough ideas to help it organise thoughts that intrude and emotions that rise within us. We all need mentors of some kind if we want to achieve. Psyche had Demeter; she was lucky. If your life is a kind of mission, then at times all you may have left is faith. And that is not a religious god, although it may be. We all act in faith ever day when we turn a switch or a tap or turn a key, for example.

Deeper still is the faith to carry on. I have known Psyches who have thrown themselves off a tower, and it was then too late to do anything about it. The capacity to tolerate such experiences is often developed with maturity and experience and, above all, support. Psyche had no experience or maturity, but she had Demeter. Underworld people are not necessarily bad in themselves. Persephone was not, but they are not suitable company for athletes either. A deal is a deal, and the instructions had been carried out perfectly up until that point. Do not compromise yourself is the message. Integrate your inner Eros is the other. We may not be in a relationship in the outer world, but women must be in relationship with the inner world of Eros.

The same thing happened to Orpheus in the myth of 'Orpheus and Eurydice'. Orpheus had that rare thing – permission to take his lost love Eurydice home from the underworld, but under one condition: not to look back at her when he walked her up and out. What did he do just before the exit? He looked back and she turned to stone and dropped away. Note here that the Greeks did not give a particular reason why either Psyche or Orpheus did what they did. Bad decisions are often banal and casual. Just like Zidane's headbutt.

Psyche got tired in the last part of her trial; she was not Artemis. Artemis got sharper as time went on, no doubt. Thankfully, Eros rescued young Psyche, and she was able to finish her mission, if slightly scathed. Sadly, there are many Psyches who end up alone with no Eros available, or their Eros turns into Hades.

You would do well to consciously write about ways you can develop your psyche along these lines. Are you organised enough? Flexible enough? Are you acting

FIGURE 6.1 Katie Webb: a twenty-first-century Artemis?

Credit: Trevor Webb.

with faith? Can you hold on when you want to give up? Psyche went on to live a rich life, ending up at the best place possible for the athlete, Mount Olympus, where all the greats live. Any young woman will do well to learn from Psyche and Artemis, for I believe they will serve you well if you ask.

What about the psyche of a young performer today? What can she say? A colleague of mine, Trevor Webb, is a long-time advocate and pioneer of youth protection and welfare in sport in England. His daughter, Katie, has two brothers who are both in professional football academy settings. As with Lily Parr, Katie has grown up competing with her brothers at sport, so she offers a good perspective on the playing field – level or not.

The current generation of female archers

Katie Webb is a county athlete who specialises in javelin and discus for Dacorum and Tring in Hertfordshire. Since first writing she has become Hertfordshire Discus Champion (4 June 2018) and Eastern Counties gold-medalist in javelin (23 June 2018).

My initial research in 2014 involved asking two groups of football players, male and female, the same questions, then comparing the two sets of answers. The following is not a piece of scientific research so there will be no conclusions drawn, but I wondered, if I asked Katie Webb the same questions, how the answers would compare when set aside the research findings from my last book. Katie answered the questions remotely.

1. Tell me about a time when an achievement of yours stood out for you.

    When I threw the qualifying distance to take myself to English Schools and represent my county.

2. And what was important about that event for you personally?

    It was very important to me when I completed this achievement as I had put in a lot of hard work and trained very hard for it.

3. Can you describe a dream you have for your life?

    One of my dreams is to place in the top three in English Schools and get a medal.

4. Is being on a team like being in a kind of family?

    In my athletics team we support each other a lot and want each other to do the best we can and achieve all our goals. We also don't want to let our team down as they are like a family to us.

5. What does it feel like to lose?

    I feel very annoyed and frustrated at myself when I lose; however, it makes me want to work harder and win my next competition.

6. What does it feel like to win?

    It feels really good when I win as it makes me think all this hard training I'm doing is paying off.

7. What is different about being a female rather than a male competitor?

    I personally don't think there is any difference between being a male competitor or woman because they both want to achieve the same goals and are willing to work the same amount of time.

8. Is there anything else you would like to add about being a young female athlete?

    It has been a great experience that I will never forget, and I wouldn't change any of it.

When I read Katie's responses it is apparent how dedicated she is to her craft. She is able already to express no regret about her choice in life, so she does appear to be receiving some life-affirming experiences and relationships. She appears immersed in her sport, which must be natural and necessary at her age and level. Katie didn't indicate any differences between the sexes in her sporting world. She is not a victim in any way. Katie added that she trains with older players, which also inspires her.

In keeping with the research in my study, Katie also sees her teammates as a family, referring to them as a reason to keep her standard high. Katie appears to take a stance of self-responsibility as a response to losing, natural as an athlete that competes on her own. My research indicated that women tended to internalise their negative feelings more than men, who tended to expel their emotions, cursing defeats using what we called 'Shadow language'. Women took responsibility more often, and were able to process their feelings much better as a result. Men appeared to need the group more; women appeared more responsible to it.

In the context of the original study, female co-researchers did appear more intuitive and self-searching when confronted with failure and challenge. It may seem stereotypical, but it does help explain why in Greece women held the important role of *pythia*, or oracle at Delphi, interpreting and intuiting the messages from the gods. Now it might be controversial to connect any attributes to a gender, but as we have seen that can be a recipe for epistemological violence and women have had enough! Women consistently appeared better at processing emotions in team cultures. Those of the future should reflect those changes in the way they work. The England women's Lionesses apparently had two sport psychologists, so it shows they are not averse to this idea, and that the future is bright for both worlds.

References

Arnot, C. (2011). 'English Women's Football Aims to Score Again', *The Guardian*, 12 April.
Beilock, S. (2010). *Choke: What the Secrets of the Brain Reveal About Getting it Right When You Have To*. New York: Free Press.
Callimachus (1921). 'Hymn III to Artemis', in *Hymns and Epigrams* (A.W. Mair and G.R. Loeb, trans.), Classical Library Volume 129. London: William Heinemann.

Castillejo, I.D. (1974). *Knowing Women*. Boston, MA: Shambhala.

Dasgupta, N. and Asgari, S. (2004). 'Seeing is Believing: Exposure to Counter Stereotypic and its Effect on the Malleability of Automatic Gender Stereotyping', *Journal of Experimental Social Psychology* 40: 642–658.

Dasgupta, N. and Dennehey, T. (2017). *Female Peer Mentors Early in College Increase Women's Positive Academic Experiences and Retention in Engineering* (S. Cheryan, ed.). Seattle: University of Washington.

De Beauvoir, S. (1968). *Force of Circumstance*, Vol. III (R. Howard, trans., 1963). London: Penguin.

Eller-Boyko, D. (2017). 'Longing for the Feminine: Reflections on Love, Sexual Orientation, Individuation, and the Soul', *Psychological Perspectives* 3 (C.G. Jung Institute of Los Angeles).

Homer (1896). *Iliad* (A. Pope, trans., 1896). New York: American Book Company.

Homer (1938). *The Odyssey*, VIII (W.H.D. Rouse, trans., 1938). New York: Signet Classics.

Isenberg, N. (2008). 'Review: Her Best Shot: Women and Guns in America by Laura Browder', *The Journal of Southern History* (Southern Historical Association) 74(1): 175–176.

Keegan, M. (2014). 'Wembley Attendance: FA Must Act on Low Turnout, Warns Davies', BBC.com. Online. www.bbc.com/sport/football/29069804 (retrieved 3 January 2017).

Nande, A. (2017). 'Lily Parr: The Gun Which Dodged Bullets to Pioneer Women's Football', footballparadise.com. Online. www.footballparadise.com/lily-parr/ (retrieved 12 February 2018).

Pankhurst, E. (1913). 'Freedom or Death', speech delivered in Hartford, CT, 13 November. *The Guardian*. Online. www.theguardian.com/theguardian/2007/apr/27/greatspeeches1 (retrieved 29 June 2018).

PBS (n.d.). 'Biography: Frank Butler'. Online. www.pbs.org/wgbh/americanexperience/features/oakley-butler/ (retrieved 28 December 2017).

Riley, G. (1994). *The Life and Legacy of Annie Oakley*. Norman, OK: University of Oklahoma Press.

Rose, H.J. (1959). *A Handbook of Greek Mythology*. New York: Dutton.

Rowland, S. (2017). *Remembering Dionysus*. London and New York: Routledge.

Shirl, K. (1992). *Annie Oakley*. Norman, OK: University of Oklahoma Press.

Simpkin, J. (2014). 'Dick, Kerr's Ladies', Spartacus-Educational. Online. http://spartacus-educational.com/Fdickkerrs.htm (retrieved 3 January 2018).

Singh, S.S. (2004). *Spirituality of Sport*. Cincinnati, OH: Saint Anthony Messenger Press.

Solomon, M. (1995). *Mozart: A Life*. New York: HarperCollins.

UEFA (2016). 'UEFA Report: Registered Female Footballers on the Rise', UEFA.com. Online. www.uefa.com/insideuefa/football-development/womens-football/news/newsid=2516070.html#/ (retrieved 1 January 2018).

UEFA (2017). 'Qualified Female Coaches: 17,550+, a 31% Rise Since 2015/16', UEFA.com. Online. www.uefa.com/insideuefa/football-development/womens-football/news/newsid=2431355.html#/ (retrieved 1 January 2018).

West, R. (2005). *The Young Rebecca: Writings of Rebecca West, 1911–17*. London: Royal National Institute of the Blind.

Williams, J. (2003). *A Game for Rough Girls? A History of Women's Football in Britain*. London: Routledge.

Zdanowicz, C. (2015). '10-Year-Old Shooter: I Want To Be an Inspiration', CNN. Online. www.cnn.com/2014/10/17/living/10-year-old-competitive-shooter-irpt/index.html (retrieved 28 December 2017).

7

NUMBERS, PHASES, AND MYTHS THAT SPEAK TO SPORT

Mental fitness, archetypal phases, threats, and opportunities

We are still in the middle section of the book but, then again, that is not quite accurate. The middle has its own beginning, middle and end. We are heading towards the end of that middle. That still means here a commitment to knowledge for the aspiring athlete who is in opposition to something. Hopefully now we can take off our shackles and go onwards and upwards. No mountain is a straight path upwards; sometimes we go down. Life is not linear. As we progress through any real challenge in life, different qualities are required at different times. Paying attention to phases is one way of developing the psychic condition of someone able to go the distance.

Lately, I have been reading quotes about writers who get tired during a project. It is a hazard; the writer becomes prey to worry, boredom, irritation or a host of other distractions. Distractions happen to us in lots of different ways; they are a form of what we in the clinical world call dissociation. As a performer of one kind or another for all of my professional life, I also know that being tired can be a great opportunity to distinguish oneself. If this book were a marathon of 26 miles, we are approaching mile 20. The last chapter is not far away. I am conscious that there remains much to share if we are to have any chance of capturing this elusive soul we are seeking. I suggest to the athlete again: be different and be courageous with your inner life. To survive and thrive in these later spells we must use our imagination, intuition and inspiration, from wherever we can get it. To seek inspiration, find chemistry from somewhere, somehow.

When I first decided to write this book, a section about the number seven was the first I had in mind. This is a romantic idea; but first, an important reprise. We have now introduced the fundamental concept of the Shadow and Animus, and a sense of how powerful these forces can be. Both are potent and potentially destructive instinctual expressions housed deep in the unconscious soul of us all. We can witness how successful athletes (and leaders anywhere) have the capacity to connect with them and use them to their own advantage. Elite performers are also able to develop and excite these potentialities when they need them. At the same time, they must restrain them, convert them and use them to their advantage. These are also the essential principles of alchemy and alchemical transformation.

Later we shall meet one of the chief alchemists, Merlin. Call it inspiration, drive or dopamine, we must be able to summon these spirits like a Shaman calls the spirit of the animals. I would put it to you that athletes especially cannot afford to lose their inner animal. The animation of performers is most often what captures our attention. Like it or not, it seems any athlete will have to find a place in their house for the dodgy relatives – conviction and commitment. Thankfully it seems that if we give them a job to do, like sport, they help us. They know how to create chemistry, sparks, motion, which is when change happens. It is the realm of the quixotic, the original 'X factor'. This section is dedicated to the athlete who wants to win. Myths are not meaningless; underneath they illustrate key themes, the prize insights in psychotherapy and interior growth in sport. What follows at the end of this chapter is a series of stories, but do not be fooled. All convey the deadly realities for any achiever. All fairytales have within them life and death, the intimate territory of our friend Dionysus.

Winning is always possible in life if we can learn how to keep coming back. Some young players in sport do not make it, but I often get a sense that they are going to be amazing at some point in their lives. They will one day play some game, some job, some mission to a high degree. I can see it within them. Whatever we want to happen may not always happen *when* we want. Life can be cruel in that way, and in my experience it frequently is. Regardless, there is the deal and the mission, the deal the athlete must make. If you choose something as a target, a goal – like me writing this book – then it is up to you to chase it down like a wild rabbit and not give up until it is accomplished.

We are moving towards the dusk of this book, so to speak; I must stay awake and not get drowsy. Distractions can be one way of getting drowsy. Everywhere today I see people automatically dive into phones, 'zone out' and not be present. It is fine, we all do it, but perhaps it is more a case of *when*, and do we know how not to? We shall see that this is a universal but subtle theme for some of the ancient stories that follow. People go to sleep in their lives, sometimes for years on end. Sometimes they wake up just in time, like Scrooge in Charles Dickens' *A Christmas Carol*. But many do not; we must not forget them.

There are naturally times of danger for animals in the wild, throughout changing seasons as well as during the passage of an ordinary day. Dawn and dusk are optimum times for a hunter, like the lion, or a soldier because the world is a bit more ethereal, a bit more shady at these times – a bit more dreamy, even; animals may be drowsy and less alert. But not the hunter. For the hunter, this is an opportunity to strike. Every sports team competitor and performer knows that there are vulnerable passages of time during a game or play. One genius of the sport world famously demonstrated this principle, knocking out the boxing machine George Foreman in the 'rumble in the jungle' fight in Kinshasa, The Democratic Republic of the Congo in 1974. This contest was known as the 'rope-a-dope' because after Foreman's endless assaults Muhammad Ali began to flag, then awoke as if from a slumber. In a shocking whirlwind of boxing, the stunned Foreman was helpless, and fell like a tree.

Muhammad Ali once shared how he remembered thinking at that point in the fight, 'man, you have picked the wrong place to be tired'. It is not just at the end of games when this happens. There are many such phases within a contest. As a determined actor I consciously decided to be good in the first ten minutes, and not be dogged by nerves, as many actors were. I was also nervous, but I learned to overcome it eventually with drive and commitment to the craft. Dangers exist for any actor or sport team during the beginning phase, those first ten minutes, when anxieties are at their highest. If my opponent is not 'played in', then surely this is a kind of invitation?

Another phase is the period just after a team concedes a point. At that point the team that has just scored is at its most likely to lose its advantage, if the will and the spark is there to make it happen. If it is not, it will be the reverse. I have always found exploring this theme of phases with players a worthwhile exercise. Distractions can be a real kind of dissociation. Dissociation is what happens with a lot of clinical trauma cases, and is a natural reaction. The psyche learns to opt out of the present plane and goes to live on another plane inside the imagination. There it is easier to cope than in the real world. For some this may be the best option but for many of us it is just the banal practice of 'zoning out'. For others, it is the only way of protecting their psyche from all kinds of horrors.

For most us this bad habit intrudes at the wrong times. For an individual player, mental drift can happen at any moment. For an athlete, it often happens in the important moments, when under most scrutiny, such as an important save, tackle or during the chance of a goal. If not internally fit, athletes cannot retain presence and composure in crucial moments. A clear mind, a fit mind, is the vehicle that can take an athlete to the later stages of competition in the best condition possible. What can get us to those phases in that shape? What can give us the energy to get our necks ahead at this point in the race?

We know by now that an ethical attitude towards life will help. Ethics are the rules that relate to the commitment to a cause greater than ourselves. In my experience young athletes tend to grow as people when they seek inner disciplines. Within mythological narratives athletes can locate some of the deeper truths that all children who grow into adults benefit from considering. As we go on, we must draw from a deeper well, remembering the wisdom of sometimes looking in the least likely places. This chapter will encapsulate all that has gone before in important narrative stories. These stories also contain new information and ways of looking at familiar scenarios in a new light.

Ethics will help at this dangerous stage, but what is truly needed here now is the facility of our imagination. Imagination is one of the great eternal gifts and skills of the hunter, artist, thinker and detective. Everyone can benefit form a good imagination but it is a key skill for the long journeys of life. Our imagination can serve us, if we tend to it and keep it exercised. It is a problem-solver and inner guide, when given inspiring messages and a path to follow. Myths once provided a way by which early cultures could preserve ideas as if they were valuable commodities such as water. Water features in many spiritual stories as well.

In the past, communities will have had certain members who travelled. As hunters or traders, they will have experienced at least some of the world around them, a quite meaningful attribute. Cultural stories from different groups will either have been shared, or protected as a community secret. We know travelling and trading did Greeks sailors and artists no harm. No doubt they will have shared their experiences and the resultant knowledge with other members of the community. A literal journey somewhere is a form of education, if we are willing to be open. We can afterwards hope to see our own contexts in a new light. 'Learn from the mistakes of others' was always part of the reality that our ancestors had to endure. We have to learn how to make the right mistakes at the right time – as any gambler knows.

Lucky number seven and sport

The first chapter I envisioned for this book related to the number seven and luck. Ask any mathematician – numbers are important in life and sport. We all need numbers in order to be found – either for or houses or our phones. But numbers can go too far sometimes. 'I am a name not a number!' is the constant refrain of angry people who feel dehumanised. Millions in concentration camps during World War II had their numbers tattooed onto them by Nazis. We must watch numbers; the power of data is on the rise in the West and will affect us all. The good side of anything must never take our attention away from the bad.

Numbers also have other, deeper relationships with the natural world. As we have already noted there is a trinity within life and sport; beginnings, middles and endings. There are also principles and motions in the physical world that cross over

FIGURE 7.1 A twenty-first-century Dionysus, Eric Cantona.

Credit: Denis Makarenko.

and combine matter with numbers. Any surfer will tell you that waves at sea arrive in threes. But why is it seven years' bad luck if you break a mirror?

Seven is a mysterious and unique number. The opposite ends of a dice always add up to seven. In Japan there are seven lucky gods who sail a treasure ship that, like Father Christmas, comes once a year and gives gifts. Seven carries a certain mystique. Seven is an important number in sport, and in football in particular. Three of Manchester United's greatest ever players wore the number: George Best, Eric Cantona and David Beckham. It is a number of the mysterious, the individual and the quixotic.

Many sports performers who have wilder Dionysian sides appear vulnerable to drink or drugs. This is what the French call 'la grande folie'. But not necessarily – as in the case of Frenchman Eric Cantona. As a soccer player he lived his game on an edge of ferocious intensity and skill. Elite sport is a world where those with edge can thrive, and Cantona had the 'X factor'. He was an authentic agoniste, and now unsurprisingly a successful actor. Like Socrates the Brazilian, he is a wild, romantic spirit who defies authority and conventions. He is an archetypal Dionysian figure in sport. There are not so many, but you can find them if know what you are looking for.

Eric Cantona had considerable strength of character as a man and was not afraid of controversy. He knew how to stand alone, and like Dionysus he naturally defied conventions and rules. Cantona embodied everything we have described previously regarding the potential of the Shadow. He was not just wild; he was disciplined and religious about his practice and technique. He once bemused a pedestrian press in England by comparing poetry to some of the great goals scored. Like Zidane, Cantona could be volatile, once notoriously attacking a foul-mouthed belligerent supporter in the stands.

He was unpredictable and fiery, but there was also a natural logos at work. Cantona once famously stood like a statue after scoring a magnificent goal, surrounded by chaos and ecstasy. Like a matador bullfighter in Madrid he demonstrated his transcendent power over the forces of darkness. Like a bullfighter the poise indicated a clinical term: core strength. Like a tree standing straight in a gale, all his fans screamed while he stood still with his hands on his hips. Cantona was known as 'King Eric' and was voted the most popular player in Manchester United's history.

David Beckham also wore the number seven shirt for Manchester United. At one time he was one of the most famous people in the world. Beckham showed he was capable of containing the vast public projections that were once aimed at him. He was able to be a god like Hercules, and keep his feet on the ground. The Greeks would have approved. Like Eric Cantona, he has been able to come out of soccer fame smiling in life and on top. It can be done.

David Beckham was a notoriously tidy person and figure, manicured and precise. Apollo, the brother of Artemis, also carried a bow. Beckham took the freekicks and scored some of the great goals for England, and – crucially – at the right moments! Being a freekick taker, he was a kind of archer, making Beckham an Apollonian kind of archetypal figure. Cantona is a Dionysian figure, Apollo's brother. When the two forces work together, magic often happens.

The archetypal figures remain. It is the people that inhabit their thrones that change. We all have our moment on the stage, as Shakespeare said. Now the stage is set for the next new kings and queens of world soccer. Like Aphrodite, the old and established will have to accept that the new young Psyches will come. If the ephebes are treated properly, they will. And like Aphrodite, the current stars don't have to like it, or give up without a fight.

The ancient archetypal forces of progress are embodied in the eternal process of breaking down old patterns, systems and structures. If you look at any derelict house, nature finds its way back in through every crack and pipe until one day the house falls down. Dionysus is also the god of vines, meaning dirty old nature breaking things down. Scientists predict that eventually the sunken Titanic will just be an orange stain in the mud. But some things will remain down there, because they are indelible.

Seven is a magical number that cannot be divided unto itself. Consequently, this is perhaps why it has gained singular significance as the symbolic identity of the individual. As we know, individuality and undivisibility are crucially important principles for us as human beings. Seven is everywhere. Originally it was thought there were seven planets in the solar system. Newton discovered there were seven colours in the light spectrum. 'Seventh Heaven' is a term often used to denote the level of God's realm. There are the seven deadly sins. In the Bible, God rested on the seventh day, and of course we have seven days in the week.

Research shows that seven is an important number for the brain itself. It was realised in the 1950s that there was an intimate relationship between the number seven and the workings of the brain. Seven represents a numerical threshold in the capacity of the brain to process information. You can only hold seven things in your attention span. It seems that, for basic physical reasons, normal brains cannot function any better than that. When I learned about this I wondered if seven was the optimum size of early hunting groups.

Myths that speak to sport

Like this book, often before the beginning of a film in a Los Angeles theatre, an announcer walks to the front and gives some notices and protocols before the film begins. Before you read these stories, there are some things to cover.

I shall humbly take it upon myself to distill the essential meanings of the different myths for you. There are many versions to each, and perhaps many perspectives that differ from mine. I do not want to lose energy or momentum by detouring into questions about the original meanings or elaborate renditions of the different interpretations. In keeping with the Dionysian spirit, there will be no citations in this chapter. These citations are for Apollo, and there have been many by now. We shall let the stories stand for themselves and then deduce the salient meanings afterwards.

We are still in the opposition section of the book, so the stories that follow have been chosen to in order to benefit the athlete. I shall share the meanings as I see them, so please forgive the subjectivity. Perhaps I can at least be a voice of experience. All of the following myths have been shared in a sporting environment by me and they seemed to fit. Remember Jung's advice that we cannot be too schematic when considering the psyche – not if we want an accurate connection with it. I have chosen myths with origins from all over the world relating to men, women, children and the elderly.

Japan: 'The Magnificent Seven' (as we know it now)

'The Magnificent Seven' is a classic Western film released in 1960, directed by John Sturges, about hired gunmen in the old Wild West. Los Angeles is a special place in part because of the city's Mexican influence. In the 2018 Football World Cup, Mexico beat the world champions Germany, leading to much joy and celebration in Los Angeles. I have had the honour of working with some Mexican soccer players who played with Spanish flair and English doggedness. I have chosen to highlight this story because it involves many of the crucial skill areas that just have to be in the athlete's toolbox. The higher you want to go, the more important they are. Indeed, little about that has changed since the birth of organised sport at the Olympics. Athletes are a kind of hired gun, just as actors and musicians are the same kind of professionals.

Life on the road for the performer has always meant going from venue to venue and trying their luck. Most athletes recount to me the perennial effort of trying to build some rhythm into their fastest time, game, personal best. Contests are an invitation, a gathering of athletes and spectators and a piece of research. By the end the athlete will be paid his of her dues, or not. We who care join the gunfighter or the gladiator in the shared experience, and we want to be the ones left standing by the end.

Like all good myths, 'The Magnificent Seven' is also a film about violence and killing. Dionysian themes are inextricably linked to the process of life and death. When an actor forgets their lines, it is also a kind of death. With guns and fighting, there is no room for flops, nervous breakdowns, the jitters of a bad day at the office. You need to be mentally fit in order to survive battles of any kind. I remember an old man in England sharing with me an interesting problem faced by pilots in World War II. He told me that they had to rest, stop, be at peace in some way in order to survive. As worried and anxious as you may be, you cannot afford to get tired or too worried. Performers inflicted by this become a paradox. The thing we fear the most becomes the most likely outcome.

Like a poor animal, the psyche becomes stalked and trapped. There are antidotes. One is restoration, otherwise known as rest. This is a primary skill for the competitor. Worry is most often a sign of tiredness or loneliness for the professional. The ambition of pilots at all times was not to kill their opponent. The imperative was to stay alive and come back tomorrow. In a race you must be mentally and spiritually fit if you want the best chance of coming back another day. It was always ever so for the mercenary gun for hire.

The issue for the performer is that they cannot hide; they must be out in the world being observed. Problems come from strange directions. 'The Magnificent Seven' opens with an exposed Mexican village being raided and robbed by a group of local bandits. Exasperated villagers leave town in search of gunmen who can help them rescue their home. They meet Chris, an ex-gunfighter played by legendary actor Yul Brynner. They ask him to fight for them, but initially he is uninterested. He has had enough of guns and wants to retire in one piece. One of the villages then produces a handkerchief with a few rings and bangles and coins. He says he is holding everything of value owned in the village. Chris is moved and surprised by this and responds compassionately. Chris is not just a killer, and he joins the villagers in their struggle.

We follow the fortunes of the gunfighters as they set off on their mission to vanquish the bandits and save the village. The film is a great example of the 1960s action-adventure genre that Hollywood specialised in, and that only Hollywood could produce. The film also has a cast of great screen actors, such as Steve McQueen and Charles Bronson, all in their prime. Special fighters are trained to be individuals, of course, but they must also be able to work in teams. The greatest teams are often like Acteon's dogs, all individuals with their own identity and specialisation. They have a 'feel' to them. Character is a visible trait, by definition. You see a lot of character around you when talent is gathered together.

The Magnificent Seven themselves were a great team, individuals captured and embodied by these great actors, who contained their Shadow and so well portrayed a team. All individuals, in my experience, have a subtle quality that they seem to share: unpredictability. Experienced professionals need only be predictable in terms of our companions' conviction and commitment. But as we know when things get tough, we are going to need more.

Early on in 'The Magnificent Seven' there is an important scene; a young Mexican hopeful arrives wanting to join the team. Chris is looking for masters with a gun, and is not taking just anybody. Consequently, he tests Chico's gunfighting skills and speed. Chico ends up humiliated as he cannot even attempt the test before him. As we know from Erikson's stages, for young Chico this is a horrific experience. He feels shamed, and storms off in embarrassment.

Sure enough, Chico later comes back, but obviously after drinking rather than thinking about what happened. He nearly loses his life in a drunken stupor by resentfully taking on the master, Chris, in a bar. He eventually collapses to the floor drunk and is fortunate to survive the incident. Chico could have just gone away defeated with a hangover; many do. But when the gunfighters saddle up and leave for their mission, he follows. As the days pass, he keeps up with them on the trail. Chico keeps a respectful distance and stays just far enough away while being in touch, demonstrating his independence and competence.

Then for a time he disappears. The gunfighters have become used to his presence, and become puzzled as to his fate. This time Chico is ahead of them, eating the cooked fish he just caught, sitting comfortably by a well-made fire as they arrive. Chris is amused; they all laugh. He beckons Chico over as a gesture of acceptance. Chico refuses, no, he beckons him to come his way, not theirs. He has generated their respect and is welcomed into the group. For all purposes, a kind of initiation has taken place for Chico. He is now one of them.

The West is the only region in the world today where there is no formal path of initiation for the young. My research for my previous book showed that initiation is a crucial life experience in any athlete's career. Debuts in older-age or bigger professional teams and first goals often represented significant initiations for young soccer players when asked. Chico could have run off with his wounded ego and that would have been the end of it. His wounded ego instead did something different – he discovered for himself a mission. He wanted to prove himself and put actions to his feelings.

A top talent scout once told me that he noticed that young athletes have one of two responses to bad situations. Bad situations mean bad games, humiliating misses, doing badly or being heavily criticised. He said that 50 per cent go off into their shells, so to speak. They get wounded. Those 'in their shells' might become isolated, lose their confidence and disappear. It could be a while before they play well again. Some never do, of course. But here we are describing something different. Part of the human genius is the way we can adopt an attitude, a perspective, a belief that will set us on a better course. The word 'determination' comes from this principle. It is the Axial-Age idea that we can change our world by what we tell ourselves and how we act.

Chico is determined to change his world, and he comes back, different. He represents the other kind of young player the scout described. This second type can become just as upset and vexed as the first. However, they come back fighting, so to speak. They recover themselves and set about living in the solution rather than living in the problem. Both get hurt, but respond differently. Whenever this 'come-back-fighting' type eventually find some kind of form, by winning or playing well, they often look at the coach disdainfully (but also respectfully), as if to say 'See?! What are you on about?! I can do it!' That look is an ancient look, from man to boy and boy to man. It is surely from our beginnings.

Chico also shows he can live off the land and be comfortable in nature. For most of us city dwellers, living outside means being somewhere rural in a tent or a camper van. However, this remains the stock-in-trade of elite military forces such as the SAS and the Green Berets. Living in nature means you have to live with your own nature; you are independent with nature as a whole. It is not simple or safe, it requires knowledge to survive. Hunters of the past will have had to contend with the same survival realities.

In the movie Chico is the apprentice amongst elite performers. He gets to join them because he demonstrates his flexibility, his personality, by redirecting and channeling his negative emotions. This is a real key for a performer. He has conviction and commitment and those qualities get him accepted. His gun skills probably aren't any better than at the beginning, but he shows that every team has room for a junior apprentice who cares passionately and shows independence and promise.

Chico shows the group that he has 'ego strength'. He no longer projects his Shadow anger outwards onto the man who had initially rejected him. I have noticed in psychotherapeutic relationships there are necessary archetypal conditions that make emotional growth possible. When adults endure painful feelings without drinking, dissociating or numbing them away in some other way I see growth happening. The tendency to blame diminishes or becomes absent completely. This is why victimhood is to be avoided if at all possible (and sometimes it is not until certain conditions are met). It is because we cannot naturally make the full emotional journey we need to make when emotional capacities grow. Athletes must be allowed to feel, and sport is an emotional world where emotions are needed.

It is not commonly known that 'The Magnificent Seven' had a predecessor, originally in Japan called 'The Seven Samurai'. In 1956, director Akira Kurosawa wrote the film, which used 'Ronin' instead of gunfighters. Ronin were Samurai warriors that did not have a company or a group; they were freelancers. The film was a huge box office success in Japan and then as 'The Magnificent Seven' in America, becoming one of the most respected films of all time. The success of the adaptation was thanks to Yul Brynner's original intuition that the film contained great universal meanings beyond time and culture. This is why we do well to learn about them, and one of the contributions that Jungian depth psychology can make to sports is having a language that can define it.

For the athlete

When athletes develop the capacity to take responsibility for feelings (containment) without needing to eject them outwards (blame), growth also tends to occur. They tend to be the athletes that are still standing in the end. Those that develop self-containment, alongside a passion so strong that it needs containing, perhaps? Passion is an excellent quality for the competitor; it is a primary requirement and is a rarer quality than one might imagine. Psychotherapy, remember, is not about being happier; it is about living more fully. Passion stored within our individual Shadow complexes can move us forward in life. Chico transcends something within himself, showing he is ready for the next step, but it is not 'pretty'.

But what is the point of this? What is the reward; why not 'act out'? As it happens, there is a benefit from 'feeling' things. That is, the next time something bad or painful happens (and it does), by bearing it, the athlete can develop an enhanced capacity to tolerate the situation. Leadership is sometimes the capacity to tolerate and bear negatives. Inner leadership is also about these things. The lesson is not that the successful don't feel loss; they do. But we do see that they can move on quicker.

That is often appreciated by team members alike, of course. This is what emotional growth represents, the capacity to heal. It is an ancient emotional truth ignored by many today but it remains a hidden key to building a future in the field. Chico lives in the solution and not the problem, and he finds himself a dream and a cause.

A dream is a common term used for an individual quest or mission. Somehow, we sense a destination, a calling for our lives (if we can hear a calling) and then we set about finding a way to get there. But as this book has relayed on many occasions, there are rules. Elite athletes develop a strength of character that can also bear the blows, struggles and strains that come with victories. Become like a gunfighter, poised and ready to live in the moment.

In short

Focus: find a mission and strive for it.

Containment: have fire and passion that is not self-defeating.

Independence: be able to survive in the wilds of life.

Persistence: keep coming back to prove a point.

Maturity: have the capacity to heal.

Presence: live in the solution, not the problem.

Connection: find your group, your family or your clan.

USA: Mickey Mouse, 'The Sorcerer's Apprentice'

Walt Disney (1901–1966) surely deserves a place in the pantheon of storytellers alongside Homer, Shakespeare and Dickens. That may be a controversial idea; he was a divisive figure in his professional life. However, few can claim to have reformed and revolutionised an entire genre, but he can. Before Walt Disney, cartoons were essentially elementary pedestrian productions using basic comedic forms such as slapstick or pathos. Disney introduced sophisticated artwork in his animation, combining deep mythological narratives into his productions.

There was another Disney innovation: a visceral and emotional connection with the audience. Another 'seven', 'Snow White and the Seven Dwarfs' (1937) had a scene representing the bleak funeral of the heroine Snow White after being murdered by the Wicked Witch. This was a first. Disney had confidence that children in a cinema could bear the emotional realities of the contexts he portrayed, and he was right. Soon after 'Snow White' there was another example, when 'Bambi' (1942) was left exposed and helpless in the forest after hearing his mother get shot and killed. As with the character Mowgli in Rudyard Kipling's *The Jungle Book* (a live-action film was also released in 1942) we could all perhaps identify with the boy, like Adler's inferior organ, helpless and in a deep forest, full of beasts, good and bad alike. It is worth noting that the world was at war when the film was released, and for many this was the ghastly truth and reality.

FIGURE 7.2 Mickey Mouse learns what it means to wear a golden hat with stars.
Credit: Debby Wong/Shutterstock.com.

Disney was bold, brilliant and a clever marketing man. One of his most famous creations was the cartoon character Mickey Mouse. Jung noted how all religious traditions appear to have a 'divine child' and in 1928 this one came from the United States. Mickey remains a popular figure today and is appreciated all around the world. He qualifies as a divine child because he is a figure of innocence. He never harms anyone and is eternally good, like his sister Minnie. We do not often see Mickey being 'naughty' but the film 'Fantasia' (1940) is unusual because that is indeed what we see. It was not regarded as one of the great Disney films, but it has a great scene within it − Disney at it's best, involving another archetypal figure, Merlin.

Merlin was King Arthur's famous wizard who features in many English medieval myths. Merlin is a familiar archetypal identity, the wise old man like Yoda in 'Star Wars'. The archetype of Merlin features at the beginning of many stories, like *Harry Potter*, and is here at the beginning and the end of this cautionary tale regarding the human psyche. So far, we have described psychic forces in the world that exist, whether we are conscious of them or not. Some of these are Shadow forces which, when we go unconscious, can put us in real peril. As we just described, Disney knew how to connect the Dionysian themes of life and death in his stories − and one scene plays the battle of those tensions in graphic detail.

In 'The Sorcerer's Apprentice', a chapter from 'Fantastia', we first see Mickey carrying pails of water down a stone passageway inside a castle. The old spiritual phrase goes 'chop the wood, and carry the water'. Mickey has his work to do but in passing notices Merlin hard at work. Merlin is focusing his concentration on a pulsating ball of light on his table. After coaxing it to life, he is able to conjure up a magical coloured butterfly that fills the air, out of nothing. Mickey is captivated by the beautiful sight. Then, boom! With a flash of light, it is gone. Merlin has finished, and we see him put his hat down as he retires for the day. Mickey blinks, a little bewildered by the awesome spectacle he has just witnessed.

Mickey investigates a bit further. He knows he is alone and cannot resist putting the hat on his head. He tries a trick, and is delighted to discover that he can move the broom on command. Mickey orders it to work, so it dutifully carries the water for him, obeying his wish. Joyfully he develops a little mastery and soon lots of brooms are climbing the stairs for him, fetching the water. We see Mickey enjoys this immensely and feels very happy about it. At one point he takes a breather and sits down in Merlin's chair. We see he gets a little dozy and soon he falls asleep. For a moment and we can see inside his ecstatic dreams. He is outside, up in the air, with a magic wand making stars appear in the sky. What fun; it is all so easy.

Mickey wakes up from his dream. To his horror, he sees an endless line of brooms carrying water and now the place is beginning to flood. He tries to stop them, but he cannot. There is no way he can undo the spell he created, and he starts to panic. The rising water creates a vortex, and we see Mickey getting caught by it. Half-afloat, he reaches for the magic book as he desperately flicks through the pages, looking for the spell that will undo it all. Mickey is dying, and begins to drown as the vortex begins to take him under.

At this point Merlin returns and is able to command the deluge to clear away. With the water gone, an embarrassed Mickey is uncovered, looking up at a very cross Merlin. Mickey gives his charming smile, but Merlin is having none of it and only furrows his brow. Mickey respectfully hands him the bucket and broom back, offering again nothing but his sweet smile. Merlin is still unamused. In fact, he gives Mickey a thwack on his backside as Mickey quickly scurries off back to his chambers.

For the athlete

So much happens in this animation, but not a word of dialogue. There are some archetypal themes here worth developing. Mickey could not resist the temptation of getting something else to do the work for him. Many chemically addicted young people never experience life without the feeling of some mind-altering chemical of one kind or another. The chemical does the work for us, or pretends to. The athlete and performer has to be very cautious about substances as they must be able to locate their own highs and lows, uppers and downers. The archetypal pattern and roots of addiction are portrayed here, but more than that for the athlete.

As we saw at the beginning of the book, the magic hat is that ancient symbol of wisdom and human practice. In Merlin it represents the capacity to make a butterfly out of nothing, a capacity which takes time. The butterfly represents the Protean spirit of transformation. With transformation there is a simple but effective formula for the athlete (and anyone else, for that matter).

application + information = transformation

Mickey had plenty of application, but he lacked restraint. He was alone and not with his master, and he could not resist temptation. 'When the cat is away, the mice will play', goes the ancient archetypal truth. Character is the capacity to 'delay gratification', which means to offset something good now in order to get more later on. Mickey did what so many do: he looked in a book to try and save himself at the point when it had become too late. By then he had started something he could not stop. It has been said that character is revealed by the things we can resist; Mickey could not resist, and we can see the result.

Mickey is just an apprentice; like Chico in 'The Magnificent Seven', he is still young and inexperienced. A little success is a dangerous thing for an athlete. Mickey thinks he has the power, and we witness how narcissistic, seductive ideas of omnipotence develop. This feeds a false sense of power within the self. Narcissism always says 'I am god!' This is often a precursor of trouble for all humans, often known as 'hubris', and especially so for the young. They are not Eric Cantona yet. Mickey needed his Merlin; he was not Merlin.

To become Merlin takes time and practice. Evidence shows that only when you are a Merlin, a Cantona or a Beckham can you handle the forces you do. Cantona and Beckham both had their own Merlin – Sir Alex Ferguson. Only then could they throw away the rule book and make magic happen. Many young people in sports think they have to be a Merlin from the beginning. We need our mentors and relationships of humility with our higher powers. Mickey is lucky; he gets away with it. Most people who get seduced by these forces never escape; if they are alone in the world, they die and we never hear of them.

In short

Mickey lacks humility and forgets his limitations.

Early success can be a dangerous thing.

Narcissism means getting ahead of yourself and forgetting your teachers.

Mickey makes a bad choice and other forces take over.

Mickey looks at the book when it is too late.

Excellence takes time; it is built brick by brick.

Chemistry is important if you want to make a butterfly.

Transformation is information plus application.

Greece: 'Atalanta and the Golden Apples'

Earlier, we featured the deity Artemis, and hopefully you have a sense of her by now. She was regarded as the queen of the hunt and of the forest. The forest does not mean the same today as it once did. Forests were once places where it was easy to get lost, became disorientated and not come back. They were naturally lawless places where real dangers existed from human and non-human sources. Artemis was therefore by implication a very powerful deity and had to be recognised and honoured. It was a bad idea to ignore her or, worse, creep up on her while she was bathing.

In Greek mythology, King Oeneus made just such an error by once forgetting to make a sacrifice to Artemis. Worse, he had made sacrifices to all the other gods, but forgot her. That kind of behaviour sounds like a challenge to a god like Artemis. Artemis is traditionally connected to boars, and sent one to Oeneus' kingdom as a punishment. Boars are known as tough, pugnacious animals who fight viciously if needed. Soon the boar caused mayhem in his kingdom, beginning with the orchards and planted areas. It became known as the *Caledonian Boar*, and the men who tried to stop it were killed, one after another.

King Oeneus had a big problem, so he asked his son Meleager for help. Meleager was one of the Argonauts, and was already known as a great hunter and warrior (and features in many Greek myths). Meleager set up a team to catch the boar; one of the crew was Atalanta. Sculptures and images of Atalanta today bear a distinct similarity to Artemis and our other archer women. Like Psyche, she was not a deity. She had mortal parents and was not a goddess like Artemis. But she was brilliant and Artemis favoured her; she was her kind of woman. Atalanta felt the same, and gave a vow of chastity to Artemis.

In a separate myth, Atalanta had previously killed two men who had tried to rape her. As with our earlier figures, mythological or not, Atalanta had her place on any team not because of her renowned good looks but her skills and capacities as a warrior and hired problem-solver. She initially met Meleager the Argonaut with Jason, and is shown on pottery found defeating the King Peleus in a wrestling match.

If anyone on Earth was ever to face Annie Oakley on the battlefield, we know by now it would not turn out well. To be sure, Atlanta was this kind of opponent. Meleager chose her for this mission in particular because of her extraordinary speed on foot. During the hunt it was Atalanta that speared the boar first, then Meleager finished the job. Full of admiration, Meleager fell in love with Atalanta, awarding her the head of the boar and its hide. In another version of the myth, some were upset about this and stole the hide for themselves. It ended badly for them, and for Meleager too, as he did not succeed in capturing the love of Atalanta. She wasn't particularly interested in men, and many died trying. Although, note: her world is full of men. Happily for her, catching the boar reunited her with her lost father, King Iasus, who had initially abandoned her as a baby.

The name Atalanta comes from the original Greek word for 'balance' (*atalante*), perhaps representing the equality of her skills with men. Those who wanted to marry her were invited to compete in a foot race. Running was a Greek tradition and lots of men tried to capture her this way. As she passed them, and she invariably would, she would stab them with a spear. She had a tough side alright. Atalanta was originally an orphan, abandoned by her father and raised by a mother bear. A group of hunters were said to have found her, from whom she developed her naturally honed skills. Atalanta was like all of the heroines we have featured – more skilful than the men.

Like lots of men before him, Hippomenes fell in love with her. He admired the way she kept her virtues while surrounded by so many great men. Hippomenes had something different about him; he used his imagination. How could he could take on this formidable beauty and make her fall in love with him? After all, she did all the 'men things' so well; what a prize she was to a man like him. Who best to go to? Psyche would have guessed the answer. Hippomenes went to Aphrodite, and asked her how he could capture Atalanta for his own. Aphrodite was delighted; of course she was happy to help him. Atalanta the archer may well be cast from the same mould as Artemis, but that did not mean she was Aphrodite's kind of woman.

Aphrodite told Hippomenes to wait until the crucial moment and then roll a golden apple at her feet. Aphrodite was a good person to ask about the feminine psyche, and Hippomenes had his chance. Atalanta's races by now were a big spectacle in Greece and many people came to watch the drama. As the two racers prepared for the start, Atalanta was like an Olympic champion out for a jog around the park – calm as you like and all smiles. She had fans everywhere she looked, and she liked it too. Hippomenes had his golden apples, but all the same he looked a bit sheepish compared to her.

Atalanta gave him a head start, twinkling at her admirers all around. With hands on hips she studied him for a moment as he raced off into the distance. Before she settled down, Atalanta gave one last wave to her followers all around. It was as if she wanted to leave it just that one bit longer – she was that confident – and like Annie Oakley she was a great public performer who liked to tease the audience and create her own tension. Then demeanour changed, and she prepared herself. At this point the crowd became silent, knowing they were witnessing a prodigy in motion. Everyone was helpless, captivated by the awesome sight of her beauty, grace and power all in one package. Like some massive spring, her body contained extraordinary torque and tension. Like a beast of prey, she narrowed her gaze onto the object of her intentions. In a flash the spring was released.

Atalanta was an awesome sight; efficiency of motion is always graceful. It didn't take long before she was up behind Hippomenes. As she drew close, Hippomenes surprised her and made his move. The assembled crowd shrieked as they saw Atalanta deviate her course and follow the path of the bouncing apple. She eventually caught up with it and stopped for a moment, admiring her new prize and a little delighted by her new acquisition. She looked up at Hippomenes and smiled; she could see he was tiring, as she was just beginning. Atalanta was still fully confident she could catch him, and she did. As she neared him, he rolled another golden apple. She was not so captivated by the second, and even less so by the next. As she fetched her third, she had lost the casual airs and was no longer as certain. She knew she has a contest on her hands.

Hippomenes really wanted this prize, as well as to stay alive! He found another gear in himself and crossed the line first, in a mixture of exhaustion, ecstasy and huge relief. Atalanta had lost, for the first time. However, she wasn't upset. She remained dignified about her defeat and magnanimous about the situation. She was impressed with Hippomenes, and liked the way he thought. Some accounts say she was partly relieved not to have to kill a man again. She was amused and curious, and definitely appreciated her gift of the golden apples; they were something worth appreciating. Marriage to a man like Hippomenes might not be so bad after all.

Greek myths are not like modern entertainment stories and sadly this one does not all end happily. All accounts have Atalanta and Hippomenes falling in love with each other, but then they both made a mistake. All versions I know of suggest that after their race, they did not send their thanks and appreciations to Aphrodite. Some versions suggest they were then turned into lions for this mistake. Being youngsters, they just rushed off and had a wild time together. Other accounts suggest that they insulted the deity Cybele by making love in her temple.

For the athlete

Hippomenes did not have to pay Aphrodite for the apples; they were a gift. Atalanta was a great team player and woman to have around, but she had blind spots. It is when self-belief turns into narcissism that a blind spot forms. Whatever they both did wrong, they did not pay enough respect to the gods – and this was terminal, just as King Oeneus didn't thank Artemis at the beginning of the story. That might seem irrelevant then in the twenty-first century, but it means the same now as it did then. We all have gifts and if we take them for granted then we may be on the way to a crash. Good things tend to happen to those who pay their respects, however one chooses to do so.

Atalanta is a woman who was surrounded by men, but not romantically available to any of them. Those that tried, died. Perhaps she was understandably angry with men in general after her father, King Iasus, had abandoned her as a baby. Atalanta perhaps made a point about being better than men as a way to compensate for feeling so emotionally vulnerable to them. However, she was importantly reconciled with her father after her fame from spearing the boar. Perhaps this reunification was what enabled her to finally risk enough to be with Hippomenes. But as is so often with the Greeks, it was her blind spots that undid her in the end.

This is one reason why so many athletes benefit from taking a therapeutic look at themselves before it is too late. The advice would be to watch out for inevitable distractions that can take you off your course. Ways of making it in the world when you are young do not apply when you are older. Much therapy happens because of this, and athletes also need to make this transition. If you are in a sporting environment then you are in a castle, and Merlin is somewhere! Particularly if success comes your way, the distractions can be attractive and valuable. But if you become diverted, the myth of Atalanta and the golden apples suggests you will risk losing the race. Always remember your gods when you are victorious, as well as in defeat.

Even if you have no gods you can always thank your parents. If it is not possible to do that, then you can thank the world for your gifts. In my experience, integrated inner masculine and feminine aspects of the personality tend to produce longer sporting lives in the long run.

In short

Gratitude: actively give thanks for the things you have. Neither Atalanta nor Hippomenes gave their thanks, and this is what undid them. (A moment please; this is a very mysterious phenomenon. I have seen lives change and great things occur when individuals practise this. I have separated this text as a way to try and convey the importance I place on this mysterious force. Practise it everywhere you can and see what happens.)

Focus: do not be put off your course if someone throws you a golden apple.

Research: Hippomenes won because he used his imagination. He stayed alive because he researched and chose a good person from whom to ask for advice.

Boundaries: be firm with your boundaries, whatever you choose them to be. It is a theme for those with loose boundaries to get into trouble.

Germany: 'The Pied Piper of Hamelin'

Sources place the origins of this familiar German myth as most likely the town of Hamelin in Lower Saxony. The myth is old, a stained-glass window in the town's main church portrays these scenes, and is dated at 1300. This is a myth I have shared in football environments and it contains important messages for athletes. Hamelin lies on a river, and had originally become very successful as a trading port. Consequently, the town had a lot of food at certain times stored away in large dockside barns. If you were to ask a rat what heaven looked like, it might describe the dockside at Hamelin – mountains of grain in big storehouses all along the riverbank.

As most of us know, the story tells how Hamelin consequently become plagued by vermin. At first, the townfolk didn't take care of the problem. 'Pull weeds early' is a useful phrase for youth development in sport. Some habits are bad habits and, like weeds, they become ingrained in the personality. The rat population became ingrained in Hamelin, alright. People in the town became anxious and angry, so

FIGURE 7.3 The Pied Piper in Hamelin today.

Credit: Marc Venema.

they developed teams of local citizens to go and beat them away with sticks and maces. Brute force was the method they chose of removing the rats.

At first, many of the locals turned out as volunteers, but it was hard labour. Rats are tricky opponents, they keep coming back! (Remember that 'negative systems will avoid change'.) Most people found this to be horrible work and became tired of it. Therefore, teams of men were employed by the council to beat the rats away, once and for all. However hard they tried, the rats would return, or just simply move from one area to another and back again. Every night in Hamelin, gangs of men could be heard shouting with their barking dogs in the smoky night air.

This was costing the town a lot of money. The men were happy to be paid for the work but it was not changing things, so the town council had an emergency meeting to discuss what to do. A child interrupted the meeting and told them about the miracle man called the Pied Piper. The mayor learned that the man really existed, but no one knew where he could be found. The mayor enthusiastically called for the word to be out – 'Let him him know we want him! We will pay him handsomely if he can get rid of the rats!'

That kind of news gets about fast, and in a few days time the Pied Piper arrived before the council. He was a curious figure. He was of slight build, was dig-nified and stood upright – quite a sight compared to the grey-looking council members. He was confident; he had presence about him. The word pied means 'many-coloured'. In many places in the middle ages it was not possible to wear many-coloured clothes. This symbolises for us his importance and that he was of high rank and status.

The mayor was not so impressed, and studied him a moment . . . they weren't used to having people like him in the chambers.

'Can you really do this?'

Resolutely, the Pied Piper answered with a broad smile, 'Yes, I can'.

The mayor was still a bit cynical; 'How?'

The Pied Piper said nothing; he just reached for his pipe and played them a beauti-ful melody. It was a sweet, attractive sound which filled the council halls like a kind of perfume. As he finished, there was only a stunned silence; people didn't know what to do. A couple of the attending council members weren't so impressed, and began to laugh at him. The Pied Piper looked around the room and just smiled at all of those that laughed. However, not all the council members felt this way, and voiced their disapproval at the disrespect.

The Pied Piper appreciated this, and informed them how much he wanted to be paid. Some were shocked, but they were in such need that they agreed and cut the deal – half of the money now, half when the job was done. The Pied Piper signed on the dotted line, assuring them he would be back in the morning. He took his bag of coins, bowed graciously, and bid them farewell. Right from the start some council members didn't like the situation at all. They thought they had just been swindled, and that they would not be seeing him again. After all, he didn't say where, when or how he would complete his task.

At dawn, sure enough, he appeared at the edge of the town. He walked his way down the empty mud streets right into the town's central square. Quite alone, he let out a shrill note on his flute followed by a magical harmony. Lovely sounds began to fill the town as he played his music. Some early-risers looked out of their windows and stared, puzzled.

Then, all of a sudden, the Pied Piper stopped. There was nothing now but an eerie silence. He sniffed the air, and turned his head as he strained to detect a noise. He noticed something, a rustle, more rustling, and soon the Pied Piper started to smile. The rats appeared, popping up out of the sewers, drainpipes and down from the thatched roofs. Like the ants in Psyche's trial, the rats appeared from nowhere and were all moving into the square.

By now some of the locals began to cheer out of their windows as they saw the rats, of all sizes, grey and brown, gathering in the square. The rats all together like this made for a curious sight. Soon a grey shiny swirl formed around the Pied Piper. Some of the locals watching from above shrieked. Was this a kind of witchcraft or a saint in action? No body knew what was going on, but soon hundreds of eyes around the square were watching in awe. Careful not to tread on any rats, the Pied Piper walked out of town and up towards the hills. As he moved through the town, rats from the side streets joined and soon thousands were all moving in motion together like a big silky grey-brown snake. When he had gone, and the sound of the music could no longer be heard, an eerie silence fell upon the town.

Then after a minute folk came out of their houses and greeted each other, marvelling at what they had just witnessed. Soon a big gathering of jubilant people took over the square. Their nightmare, it seemed, was over. People cheered up at the mayor, who was smugly waving from his office. Later that day, the residents had a big party and celebrated his name.

The following day the Pied Piper walked back into town to collect his payment. He was celebrated as a hero by the locals, who patted him on the back and toasted him. A woman brought out a huge ham and presented it to him. Gracefully he declined, assuring her he had already agreed payment, and she should eat it with his blessings. He stopped and raised a glass full of punch, given to him by a local, to a big cheer.

From up above in the council chambers, the councilmen could see the adulation he was getting. They were a little jealous. They had to make the tough decisions in life; he was just a clever musician. One of them complained that it was a ridiculous price to charge for a piece of mass hypnotism. One agreed – 'Anyone can do that!' The town was indeed half-bankrupted as a result. 'Besides, they could come back, what then!?' The mayor had heard enough. He agreed; what could he do, anyway? He refused to see the Pied Piper. He instructed his clerk to go out and tell him to leave.

'The Mayor has been called away on business, sorry about that. And er, we had a few unexpected fiscal issues mature in the financial sector, yes, causing a deviation in the interest rate charge – so we don't have the equity we had intended. Dreadful calamity . . . didn't accrue with the usual marginal ratio. Before you object, clause 781, B7a in the contract you signed clearly allows for this, you know. But anyway, we have to say: we think you have been very well looked after with what you have already been paid. So, thank you so much; goodbye.'

A mean-looking military bruiser approached and stood behind the clerk. The clerk felt emboldened; he blurted out:

'You've had enough! Be on with you!'

The Pied Piper said nothing; he bowed his head, turned around and left the building into the rainy streets.

The mayor studied him from his chambers as the Pied Piper walked away. He laughed it off, comforting himself with some inner bluster; 'I have 200 soldiers who could see to you, fool!' It was true. The mayor had always liked to see himself as an important person, an official worthy of respect – not a foolish-looking idiot like the Pied Piper, with his colours and musical acts.

People tried to celebrate the Pied Piper as he left town, but he had a serious look on his face. That night as the town slept, he played his flute again. His sounds filled the air, and as most of us know the children in the town got up out of bed and began to follow the sound. Somehow, the tune he played kept all of the parents asleep and only entranced the children. Soon, all of the children in the town were gone.

There are various endings from here, but all agree that the rats eventually returned and the town suffered a considerably worse plague than before.

For the athlete

Previous chapters described the power and original influence of music for early humans. The Pied Piper was a musician, a natural source of energy and connection. In this story, it was song that cleared away the rats, not bullies or mercenaries with their whips and fire. This story testifies that bullying and force are incapable of creating healthy change; these techniques are also inflexible, offering only the same message again and again. The use of force on the rats did not work for long.

In performance cultures, repetitive heavy-handed messages are not going to produce the change an athlete seeks. Self-critical messages can be like us hitting out at the rats. The rats live not in the open but between the walls, like shadows. Self-abuse can be like this, and like all abuse it is done in secret. It was the song that brought the rats out and away.

Athletes must sometimes be tough with themselves if their performance slips or they catch themselves being lazy. Athletes need to use other kinds of messages at other times. As we can all see, commercialism is reaching younger markets and age ranges. I sense a danger that the rats will follow the children as commercial targets. The young, undifferentiated mind is often too harsh and critical on itself if left on its own in the world, without a mentor to help nurture it. Progress for an athlete is very often being able to desist from such basic internal voices. Like a radio station we can be out of tune, and a clear frequency is the goal of the athlete and internal alchemist. Odysseus had his sailors plug their ears with beeswax so that they didn't fall prey to dissociation and distraction by the Sirens, which can lead to negative states of fear and panic.

Football managers perhaps become good at their jobs because at times they have to tell themselves these kinds of inspirational messages. Whatever their content, the inspirational messages are rarely harsh. If we forget them entirely the rats are likely to stick around. As Queen Elizabeth I showed when facing the Spanish Armada, powerful messages are not harsh. She was harsh about the enemy, but not about her subjects. Harshness has a limited power. Like a radioactive substance, it has a halflife. Every time it is repeated, it has only half of its influential power.

'The Pied Piper of Hamelin' also provides a lesson about underestimation. The piper is not taken seriously by most of the politicians, but the townsfolk did not underestimate him. The mayor was a materialist, in that he believed only in force and money. Kindness was interpreted as weaknesses; spirituality was misunderstood and feared. Ultimately, the divine child, that crucial voice that creates so much, was lost. Hamelin paid bitterly for its underestimation.

In short

Materialism is an over-dependence on objects and finance (the opposite of your friend, Animism!).

Some thoughts can be like rats.

Song is powerful; a lyrical message can lead away the rats.

Inspiration is more powerful in leadership than degradation.

Inspiration and a natural approach beats self-criticism.

Underestimation of the spiritual can bring disaster.

The Kalahari: 'The Young Man and the Lion'

Laurens van der Post (1906–1996) was a recognised authority on the peoples of the Kalahari in Southern Africa. He was also mentor for a time in Africa to a young Prince Charles, in line to be the next king of England. Van der Post wrote a book about the bush peoples he met in Africa called *The Heart of the Hunter* (1961) and

FIGURE 7.4 A young hunter in the Kalahari today.

Credit: Oleg Znamenskiy/Shutterstock.com.

dedicated it to Carl Jung. Like Jung, van der Post was interested in the soul, something of which he felt he had discovered in the Kalahari peoples.

Like so many in this chapter, he was a controversial figure and I hope that need not detract from the telling of this important African mythological story. This one has been a central theme in my work with young people who do well to know about lions, as in England they are on the flag of the country's national football team. During World War II, van der Post was a Commando, a soldier that had been taught to live in the wild, and in the shadows, in accord and in harmony with nature. He was not the only soldier after war to have left urban life to live in 'the wilds'. In America, many Vietnam veterans went off to live in the Appalachian mountains. Van der Post went to live with the Kalahari, who told him the myth of 'The Young Man and the Lion'.

Kalahari mythology and folklore normally centred around a being called the 'Mantis'. It is absent from this particular myth, which focuses on challenges we all must take on alone. This myth features an important animal for sports, the lion. Before his telling of the story, van der Post outlined why the lion was regarded by the bushmen as the king of the plains. Compared to the lion, all other animals have obvious limitations. For example, an elephant has poor eyesight, a hyena is light, but the lion has strengths in abundance and in all respects. It is smart, can hunt day or night, is strong, agile and has great vision. A lion was therefore divine in stature for the Kalahari. It was also a given for the Kalahari peoples that the lion is a quixotic and dangerous animal to predict. Even if you think you knew a lion well, it will surprise you. It is the ultimate symbol of the individual with strengths in every sense, which is one of the reasons the symbol of the lion is still so ubiquitous.

The Kalahari are a hunting people and their myths relate to our challenges to be individuals, to 'individuate', in the same way that Jung would have put it. The Kalahari predate Homer, therefore they can hold vital clues as we search for the soul of the athlete. In terms of a search for the soul, we cannot go to a much better place than the Kalahari people. DNA evidence clearly shows we all originated from this area. This means that we, as a species, were at one time all black. This, then, might be a little closer to the soul of the athlete we seek. The hunters who told van der Post this myth said it was from the 'early peoples', meaning it must have a truly ancient lineage. We cannot know how old it is, but it is unlikely there are many older stories in the world.

A young hunter was a popular figure in his village; he wanted to contribute, worked hard and people liked him. One day he went out hunting as normal, but this day he felt drowsy. He could not shake it off, so he decided to lean himself up against a tree and soon fell asleep. Kalahari folklore warns that hunters can become hypnotised by animals, being seduced into a kind of a trance. The greater the animal, the greater the trance, and the greater the danger. Sure enough, a passing lion discovered the young man asleep. Lions do not tend to turn down an opportunity and the young man was in big trouble. The hunter became aware of his danger, but too late. His only chance was to feign being dead already, and then just hope for the best. He took a deep breath and waited for what was to come next.

Hauling an animal up a tree is normal practice for lions in Africa, and this is what happened next. With great fortune for the hunter, the lion hauled him up by his robe and he managed to get to the top of the tree in one piece. He was alive, but in great pain; despite his agony, the hunter resisted crying out. He held his nerve, and the lion remained unaware that the man was quite conscious.

The lion then hesitated; he was not sure whether to go and take a drink or stay and eat the man first. He concluded that a nice drink would be better first, and so went to leave. But as he did so, the lion noticed some tears in the hunter's eyes. As if enjoying some fine delicacy, the lion gently licked them away. Perhaps he enjoyed the salt in them. The lion then set off in earnest on his original mission for water.

With the lion finally out of sight, the young hunter took his chance, and ran home as if his life depended on it. Badly cut and in pain, he used all his strength to make it back to the village. He tried everything to clear his tracks; at one point he went through a stream so as not to leave a scent for the lion to follow. Exhausted and in terrible shape, at dusk he finally made it back into the welcoming arms of his kin. All of the villagers were very happy and relieved to see him. That soon changed, however, turning into kind of creeping fear when he told them what happened. The older folk all knew it would mean the lion would come looking for him and that he might soon arrive. Terrified, they wrapped the young man in animal skills to try and hide his scent. They waited, helpless, in the hope that the lion would not come.

Returning from his drink, the lion soon discovered the man gone. The lion was furious to lose his prey. Immediately, he set about tracking the hunter down, as if his own life depended on it! Lions are relentless when angry, and it used every skill it had to track him down. At first it was easy; there was and blood and sweat to follow. The lion reached the stream and guessed rightly to go in the direction of the village. He easily found the place where the hunter had left the river. He arrived at the boundaries of the village. The villagers shrieked as the lion eventually came into view. This was a bad situation.

The lion was the king, and they were its subjects. These folk were all impotent – they would have agreed with Adler – compared to a lion like this; they were totally helpless and inferior. The lion demanded his prey. Some of the villagers attempted to save the young hunter, but the lion was adamant; he wanted his prey. There was no alternative; nature must take its course. Eventually, and with much wailing, they had to surrender the hunter to the lion. The villagers had to accept that their own survival was dependent on a real relationship with nature. They knew that to withhold the young man was wrong. The laws of nature had to be obeyed, otherwise they would all be destroyed. The hunter was given over, and was killed by the lion. Then the lion, in turn, offered itself to the villagers, and was killed by them.

For the athlete

Mickey Mouse also became dozy, remember – he fell asleep when he should have been awake. As with Atalanta, distractions and aversions can captivate a person and take them from their path. In my clinical experience of group therapy over ten years I have often experienced this issue. Some patients cannot attend the session without becoming drowsy. It is as if some kind of hypnotist is putting them to sleep. It is not about being relaxed; such folk often suffer from acute anxiety. Despite being worlds and ages apart, the Kalahari would naturally understand the danger these Western patients are in. 'The greater the drowsiness, the greater the danger' is true in clinical settings and it means the same thing in the wild; it is life and death.

The sharing of tears was an important feature in this story for the peoples of the Kalahari. This symbolised that the hunter and the lion were now forever united; for good or bad, they were part of the same thing from this moment on. For the Kalahari this means that once they have been through a few difficult emotional experiences with each other, things change. They become brothers or sisters, for good or bad. In my experience, when we share our vulnerable sides most often healthy bonds are created between people. I have noticed that, clinically and in sport, when extreme emotions are shared safely, confidentially, the relationships between people change and develop. Confidence is *confide*nce, remember.

The young man tried to cover himself in the skins of other animals. The bushmen believed that this myth symbolised the importance of an individual not hiding within community cultures. They recognised the need for a young person to meet their inner animal selves, which is also a common theme in this book. Today that means first that we cannot grow up online. I have met those that have tried, and from my perspective it does not work. Separating ourselves too far from any nature into a computer reality is not going to help develop important neural networks and capacities for interpersonal relationships and connection. There are matters wherein you cannot hide forever wrapped up in the community. An athlete must be out into the open and connected to nature; by doing so, we can find ourselves.

In short

The lion is king because it is skilled in all areas and it develops each one.

Individuality is a supreme expression in the quest for the human soul.

You cannot defy nature's, nor live online.

Individuality is realised when we meet our inner animal and we become indivisible.

It is dangerous to become dozy in the wrong place and at the wrong time.

When pain is shared with a teammate or coach, the relationship grows.

The seven deadly sins for the elite athlete

Laziness: not attending to inner disciplines or your craft.

Immaturity: and an inability to heal and 'move on' quickly.

Victimhood: always blaming bad results on external factors.

Defeatism: unproductive paranoia cultivating insecurity and infidelity.

Intellectualism: 'thinking too much' at the wrong time and in the wrong place.

Disrespect: not caring for your gifts, or giving gratitude.

Distraction: going to sleep at the wrong time and in the wrong place.

References

van der Post, L. (1961). *The Heart of the Hunter.* New York: William Morrow and Co.

The ending

8

REPAIR

The return to Freud

Good stress or bad stress in the twenty-first century

This book began at the human beginnings, so where are we now? In 2018, Los Angeles has in parts become a desolate, lawless tent city where squalid conditions breed primitive realities for those trapped there. The world hasn't come so far since the early days of Greece and city life then, it would seem. And now, worse, in a shocking piece of news, Edward Helmore cites a US federal study on suicide stating: '25 states have recorded increases [in suicide] of more than 30% since the late 1990s' (Helmore, 2018). Something in the Western psyche appears to require healing and repair. Psychotherapeutic, mindful models are one way that will help.

Crisis is a feature and central characteristic of elite sport, which is why the capacity to repair remains so essential for the life of an athlete. They must stay alive, keep focused and keep coming back. London Jungian analyst and psychotherapist Cathy Bor has written a fascinating portrait about Lionel Messi (Bor, 2015), one of the world's greatest players; but for all of that, he is not able to escape ignominy, failure and defeat. He had a miserable Football World Cup in 2018, along with his home nation Argentina. Proud footballing nations such as Germany, Portugal and Argentina all had to leave the tournament early in 2018, and now have to think again. Another two powerhouses – Italy and the Netherlands – didn't even qualify, nor did the USA.

Life can be tough. At the beginning the book we covered the early Greeks and their home terrain of caves and rocks, which forced them to use their imaginations to survive. As I type this ending, dramatic news is emerging. A soccer youth team aged 11–16, called the Wild Boars, have become trapped after torrential rainfall in the Tham Luang cave complex in Thailand; 12 boys and their coach are stranded and their future is uncertain; they may yet still drown. Heroic divers from many countries, including two Britons, Richard William Stanton and John Volanthen, volunteered to try to find the group and now, after ten days in the caves without food, they have just been discovered alive. Reports are suggesting that the young coach practised group meditation to help them cope with the perpetual darkness (*The Hamilton Spectator*, 2018). Meditation rarely means the difference between life and death for a soccer team, but for those dealing with addiction, mediation is a capacity also practised as a way to hold on, to not get subsumed by the rising tides.

This chapter marks the final phase and third element of the sports *trilogia* this book presents; beginnings, middles and endings. This is of course a very Jungian way of looking at things, and that does not seem as unusual as it once was. It is the natural order. Change is in the air, and I have discovered that other depth practitioners in the world are also now achieving success relating clinical models and perspectives to sport using philosophies from the East. Experience suggests this a compliment to, not a rival or alternative to, conventional methods of sport psychology. Below we can explore a recent and significant shift in sport psychology and a resurgence of value for the ineffable and unquantifiable, which mindfulness and meditation surely represent.

Jungian depth traditions can claim to have always held a space for the ineffable in research; it is not new for us. Sport psychology is an evolving science that would do well to incorporate depth clinical models and ideas as a compliment to its own epistemology. Phil Jackson is a renowned basketball coaching legend who pioneered many ideas relating to spirituality, ethics and sport. His great legacy followed on from the ideas of great legendary coaches such as John Wooden, thinking soulfully about people and cultures. Few know that Phil Jackson works closely with a spiritual guide called George Mumford, who has written a timely book called *The Mindful Athlete: Secrets to Pure Performance* (2016). Mumford's study compliments so many of the themes in this book citing spiritual teachers and philosophers and the crucial role of learning and emotional development.

In keeping with the theme of this book, George Mumford has a Master's degree in counselling psychology. He cites many familiar authors, such as Joseph Campbell, Donald Winnicott, the Buddha and Martin Buber, while describing his role as a teacher to athletes on mindfulness. He recounts how Phil Jackson's team was 'in various states of emotional distress, Phil had to rebuild a team and bring harmony to discord. That's when he reached out and brought me to his training camp to teach mindfulness and help heal the team' (Mumford, 2016, p. 30). This is one central reason why clinical depth models have integrated so effortlessly into sport, certainly in my experience. These are languages with the soul in mind; they are related to repair and healing, and will in the future find a world more in need – but also more open.

It is the role of the manager to decide if and when any healing is required from the outside, but, as with normal psychotherapy, there is a role for the specialist. Mumford's biography describes how he went on to work with Phil Jackson for his time with the New York Knicks, which demonstrates that this kind of learning may not always be for crisis situations or firefighting. Or, as this book testifies, elite sport is a world mostly in perpetual crisis, if done right.

In 2016, an important series of essays on sport psychology in a recent book edited by Amy Baltzell illustrate a seismic shift happening regarding the value of the ineffable in sport psychology. The book aims to be a kind of compendium of the brightest minds in sport psychology writing about the spirit of mindfulness and the impact it can have on performance. In his chapter, clinical psychologist Frank Gardner suggests that 'something so exciting was happening in the clinical world and its relevance to the sporting world was nothing short of striking!' (Gardner, 2016, p. 128).

Many sport psychologists refer to the mindfulness teachings of Jon Kabat-Zinn, currently professor of medicine at the University of Massachusetts. He has written many texts on mediation and spiritual principles. The more empirically attuned world of psychiatry has recently produced a couple of sport psychologists. In 2012, Dr Steve Peters, a psychiatrist in England, wrote a very successful book on sport psychology and an early contribution incorporating the unconscious (Peters, 2012). Clinical psychology and sport are inclusive worlds, and that is the spirit of this last chapter, where we shall find a space for some recent voices on the scene.

Since I began writing this project a year ago, two new books have been released by depth sport psychologists with analytical backgrounds in England and Argentina. I would like to feature them, along with a section written especially for this book by New York-based depth sport psychologist Dr Tom Ferraro. As a compliment to the Jungian emphasis, his work will take us on a Freudian path. All authors illustrate how the science of sport psychology is developing a distinctly depth-clinical wing and new connections are being made all over the world. This can only compliment the current culture of sport and welfare in general. The evidence of abuse in sport in the news of late demonstrates how much it is needed.

But who cares? In my experience, young people do. There is a thirst for the lessons of applied clinical psychology that can help lots of people with practical life skills and ways to organise their thoughts. Now is an age and time that calls on the depth-clinical world to speak its truth and share its impressions in many disciplines. This is where clinical practitioners and mental health professionals can follow my university motto and 'tend to the soul of the world' with a meaningful contribution. Sport psychologists have long been interested in these same issues and this chapter will also feature the work of one of the most prominent, Dr Mark Nesti.

Writing this book has been a marathon – a literary one – but a marathon all the same. I am approaching mile 25 out of 26, and am still conscious of a longing that wants to burst out. I don't want to miss anything, drop a stitch and miss the only opportunity I have to get it right. How can I remain focused on my challenge and not dissociate? It is the same task for a psychotherapist and throughout this project I hold a primary place for the clinical patients in my life. Throughout the writing of this book, I have been working with people who are trying to survive in the urban jungle, which kills more than the natural one. So many times, the two worlds have similar messages, but they are not the same; one is really about life and death. The other just feels like it.

Writing this book has helped new insights emerge from within me. Focusing on a task like this produces a deep reaction and response from the unconscious; if it doesn't, the writer is probably not involved enough. My unconscious has occasionally provided me with an insight worth noting. If one hears a calling, one is lucky, and I have been lucky to have a life where I can afford to listen to it. I am grateful to Dr Robert Romanyshyn, whose work on alchemical hermeneutics has been a great contribution to my work and my life. Conviction and commitment and their relationship to achievement as well as personal pathology have been recurring themes. Those two dodgy relatives want to live at the edges of our lives. We cannot dispense with them as performers; they are our bread and butter.

But what are the resources that can propel an athlete forward when they are at the final moments? For a competitor these are the dangerous times, when nerves are stretched and the mind is tired, looking for it all to stop, perhaps. By now in any elite race or competition, an athlete is likely to be in a half-mad condition. I have noticed how extreme effort over long periods produces a kind of delirium. Physical and psychic strain dominates the body, which does its best to cope by creating dopamine to try to kill the pain and soften the landings. This is also a good description of the altered state a Shaman enters into.

In my case, that dopamine has another good effect: it fires up the imagination. Any great performer knows how to use imagination as a problem-solver. I have seen it written that 'worry is a misuse of the imagination'. Perhaps worry is when the mind becomes overheated and cannot contain itself. Mechanical engines can indeed give us a clue about performance conditions. Engines hit their peak at high temperatures and stresses. The most influential engine in World War II was that used in the Spitfire and many other planes and tanks – the Rolls-Royce *Merlin* engine. This is, of course, the perfect name, the original alchemist and a perfect symbol in our search for the soul of the athlete. Indeed, Merlin can make your plane fly.

When I was a drama student, I learned that the pioneering theatre director Konstantin Stanislavski liked to work with actors when they were tired. It is when many performers give what is often referred to as an 'honest' kind of performance. In these psychological places, a boiling-down happens, a reduction. As any good chef will tell you, this is always the way to make a rich stock. To be precise, the correct term in this case is 'redaction'. This is the name given to the repetitive process of continually editing and refining any good works. For an athlete, elements are continually revisited, revised and ultimately reduced to their essence and played out in the moment by the great artist. It is the Philosopher's Stone, continually rubbed and revisited.

This is profound, and why Plato and Socrates were so interested in this subject and the eternal truths of what makes for good or bad outcomes. The Philosopher's Stone is made from the *Prima Materia*. It is eternally visited and tended to, the mark of psychological integrity that distinguishes the great from the good. Sport and spirituality share many elements and this relates to our past relationships with similar states that rely on the interior, like hunting.

What are the ingredients, then, the components of this state of mind? What is it about the psyche that can fly at this height, play at this pressure and live at this altitude? It has historically been a difficult task for humans to escape the forces of gravity. Conviction and commitment will get you high, for sure. But we know the athlete needs more. Many in society try these two characteristics on their own and never come back. If drugs are your way to get high, and you have conviction and commitment about it, then death, prison or an asylum may be the only destination at the end of the line. We cannot count on Merlin showing up at the right time, as with Mickey Mouse.

We humans need to come back to Earth. That is a human skill and quality that can be lost. As well as the Buddhist devil Mara, and the 'voice of doubt', there is another Western name for Lucifer: 'Dis'. Dis is another ancient name for the Devil. This devil is an enemy of sports, found in disharmony and disconnection, as well as disgust, disdain, disbelief and disrespect. These are all words that imply a kind of separation. I am grateful to Dr Donald Kalshed again for his works on the inner world of trauma and soul.

The opposite side of this separation is the sprit of joining. This, note, is also a virtue and characteristic of childhood and play. Jung identified the inner child as the crucial part of us all that continually seeks to grow and 'be' in the world. The politicians of Hamelin messed it all up with materialism and lost their youth. Remembering Nelson Mandela's ideas about children in 1995: 'There can be no keener revelation of a society's soul than the way in which it treats its children'. There are important and deep connections between the soul and the world. Schopenhauer connected kindness to animals and good character, period. Like it or not, protecting our inner child and inner animal is a responsibility. It is a real task we can accept or deny. It is an act of self-parenthood, another universal task for us all.

Is anyone talking about this in general education for young people today? In my experience, general educational models have not found a language for these relationships, but depth-clinical science always has. We can neglect our inner child or abuse it with self-criticism but we know by now that athletes must nurture it. Psychotherapy is a special kind of help available to provide a safe professional environment for athletes so they can learn how to do this for themselves. Here, they can feel no pressure and be free to safely stumble in the dark towards growth as a person. It might sound frivolous or cheesy to some, but it can be a case of life or death, success or failure, winning or losing. Confidence in a person and a real relationship is what enables this growth to happen.

Over 15 years I have probably spent thousands of hours in one-to-one sport psychology meetings with young and old athletes. I would never share anything any one of them has said. But I can share the lessons this experience has given me about young people and sport. It was curious to me that my role as a sport psychologist and psychotherapist often related to the same challenges in life.

'Dis' is a word that implies separation, disconnection. But, at the same time, need stress – so what should we do? There is another alternative possible emotional state other than the 'Dis' kind of stress, the kind we need for elite performance. This is another plane, a more euphoric state that can help create the foundation for the 'afterburn' needed for extreme endurance. In a bid to refine and better understand stress, researchers in the 1970s closely monitored body reactions to pressure, introducing the term 'eustress' (Selye, 1977). Hans Selye, an eminent endocrinologist, distinguished brains and bodies that were going at top speed from those that were struggling. Eustress represented a different kind of experience – intrinsically healthy and without negative connotations.

Researchers found what the Greek ex-slave Epictetus deduced long ago, that stress related more to our perception of events and not the events themselves. If a burglar breaks into your house, then be stressed! Significantly in sport, we do not have that obligation to 'think' anything. Life is not an intellectual exercise, and they say 'attitude is altitude'. Successful people are indeed flexible with their approaches and avoid getting stuck. This is only to do what all life on earth has always done: adapt. Eustress is the higher-frequency human state an athlete must reach during the important moments of sport. Excellence is a dedication, an obsession (not a compulsion); an energy directed in this cause is likely to be rewarded by the gods of sport. *Eu* is Greek for 'good', and *euthymia* is the clinical term for a positive normal mood.

Mickey Mouse tried to make magic, but he was too young and could not contain the euphoric powers he unleashed. Dopamine and norepenipherine have been proved to be crucial balances that the athlete must produce like a chemist. Containing highs is a difficult task for all humans, and experience shows it takes years of practice and dedication in a complex world such as elite-level competition. Eustress is a plane of experience that relates to euphoria and ecstasy. These are the Dionysian realms of Mount Olympus, the first home of sport and drama. Real ego strength and temperament is made like tempered steel, with hot and cold experiences.

Knowing how to lose is a skill that needs nurturing. For athletes struggling with the highs and lows of life, psychotherapeutic relationships and approaches can help enable them to get a better command of their own inner worlds. Psychotherapeutic skills additionally enable individuals to reappraise and reintegrate some of their conditioned 'outer-world' attitudes and experiences. Some of these inevitably end in suffering and an inability to realise form or potential. There is only so much water in the well. Mental fitness relates to these capacities of integration and simplicity. The positive line is eventually the line of least resistance in sports, and Freud may agree. That means a lack of diligence over difficult matters or tasks can be easier, but cost more in the long run.

But what is the special ingredient, the approach or philosophy that will help the athlete attain eustress and not distress? That is harder to name. Sport is not a personality contests or a rational system we can unlock with numbers. But when I reflect on my own experience writing this book, I know I still love this project, this task I set myself. I care about it, I'm giving it everything, especially now at the end. My relationship with this work is based on love and faith. It is not fear-based or the slavery of involuntary obligations. But maybe this is why so many sporting greats give the advice to 'love what you do'.

Now, a vital point for anyone seeking longevity and a full life. I am also curious, which, like gratitude, is a force never to be underestimated. All the bad things of the world happen when people do not care about each other.

Carol Dweck clearly identified (2006) that the way children approach a task has much to do with the outcome. All age groups who regarded problems as challenges did much better than those with more egotistical perceptions related to ideas about their 'talent'. This dovetailed into perceptions of how things look in front of others, which is a problem. Young adults are wired that way, and of course it remains an important issue in a social setting, but this is all the more reason to learn skills to help.

However, as children grow into adults, that is not the dominant issue at stake. Nurtured learning experiences can create an anchored sense of self-confidence where self-consciousness does not rob a child of owning the dance. Like a thief in the night, the natural joy of joining in and playing is gone, only to be replaced by perceptions that are negative or victim-based. Children in society may need much more help with these issues in the future, and adults can help.

The overvaluation of thinking (rather than acting) as a way of solving problems is a characteristic and modern obsession with many young people. This is often correlated with symptoms of anxiety and obsessive-compulsive disorders. Like the words in a song, eustress will also carry on within you, even when the contest is over. But this is a feeling, not a thought. There is even an occupational hazard and crossover that the performer must learn to manage. In the theatre world it was not the first-night performance you had to fear; strictly speaking, it was the second. This was when the initial euphoria and adrenaline had gone, leaving a performer vulnerable and with a literal hangover. After a victory, elation can turn into a sweet inner wine that lasts the evening or beyond. After a defeat, eustress degrades and turns into a desolate feeling of loss and impotence. Even Winston Churchill had his depression, his so-called 'black dog'.

Now the contest is over

After the battle is over, there must be time to end and mend. If athletes could not manage to do that, we can assume they would not be in an elite sport environment. But anything is possible; people are not systems.

In clinical settings, I occasionally meet parents at the beginning of a treatment cycle who confidently expect themselves to be 'put right in 30 days', as if they would be going through a machine and in 30 days be cooked, some miraculous intervention that would change everything, revert them to as if they were children. It does occasionally happen, but that is rare. 'Systems' are the hallmark of the dominant left-brained perspective which does not do ideas of 'soul' very comfortably. But any student of sport must. Healing and growth is a long-term picture, which is why we need to nurture ourselves and our talent. Objectification tends to erode human spirits, relegating such ideas as less-than-important. We do, however, begin to search for keys, and we have to find them fast sometimes.

A friend of mine once casually shared a perspective that offered me much in terms of an insight into the human soul and psyche. I should point out that my friend is not a psychologist but an engineer, a very wise, right-brained, capable one. Echoing my sentiments about the parents above, he said 'I hear a lot of people talk about themselves as if they were a car. You know, if this part was there, or if I took this part out, then my brain would be better. I don't think it's like that at all. For me, people are more like the streams, you know, in the wetlands. When the rivers run in the right places, the animals return.'

In my ten years of clinical experience and learning, that is the best summary of the psyche I have ever heard. Psychotherapy helps the rivers flow again, or for the first time for some. The ones that get dammed up when young, or those that dam themselves up in order to avoid unbearable feelings. For whatever reason, when the rivers are flowing, people tend to mend and grow. This is the 'teleological' side of the mind we can see in motion. Patients who enter the clinic present as frozen, depressed and disengaged. In a couple of weeks, I see them come back to life; they move their arms more when they talk, they smile, laugh, cry; they are more animated.

Athletes can do what they want. They can choose to repair and grow or they can choose to cope. Most people don't change the habits of a lifetime, and try to cope. Coping is sometimes the worst strategy an athlete can choose and it is also, I suspect, the most common. The trouble with coping is that it risks ruling out the possibilities that emerge by seeking change, connecting with other people or learning that may bring new solutions or ideas. There is an implication there that we have to not cope in order to cope better in the future, which seems counterintuitive. Temperament is the heating and cooling of steel, and in my experience it is the same for the agonistes. If we defend and protect ourselves from feeling too bad, we may be storing up a dam in the river that will one day starve us.

Mentors and people are available who can help or suggest new opportunities for learning. Isolation is different from solitude, which is everyone's right. But this is something naturally to be avoided for the young athlete, who needs psychic connections. Depth-clinical psychology relates to connection to the spirit, and different people have different tolerances, capacities and attitudes regarding this subject. In sport, when people are learning, people are generally growing.

Some are cynical about these things, or naive like Red Riding Hood, or full of a wilful ignorance. For many years I have run a mediation group in a sober-living house with young men who have very limited financial resources. I do not get paid in money terms, but the work has a lot of meaning. They do not laugh at spirituality, they are passionate about mediation, their lives are at stake. They truly battle the forces of 'Dis' and Mara on the concrete streets of Los Angeles every day. They are not so choosy about ideas related to mind-calming and inner health. But they had to hit rock-bottom first and accept they needed to change inside. Now they live more fully.

The trouble for the aspiring athlete is that they might not be able to meet the demands their dreams and failures will make on them. This is a bad age to expect a mentor, but this is perhaps the best age to find one! If you are an aspiring anybody who wants to work with sport and the soul, then these books below are all key. Each one has its own identity and I would recommend all of them to the truly aspiring athlete, coach or teacher.

Emerging voices from the depths of psychology

Dr Mark Nesti, Psychology in Football

Mark Nesti is one of the most experienced sport psychologists and lecturers currently working in England. His book *Psychology in Football: Working with Elite and Professional Players* (2010) is a wide-ranging insight covering the waterfront of psychology in soccer clubs. He has written many such books; this is just one. Anyone working in a sports club (including in the USA) could benefit from the information he covers. Mark Nesti especially deserves a mention as he has the courage to use the word 'spirit'. He has a clear insight into the realities of development issues, including an illuminating section called 'Developing the Spirit' where he follows the same spirit as this book. That is, he uses a wider lens in order to see some familiar words and subjects more clearly, which I consider to be good science.

This is a comprehensive and detailed examination of a sport culture, in this case football. Nesti covers all of the ways a sport psychologist can usefully work in a club. Nesti has much experience in professional football, and he also has the courage to write about the soul of things. That is not easy in the English sport world. He is very attuned to English football culture and recognises missing links in the psychological culture of sport.

He writes about a forgotten worker in professional football clubs: the chaplain. It is revealing what he says: 'Sports psychologists share a personal identity with chaplains, again, irrespective of their own attitude towards religion and belief. Players in particular will tend to see similarities between chaplains and sports psychologists; one deals with the soul, one with the mind' (Nesti, 2010, p. 175).

Nietzsche worried about the future of us all when he identified the diminished role of the church and religion in people's day-to-day lives. The chaplain may be the best available to help with religion, but the soul also has a qualified friend in depth-clinical psychology. This is another option available for the athlete who indeed must work with the soul. It may be their only chance.

I want to add in all sincerity that every player should meet the chaplain at a club; they might indeed be a secret Yoda waiting patiently for the student to arrive. Many players also identify with religions and clubs may have someone very experienced or knowledgeable in place who performs that role. Athletes should be open and inquisitive about any spiritual matters; do things differently.

Many of the great coaches I work with are often the more obscure figures. They are the Merlins, the ones who can patiently coax, make a butterfly out of nothing, in a team or individual. Or is it that they know how to liberate the souls of their athletes by creating cultures that help all people grow? The great coaches are alchemists, able to conduct the chemistry and tone of the place. As in times of war, certain conditions bring such facilitators forward, and these figures almost always stay in the background.

Dr Ricardo A. Rubinstein, Sports on the Couch

Here is the first contribution from a pioneering sports analyst from Argentina. *On the Couch* (2017) is written by Dr Ricardo A. Rubinstein, an Argentinian doctor, psychiatrist and an analyst-in-training. Argentina frequently features as a culture with a rich tradition of psychotherapy and enlightened attitudes towards depth psychology. On 25 July 2017 the International Psychoanalytic Association Congress met in Buenos Aires. Argentinians make for marvellous sportsmen and psychotherapists, naturally; the country has a rich tradition of supreme athletes and football managers. One of the world's greatest ever soccer players, Diego Maradona, came from Argentina. Today, Lionel Messi is another Argentinian player who will live in the pantheon of the world's greatest.

Dr Rubinstein is able to locate the historical and cultural traditions of the culture, describing an archetypal football identity that comes form the 'Gaucho' culture in Argentina that has its own way of playing with style and dare. His book explores depth-psychological issues, developing many Freudian themes in sports. Dr Rubinstein tackles transferential relationships that exist everywhere in sport cultures but are rarely, if ever, discussed or elucidated. His understanding is clear, and he is part of the new generation of sport psychologists who are analytically and psychotherapeutically minded. Mark Nesti relates a debate over 'person first, or athlete second' for the sport psychologist, and both agree to go to the person-first lens. This is also the reason why depth-clinical models have found a home in sports.

Dr Mike Brearley, On Form

Mike Brearley was the young captain of the England cricket team while I was still at school. Some of the matches he played in have been regarded as legendary international sporting encounters at a time when many great players from all over the world were in their prime. Dr Brearley is now a practising psychoanalyst in London. I can imagine that if you are like Odysseus or Psyche, on a mission facing dangerous hounds of hell, then he would be a good person to talk to about it. I first learned about *On Form* (2017) through a radio podcast. The book connects drama, meditation and performance, and goes into detail regarding an image highlighted in my own work and sense of sport: the hunter.

Depth psychology reaches into the depths, the soul and spirit of the ethereal. I know it works, perhaps because this is such a left-brained, data-driven time that people are indeed searching that bit deeper for antidotes. Evidence at the box office and in general suggests people still connect on deep archetypal levels with sport. Cognitive behavioural models and ideas have struggled to find a language for such an emotional world as sport, but psychotherapeutic approaches can be the language for progress when all else fails.

But this understanding has one important proviso. Our Greek friend Epictetus was an early cognitive behaviourist, and the cognitive method is good! Our point is, there are other dimensions to attend to here as well, such as the aesthetic and the spiritual, something that methodology does not embrace.

In one of Mike Brearley's chapters, 'How do I know what I think until I read what I write?' (Brearley, 2017, p. 356), he cites E.M. Forster as the source of this statement regarding the unconscious, creative forces that lie dormant beneath the conscious mind. I have to thank Dr Brearley, as this was helpful in approaching the end of this book.

Knowledge of the soul is a broad universal church with room for us all, young and old alike. It is not obtuse or ethereal to suggest that these clues for living are everywhere in the world, as long as we keep looking. But the young generally need to be shown the way first, and that is our responsibility as adults who can influence these things in this modern era. So far, this new era has not been good; anxiety and suicides in the young are increasing and commercialism is reaching far into the world with its digital tentacles. But things are changing; there are many positive developments, and this is an interconnected, curious world as well as a troubled one.

I began this book by saying that each chapter could be a book in itself. Happily, these new books demonstrate that things are changing. The social vacuums that currently exist seem to be in turn creating new voices and ideas that bring deeper, more meaningful investigations and connections to the soul of the young and people in general. A successful psychotherapeutic relationship finds keys that can unlock doors. Each one of these books is a key that opens a room in the expanding new household that is depth sport psychology. Another voice, and a part of this emerging field from New York, is Dr Tom Ferraro.

For many years, Tom Ferraro has joined the dots of psychotherapy, emotional healing and sporting excellence. Much of his work has been done with individuals such as elite golfers – another reason why I wanted him to share his thoughts and contribute to this book. He is a passionate believer in the depth model and has created many successful outcomes for people on and off the field. He continues our discussion in this book's final chapter.

References

Bor, C. (2015). *Lionel Messi, Football's Divine Teacher Prepares for Glory*. Online. http://8by8mag.com/lionel-messi-football-champions-league/ (retrieved 3 July 2018).

Brearley, M. (2017). *On Form*. London: Little, Brown.

Dweck, C. (2006). *Mindset: The New Psychology of Success*. New York: Ballantine.

Gardner, F. (2016). 'Mindfulness and Acceptance-Based Models', in *Mindfulness and Performance*, A.L. Baltzell (ed.). Cambridge: Cambridge University Press.

Helmore, E. (2018). 'US Suicide Rate has Risen Nearly 30% Since 1999, Federal Study Finds', *The Guardian*, 8 June. Online. www.theguardian.com/us-news/2018/jun/08/us-suicide-rate-has-risen-nearly-30-since-1999-federal-study-finds (retrieved 25 October 2018).

Mandela, N. (1995). Nelson Mandela Children's Fund speech, 8 May, Pretoria.

Mumford, G. (2016). *The Mindful Athlete: Secrets to Pure Performance*. Berkeley, CA: Parallax Books.

Nesti, M. (2010). *Psychology in Football: Working with Elite and Professional Players*. New York: Routledge.

Peters, S. (2012). *The Chimp Paradox: The Mind Management Programme to Help You Achieve Success, Confidence and Happiness*. London: Vermilion.

Rubinstein, R.A. (2017). *Sports on the Couch*. London: Karnac.

Schopenhauer, A. (1837). *On the Basis of Morality* (E.F.J. Payne, trans., 1903). Oxford and New York: Berghahn Books (1995 edition).

Selye, H. (1977). *Stress Without Distress: How to Survive in a Stressful Society*. London: Holder and Stoughton.

The Hamilton Spectator (2018). Boys' Team Identity, Meditation May Ease Stress in Thai Cave', Associated Press, 5 July. www.miamiherald.com/news/article214351339.html (retrieved 5 July 2018).

9

FREUDIAN DEPTH SPORT PSYCHOLOGY

Tom Ferraro

This chapter will present the argument for the use of depth sport psychology for the athlete. The essential position of depth sport psychology is that without a foundation of support and insight garnered over time, any behavioural intervention will fail. This is especially true in the context of competitive sport, where the intensity of emotion is high. We do not believe that attempts at behavioural change are wrong but rather that they will only be useful after a solid foundation of support, insight and a strongly established working alliance has been formed.

The depth approach can be subdivided into a Jungian and a Freudian approach. The Jungian approach, with its use of myth, art, storytelling and the collective unconscious, is especially well-suited for teams and groups of athletes and this approach has been more than adequately presented by Dr Burston. The present chapter will focus on the Freudian approach and how it is used to treat to individual athletes, whether they are part of a team or playing an individual sport.

As of 2017, the field of sport psychology and clinical psychology in general emphasises a simplified approach to athletes by looking only at symptoms and then applying a variety of 'tools' in order to suppress them. This dehumanised approach in clinical psychology has emerged over the last few decades due to a host of cultural, political and economic forces, including the influence of insurance companies, the pharmaceutical industry and the medical profession. As a result of this time pressure, practitioners in the field of sport psychology have increasingly been expected to provide quick fixes that are symptom-focused and cost-saving. This approached is especially attractive in the fast-paced world of competitive sport, which insists that this weekend's big game must be won at all costs.

The problem with this fast-paced, symptom-focused approach is that it simply doesn't work. The athlete may experience a very short-term removal of symptoms but without doubt the athlete will soon be faced with another symptom of equal or greater significance. This is called symptom substitution.

The common reason that symptom-focused cognitive behavioural tools fail is because the patient was not given sufficient opportunity to establish ego strength, self-esteem nor insight into the causes of their symptoms. A fast-paced approach which attempts to suppress symptoms without allowing for ventilation of affect and the establishment of ego strength through a working alliance is destined to fail.

Humans are complex in nature and the emergent symptoms are multi-determined and derive from a combination of ongoing real-world triggers, an accumulation of psychological traumas that are usually repressed and unconscious dynamics within the athlete. Added to this is the unique and intense pressure elite athletes face each day and it is obvious that they need a trustworthy, objective and strong therapeutic relationship which will provide them the time to ventilate affect and eventually develop the strength to face the various conscious and unconscious issues which are producing the symptoms. These unconscious issues typically include a sense of **weakness** which causes anxiety, **vanity** producing a fear of shame, **perfectionism** which causes a fear of failure and tension, **grandiosity** which causes either uncontrolled anger or shame when failing in front of crowds, **conflicts about winning** which will produce self-defeat, **moral deficits** which put the athlete at risk of criminal behaviour and **lust, greed and aggression** which can produce acting out and a blind denial of negative consequences.

The glaring weakness of the field of sport psychology as it stands today is that the clinicians, coaches and players minimise the profound emotions that athletes must deal with. The primary reason any current cognitive behavioural psychologist is achieving a measure of success is not because of the so-called 'tools' they use but because they have either intentionally or unwittingly established a long-term working relationship with the athlete which allows the athlete to form trust, ventilate concerns, slowly explore the variety of issues at play and find some occasional insight into what is producing their choking or anger or depression. The athlete deserves a supportive relationship in order to ventilate concerns, gain some solace, get help with problem solving and uncover the issues which are producing the symptoms in question.

Depth sport psychology is unique in that it seeks to find what is hidden inside the athlete, which is thus far unconscious. Most coaches, general managers (GMs) and parents will all hope that the cures are fast and simple. The athlete will join this resistance because invariably the repressed emotions are unsettling and painful to face again. All of this denial is what the sport psychologist must face each session. And, unfortunately, most if not almost all of the field of sport psychology had joined in this denial, blithely assuming that a few sessions of positive self-talk and deep breathing will do the trick. So what we now have is a field that is in jeopardy of becoming obsolete and trivial or useless.

Currently, most sport psychologists use standard cognitive behavioural techniques which focus on the athletes' symptoms using standard suppressive methods such as imagery, cognitive behavioural therapy, positive self-talk, goal setting, various relaxation therapies, hypnosis and focusing treatments. These tools are designed to suppress or control the various emotions that are overwhelming the athlete and a review of any standard sport psychology textbook reveals that this is the exclusive approach to helping the athlete without a mention of psychoanalytic views, repression or the unconscious.

In recent years there has been some use of 'acceptance therapy', which is borrowed from Eastern philosophy and encourages an awareness of affect rather than its suppression. However, all these approaches are based upon theories which overtly deny the significance of the past and the existence of the athletes' unconscious. All these approaches give these interventions their characteristic shallowness and this is why the gains made are so short-lived and disappointing.

Psychoanalysis has been founded upon the belief that there is such a thing as a person's unconscious, that their unconscious has an impact upon their mood, success or failure and that the patient is heavily invested in forgetting or repressing this pain. The painful past as well as early childhood experiences have a major impact upon a person's athletic performance by distorting perception, creating anxiety, despair, low self-image and self-defeat. In addition, the energy it takes to repress these memories produces depletion in the athlete as well.

The typical case is the elite athlete who has enormous natural talent, a good work ethic and expert training that allows them to rise to the top of their field. But most often there is no provision for ongoing psychotherapy and certainly no such thing as a mental gym for them to attend each day. So inevitably based upon the competitive experiences they all must face, symptoms arise which relate to anxiety, anger, self-doubt or depression. This is when they are most vulnerable to either substance abuse or to injury. They turn to drugs to ameliorate the symptoms, or incur injury, which then provides the secondary gain of temporarily removing them from the action.

The standard psychoanalytic approach uses the establishment of a working alliance, free association, dream analysis, transference and counter-transference analysis and the careful working-through of interpretations in order to heal the athlete and improve performance. There is usually no attempt to suppress the symptoms presented by the athlete but rather to make sure that the athlete is helped to confront the actual meaning of these symptoms. This process has a most potent impact on the symptoms in question.

Typically, the psychoanalyst must undergo an additional four years of training to earn their degree and only through this training do they acquire the insight to treat the patient effectively and to assess their resistances and defences. The world of sport produces intense and overwhelming emotions which can break down an athlete's defences and force them to turn to a variety of drugs to cope with their affective flooding.

I will provide four case studies to give the reader a brief feel for what occurs in the typical psychoanalysis of an athlete. It should be noted that not all athletes have the ability to work in analysis since it requires introspection, good intelligence, the ability to trust another human and to be relatively free of sociopathy and drug use. Various elements in these case studies have been modified in order to ensure anonymity. The case studies involve athletes who have achieved global status or who are serious nationally recognised amateurs in their sport.

Case study 1. 'The injury-prone perfectionist', working with a harsh superego: 16-year-old, highly ranked male tennis player

The symptom picture

This patient was brought to therapy by his father, who reported that the patient would get very angry after losing a point and would then lose focus. During clinical interview the patient admitted to having a bad attitude and that he would get into rages on the court and then very quickly grow despondent during matches. The father had sufficient insight to see that the patient's body language was also self-defeating in that it encouraged his opponent to try even harder. He also was suffering with tendinitis based upon overuse. As is typically the case with new patients, the parent demanded that I teach the player different ways of carrying himself on court in the hope that this would cure his problem. These kinds of pressure-filled demands are commonly seen and the first job I was faced with was some psychoeducation so that both patient and parent had a more realistic view of the depth of the issues at hand.

Dynamics underlying the symptoms

Over the course of a five-session intake period, what became evident was that the patient had strong obsessive-compulsive tendencies which carried with them a demand that he do all things perfectly. As an example, he would spend most of his time during school scanning his penmanship for any slight irregularities, which would then lead him to carefully erase the errors and re-write the word. This tendency to expect perfection carried itself onto the tennis court, which would produce much anger as well as anxiety following mistakes, but, as is the case in all sports, he was not able to erase this error so would soon get despondent instead, slump his shoulders and essentially quit the match.

This player had an older sibling who was intellectually superior and who would taunt and ridicule the patient throughout childhood. The perfectionism was a compensation in an effort to undo the damage done by the sibling and to express underlying rage as well.

Another aspect of the symptom picture of this patient was his tendinitis in the right shoulder. As is typical of the perfectionist, he would push himself to exhaustion in all practices and proceeded through the three stages of burnout which included: 1) flat play; 2) a lowered immune system, which caused frequent colds; and finally 3) a variety of injuries as the body gave way.

Treatment

The interventions employed in this case combined: 1) education of the father so that he might monitor his son's rest and recovery; 2) insight for the patient as to why he would get so angry and then sad during matches. This is done by encouraging free association to the topic of anger, noticing when he avoided completion of his thoughts and then helping him to return to the topic. This technique leads to real insight into the nature and the causes of the anger and perfections and self-attack. The process that unfolds is that the patient will unconsciously begin to adopt the kinder and gentler conscience of the analyst and use that to replace the harsh, more primitive superego that is wreaking havoc on the patient in the form of anger. Then, and only then: 3) conscious interventions which included cognitive therapy and positive self-talk to combat the negativity and self-attack. We also did some behavioural role-modelling using George Kelly's body language coaching so that he changed his physical reaction to mistakes in a way that actually enabled him to remain confident and less encouraging to his opponents.

Case study 2. The false-self in a football player

Symptom picture

This patient came to my office during a period when I was the team psychologist for his professional football team. He presented with symptoms of migraine headaches, nausea before games, alcohol abuse and an unwillingness to do penalty kicks in games. He has been treated twice weekly for the past 16 years. His complaint about fear of penalty kicks emerged after he missed one during the Olympics. This miss prompted him to refuse any further penalty kicks, much to the chagrin of his coach and team, since he was by far the best on the team. This avoidance was cured within five minutes of our first consult with the instruction to become target-aware during his approach to the ball. Like all truly elite athletes this instruction was immediately learned and his avoidance and anxiety regarding penalty kicks was cured; it was apparent to me that the fear of penalty kicks was the very least of this world-famous athlete's concerns. His variety of psychosomatic concerns were far more intractable and included head pain, back pain, itchy and scaling skin hives and nausea. Up until the start of therapy he was using alcohol to self-medicate.

Dynamics underlying the symptoms

The anxiety in this patient stemmed from what on the surface was a benign-looking event. This athlete had declined recruitment from a particular college coach who was now his head coach on the national team. The coach's narcissistic injury was so great that he successfully encouraged the team to ostracise this player to the point where the patient felt alone and worthless. The coach used the player as a starter but never gave any credit or praise. This dynamic caused enormous upset, rage, anxiety and depression, which were initially masked by alcohol and psychosomatic symptoms outlined above.

Adding to this problem was the athlete's childhood. He was a gifted child raised by a borderline mother and without a father. As Winnicott and Alice Miller's work discussed, gifted children will often develop into false-selves as they are able to read and respond to the needs of the depressed mother. And this false-self became extremely problematic when the patient matured and was faced with a coach who actually had a vendetta against him and withheld support.

Treatment

Over several years of work in insight-oriented analysis, these dynamics were understood. We basically employed free association and dream analysis, which the patient was able to tolerate well. Dream analysis was used and the most repetitive dream was of him flying in a large aeroplane which would invariably crash and burn. The basic interpretation of that dream was that the patient saw the toxic coach and mother as equal to the force of gravity, which could never be escaped from and which would pull him down into depression. Transference remained largely positive and resistance was minimal in this case. Over time his alcohol use diminished. His various psychosomatic diseases were treated with a combination of medical interventions and insight-oriented work. The affects of anger and anaclitic depression were often somatised in the abdomen, which prompted him to seek out a variety of medical tests, none of which found positive results. This was followed by insight-oriented work which revealed deep-seated childhood depression. Skin rashes were also first treated medically and this was followed by insight-oriented work revealing both shame issues and loneliness. He retired under his own time frame and is now a successful coach himself.

One can readily see that serious psychological treatment is often needed but so often real psychological treatment carries with it serious stigma. Professional athletes embrace an ethos of action, toughness and masculine power, which is often at odds with the introspective attention to feelings that are used in therapy. The irony is that real long-term analytic work is often the only treatment which will bear fruit.

A word about psychiatric medications

Typically, the first form of treatment the athlete is offered will be standard psychiatric medications like anti-depressants. Unfortunately, many of the drugs used in the psychiatric realm have troubling side effects which slow performance and thinking or produce weight gain and even the slightest decrement in performance cannot be afforded at the highest competitive levels. When an athlete has career-threatening emotional symptoms and when they discover that medication often carries performance damaging side effects they finally turn to the sport psychologist.

Case study 3. The use of transference in the case of a professional golfer

Symptom picture

This is the case of a male professional golfer who came to the office with deep frustration because he would become anxious, tight and give away good scores at the end of each tournament. An exceedingly common issue for golfers, this is referred to as choking and may be the most commonplace neurotic symptom seen in sports. Symptoms of anxiety in athletes include panic, fear of dying, being on edge, fatigue, muscle weakness, muscle tension, chest pain, sleep paralysis, dry mouth, choking sensation, jitteriness, shortness of breath, trembling, sweating, dizziness, numbness, heart palpitations and nausea.

These emotions are not only highly unpleasant but also have the capacity to derail top-level performance. The athlete will do almost anything to avoid these symptoms through legal or illegal drug-seeking or will also remove themselves from the tension by choking, which can be an unconscious way of avoiding the overwhelming affect of being in the lead. Suppressive techniques such as deep breathing, relaxation therapy or positive self-talk are surprisingly ineffective with these symptoms, despite their widespread use. Gardner and Moore's work was the first to reveal just how ineffective these techniques are. I liken their use to using aspirin to treat cancer. Anyone who has tried to use these interventions on professional athletes under severe competitive pressure knows how ineffective they actually are. The result is that the patient is disappointed and the field's reputation suffers.

Dynamics underlying the symptoms

This patient suffered a deprived childhood. His father left home when he was an infant and contact with him was sporadic, at best. When he did meet the father, he observed that the man was weak, ineffective and a failure in life. The patient's mother was described as bitter and critical and the patient reported that by his teen years he was doing poorly in school and was depressed. I will focus in this description only on the dynamics of him and his father through a discussion of the transference.

Treatment

The concept of transference was one of Freud's greatest discoveries and he would often say the only cure is the transference cure. Transference is the accumulation of emotional experiences that a person has with his parents which become internalised and expressed in the way they present themselves to others and in how they in turn instil feelings about themselves into the others with whom they interact. Without proper training, a therapist, coach or teammate will unwittingly respond to the athlete based upon these subtle cues they are receiving. In this case I could feel the impact of the transference immediately. The patient instilled in me a feeling that he was a loser and a failure, and this was communicated by his weight, his manner of dressing and his speech.

When one is trained sufficiently in how to understand the transference feelings one is able to resist their influence and thereby provide the patient with a different interpersonal interaction. By refusing to believe that the patient was a loser who would always choke down the stretch I was able to maintain a respectful and admiring view of him, which was communicated unconsciously during each session. What slowly occurred was that he began to acknowledge his own worth and power and thereby overcame his tendency to give away leads down the stretch. The result was that his tournament income doubled within a year and this was in no way related to any cognitive behavioural interventions. This work was all about transference-countertransference insight about the patient, his father and me.

Case study 4. Wrecked by success: the case of an All-American football player

The world is aware of Tiger Woods, but may not be aware of how and why the dynamic of being wrecked by success is so common. Here is a case that reveals this dynamic.

Symptom picture

This is a segment of an analysis of an All-American football player. This section will only describe his reaction to the apparently good news that he was elected as All-American. Following the announcement that he was to receive this prestigious award, the patient began getting messages from all over the country congratulating him on this accomplishment. He got calls from his proud parents, long-lost relatives, old and new friends and all of his teammates. Over the next four weeks he became more withdrawn, sullen, would sleep all day and missed his classes in college. Needless to say, this became the central point of conversation in his twice-weekly sessions.

Dynamics underlying the symptoms

What became apparent in this case was that rather than instilling some pride and joy in the patient, the award served to escalate the pressure he was already was feeling on his team. Now not only was he expected to perform well, but he must perform so well that his team would never lose again. He felt he was now a public figure and must be the team's saviour and full-proof good luck charm. He was already a patient who was prone to guilt and depression and this award served to break through his tenuously constructed defences and left him nothing but stress and anxiety. His depression was his way to withdrawing from this pressure and surviving the stress.

I have always felt nothing but pity and worry when I witness the acquisition of fame in people I have worked with. In the mid-1990s I was in Rome with my wife on vacation, staying at the five-star Cavaliere Hotel. That was the week that the Michael Jackson world tour was also in Rome. One day we got on the bus, which was to take us from the hotel into the centre of Rome, and I noticed that a number of 20-something Americans boarded with us. I struck up a conversation with them; I found out that they were part of Michael Jacksons' tour company. They were choreographers, dancers, singers, seamstresses etc. and they told me that there were 220 of them in total, and that they had been on tour for ten months already, playing to sold-out performances every night around the world.

So here were 220 young talented professionals working for Michael Jackson, and he was putting them all up in five-star hotels each night. I met the opening act and she told me her group was paid $8,000,000 to open for him for the year. I asked them if Michael was staying at the Cavalieri himself, and they said 'Oh no, Michael rents out an entire boutique hotel just for himself so he can get some privacy'. I realised then and there that the pressure of fame and success is almost incompressible for the average person to fathom. This short story explains why famous people take drugs, hide out, do self-defeating in order to escape from the pressure and sometimes even commit suicide. Or, as Bob Dylan once said following his breakdown, 'You know, the fans can really kill you with kindness.'

Treatment

My patient was getting just a little taste of fame and his reaction was understandable. He could feel the increased pressure being put on his shoulders by teammates, parents, coaches, friends and fans. What I did was help him to explore the inevitable consequence of fame and then tried to help him to construct a defence to ease the pressure. I let him talk it out and tried to help him understand that his job was to determine exactly how much he wanted to give, and that he was the only measure of his success.

Summary

The uniqueness of the Freudian approach to the athlete lies in its effort to patiently await the emergence of unconscious data that typically confirms ones initial suspicions about the true causes of the symptoms and problems presented. This insight can only be arrived at with the use of free association and free-floating attention which does not insist that the patient suppress his or her affect.

There will always be room for and a need of the behavioural control methods but I believe that sport psychology will find its ultimate success by establishing a trusting relationship with the athlete, by being patient and non-judgmental and by exploring what lies underneath which was initially adamantly denied by the athlete. The danger that the field faces today is that it will continue to join with the athlete's resistance by minimising what is at work and by providing ineffective quick fixes under the pressure of the moment. If this continues to happen the field is in serious danger of becoming a useless joke that GMs, coaches and players will eventually turn away from. The time has finally arrived for depth sport psychology to emerge as a powerful and effective treatment for the professional and elite amateur athlete.

Anyone who has worked with athletes understands the pressures felt when you perform in front of millions of adoring fans. But what few fans and often few coaches seem to realise is that these heroes and modern-day gladiators are suffering a host of often debilitating symptoms which include panic attacks, anxiety, poor sleep, pain, fear, obsessive worry, depression and psychosomatic diseases. These symptoms will not be removed with street drugs. They will not be removed with antidepressants or tranquillisers. They will not be removed by prayer or meditation. And they will not be removed with a bit of deep breathing, positive self-talk or hypnosis. What is needed, especially for the more introspective and more intelligent athlete, is good old-fashioned psychoanalytic psychotherapy.

EPILOGUE

I was struck by the themes that athletes struggled with in the case studies outlined in Chapter 9, and how they relate to some of the clinical patients I am working with now. I hope that you can identify defences, inflations, wounds and dilemmas a little more clearly. Depth-psychological approaches are new to sport, but the language of the emotions, of the struggle and despair, has found a willing audience of athletes that can relate. All of the studies in Chapter 9 revealed subtle pressures and daemons that elite sports athletes can face; we all can. This book calls out for a caring voice able to be one step ahead, especially for the young. Computer mentors may well represent the future, but for the athlete alone that will mean a bad parent. I look forward to the future and where all this will lead: human-to-human, the old way.

Now is the epilogue, the real goodbye. As this book has always maintained, there are stages to go through in life and we shall attend to this one. Experience suggests that when we pay attention to them, things get better, and the reverse when we do not. This book is written as a wave in the world rises, the wave of e-commerce and now a new kind of agoniste, the 'e-sports' competitor. E-sports are with us, and being a such a virile form of commerce, they will not be going away any time soon. Right now, many young people spend their entire days at a computer monitor playing games while interconnected with others around the world. It sounds good in one way, but where is the soul of the athlete here?

As write this book new models and psychologically minded systems are being created to try and heal the new rising wave of pathology and distress. Disconnection and its sibling anxiety are at a new high in the West and systemised ways of thinking on their own will not solve the problem. A lecturer of mine once suggested 'the cognitive world has no realm for the spiritual or the aesthetic'. The sport world has both of these features as a central theme, so athletes, beware!

Soon football and other sport teams will have 'virtual players'. These are young people who play online and will have contracts earning large sums of money by representing a team or a brand. They are already with us. Perhaps all of us will one day be happily interconnected with each other and remote from each other at the same time. Public sporting events will no longer happen. On the other hand, this evolution has some positives.

This development has created a new kind of accessible interactive experience that is remarkably inclusive. It has meant that old-age pensioners can pit their wits against Muhammad Ali, or as Lionel Messi for Barcelona in the Champions League. You can play against Bjorn Borg in the Wimbledon final and get a sense of how that would all have been. The digital age will be kind to those who cannot get about much. The Internet is a friend to democracy and free trade, providing a route for the developed world to give to the poor in ways not possible before. I have some clients who testify to the community side of the experience and that this helps them.

On the negative side, unknown psychological consequences will come for some of those that get involved. For some that will be negligible, and for others it will be terminal. It is not the destination for young people who still have to live a life and grow somehow. As we saw earlier, there are many lives currently being damaged by compulsive relationships to computers. It is nothing like the experience of the social interaction we see in real sport, but it seems like it. If I want to be Ronaldo I may fail, but if I play football I will at least be a bit fitter for the experience, and maybe make a friend along the way. The virtual world offers less-certain benefits for the aspirants.

The world of sport has a soul. It is a good soul. It is healthy soul; as we can see, it spreads much joy to those who want to join the dance. We can now see the evidence that young people who learn how to work in teams are better adjusted to live in the world. However, it remains a dangerous world; there are new hazards that are stalking the children. I am grateful to the US football coach Bill Swartz who has taught many generations of players. He alerted me to the tragic book *What Made Maddy Run?* (Fagan, 2017), which highlights the emotional dangers and perils for the young in this modern age of super visibility. The soul is needed more than ever in the world, and we cannot be ashamed by the word or take it lightly. Every myth suggests that if we do, we are heading for a fall.

The light within sport is not dead; it was the original Olympic soul of sport that brought the North Korean and South Korean representatives together in 2018. Perhaps it is one of the few hopes for the world going forward. The 2018 Football World Cup in Russia did not have any of the terrible racism or violence predicted; it was a joining together. During the Belgium *v.* England match on 28 June 2018, it was noticeable that the supporters in the ground were mixed up as one; there was no distinguishable colour, just supporters.

George Leonard (2001) believed that a mind-body-spirit split has happened for us in the West. Perhaps the flame is still alive somewhere. Lily Parr and Annie Oakley were not from the financial elites, but they were from the spiritual and sporting kind. They knew how to climb Olympus and come back to Earth safely. The Greeks harnessed a spirit, and knew how to give it a home to roam safely in the world of sport and entertainment. They realised that we the spectators can also join this ancient pleasure of being carried along with the athletes for a while, win or lose.

When we look to define the ineffable, something like the soul, perhaps we might be doomed to failure. Words are never enough on their own. But here we have a kind of blueprint of the soul, one bestowed upon us by nature and acted out for us by the athlete. This may be the footprint in the mud we suggested at the beginning. This is the blueprint, an outline we can rely on as we forge ahead with our future, win or lose.

The soul of the athlete

Understands beginnings, middles and endings.
Inclusive, it replaces war and brings people together,
Has a life on the road, in the field,
Is able to suspend itself,
Is able to play freely,
Always returns to earth,
Is conscious, and awake to the world,
Is ethical,
Nurtures and protects its inner animal,
Nurtures and protects its inner child,
Is an alchemist,
Is a landlord for our dodgy relatives, conviction and commitment,
Has restraint,
Never gives in,
Is able to heal,
Comes back the next day, wiser.

References

Fagan, K. (2017). *What Made Maddie Run?* New York, Boston, MA, and London: Little, Brown and Company.
Leonard, G. (2001). *The Ultimate Athlete*. Berkeley, CA: North Atlantic Books.

BIBLIOGRAPHY

Adams, L. and Russako, D. (1999). 'Dissecting Columbine's Cult of the Athlete', *The Washington Post*, 12 June. Online. www.washingtonpost.com.wpsrv/national/daily/june99/columbine12.htm/ (retrieved 29 January 2010).

Adler, A. (1917). *The Neurotic Constitution* (B. Glueck and J.E. Lind, trans.). New York: Moffat Yard.

Adler, A. (1930). 'Individual Psychology', in *Psychologies of 1930*, C. Murchison (ed.) (pp. 395–405). Worcester, MA: Clark University Press.

Albert Camus Society, UK (2012). 'Camus on Football'. Online. www.camus-society.com/camus-football.html (retrieved 14 November 2011).

Armstrong, K. (2005). *A Short History of Myth*. Edinburgh: Canongate Books.

Arnot, C. (2011). 'English Women's Football Aims to Score Again', *The Guardian*, 12 April.

Baltzell, A.L. (2016). *Mindfulness and Performance*. Cambridge: Cambridge University Press.

Batchelor, S. (2005). *Living with the Devil: A Meditation on Good and Evil*. New York: Riverhead.

BBC 5 Live (2017). 5 Live Sport Specials, broadcast 22 December.

Beilock, S. (2010). *Choke: What the Secrets of the Brain Reveal About Getting it Right When You Have To*. New York: Free Press.

Benjamin, J. (1995). 'Recognition and Destruction: An Outline of Intersubjectivity', in *Like Subjects, Love Objects: Essays on Recognition and Sexual Difference*. New Haven, CT: Yale University Press.

Binswanger, L. (1960). *Melancholia and Mania: Phenomenological Studies*. Pfullingen: Neske.

Bly, I. (1990). *Iron John, A Book about Men*. Reading, MA: Addison-Wesley Books.

Bohr, N. (1954). As quoted by Edward Teller, in 'Dr Teller's Magnificent Obsession', Robert Coughlan, *Life* magazine, 6 September 1954, p. 62.

Bor, C. (2015). *Lionel Messi, Football's Divine Teacher Prepares for Glory*. Online. http://8by8mag.com/lionel-messi-football-champions-league/ (retrieved 3 July 2018).

Brearley, M. (2017). *On Form*. London: Little, Brown.

Brown, M. (2017). 'Trees Talk to Each Other, Have Sex and Look After Their Young, Says Author', *The Guardian*, 31 May. Online. www.theguardian.com/environment/2017/

may/31/trees-talk-have-sex-look-after-young-peter-wohlleben-hay-festival   (retrieved 5 July 2018).

Brown, S. (2007). 'Animals at Play'. YouTube. https://m.youtube.com/watch?v= iHj82otCi7U (retrieved 1 December 2017).

Burston, D.H. (2015). *Psychological, Archetypal and Phenomenological Perspectives on Soccer*. London and New York: Routledge.

Caillois, R. (2001). *Man, Play and Games (Les jeux et les hommes)* (M. Barash, trans.). Chicago, IL: University of Illinois Press (original work published 1958).

Callimachus (1921). 'Hymn III to Artemis', in *Hymns and Epigrams* (A.W. Mair and G.R. Loeb, trans.), Classical Library Volume 129. London: William Heinemann.

Calvin, M. (2017). *No Hunger in Paradise*. London: Random House.

Campbell, J. (1988). *The Power of Myth* (B.S. Flowers, ed.). New York: Doubleday.

Castillejo, I.D. (1974). *Knowing Women*. Boston, MA: Shambhala.

Churchill, W. (1942). 'Now is Not the Beginning', Mansion House speech, London.

Claxton, G. (2005). *The Wayward Mind: An Intimate History of the Unconscious*. London: Abacus.

Collins, D. and MacNamara, A. (2012). 'The Rocky Road to the Top. Why Talent Needs Trauma'. *Sports Medicine* 42(11): 907–914.

Conn, D. (2017). 'Football's Biggest Issue: The Struggle Facing Boys Rejected by Academies'. *The Guardian*, 6 October 2017.

Conquest, R. (1991). *Stalin: Breaker of Nations*. New York and London: Penguin Books.

Cooper, A. (1998). *Playing in the Zone: Exploring the Spiritual Dimensions of Sports*. Boston, MA: Shambhala.

Cousineau, P. (2003). *The Olympic Odyssey: Rekindling the True Spirit of the Great Games*. Wheaton, IL: Quest.

Cross, G. (2008). *Men to Boys: The Making of Modern Immaturity*. New York: Columbia University Press.

Csikszentmihalyi, M. (1990). *Flow: The Psychology of Optimal Experience*. New York: Harper & Row.

Dasgupta, N. and Asgari, S. (2004). 'Seeing is Believing: Exposure to Counter Stereotypic and its Effect on the Malleability of Automatic Gender Stereotyping', *Journal of Experimental Social Psychology* 40: 642–658.

Dasgupta, N. and Dennehey, T. (2017). *Female Peer Mentors Early in College Increase Women's Positive Academic Experiences and Retention in Engineering* (S. Cheryan, ed.). Seattle: University of Washington.

De Beauvoir, S. (1968). *Force of Circumstance*, Vol. III (R. Howard, trans., 1963). London: Penguin.

Diamond, S. (1999). *Anger, Madness, and the Daimonic: The Psychological Genesis of Violence, Evil and Creativity*. Albany, NY: State University of New York Press.

Diver, K. (2005). 'Journal Reveals Hitler's Dysfunctional Family', *The Guardian*, 4 August. Online.www.theguardian.com/world/2005/aug/04/research.secondworldwar (retrieved 2 July 2018).

Dussault, J. (2015). 'Did North Europeans Resist the Rise of Agriculture?' *Christian Science Monitor*, 8 April. Online. www.csmonitor.com/Science/2015/0408/Did-Northern-Europeans-resist-the-rise-of-agriculture (retrieved 10 September 2017).

Dweck, C. (2006). *Mindset: The New Psychology of Success*. New York: Ballantine.

Eller-Boyko, D. (2017). 'Longing for the Feminine: Reflections on Love, Sexual Orientation, Individuation, and the Soul', *Psychological Perspectives* 3 (C.G. Jung Institute of Los Angeles).

Epictetus (1865). *The Enchiridion* (E. Carter, trans.). Boston, MA: Little, Brown and Company.

Fagan, K. (2017). *What Made Maddie Run?* New York, Boston, MA, and London: Little, Brown and Company.

Feynman, R. (1965). *The Character of Physical Law*. Boston, MA: MIT Press, Modern Library.

Fichte, J. (1799). *The Vocation of Man* (Die Bestimmung des Menschen) (W. Smith, trans., 1848). London: John Chapman.

Gadamer, H. (1980). *Dialogue and Dialectic: Eight Hermeneutical Studies on Plato* (P.C. Smith, trans.). New Haven, CT: Yale University Press.

Gardner, F. (2016). 'Mindfulness and Acceptance-Based Models', in *Mindfulness and Performance*, A.L. Baltzell (ed.). Cambridge: Cambridge University Press.

Gimbutas, M. (1996). *The Goddesses and Gods of Old Europe 6500–3500 B.C.* Berkeley, CA: University of California Press.

Green, C. (2009). *Every Boy's Dream*. London: A&C Publishers.

Grof, S. (1988). *The Adventure of Self-Discovery*. Albany, NY: State University of New York Press.

Harari, Y. (2011). *Sapiens: A Brief History of Humankind*. London: Vintage.

Helmore, E. (2018). 'US Suicide Rate has Risen Nearly 30% Since 1999, Federal Study Finds', *The Guardian*, 8 June. Online. www.theguardian.com/us-news/2018/jun/08/us-suicide-rate-has-risen-nearly-30-since-1999-federal-study-finds (retrieved 25 October 2018).

Herodotus (1920). *Histories* (A.D. Godley, trans.). Cambridge, MA: Harvard University Press.

Hillman, J. (1983). *Healing Fiction*. Woodstock, CT: Spring.

Hoare, C. (2011). *Erikson on Development in Adulthood*. New York: Oxford University Press.

Hoffman, P.S. (2014). 'On Acting: An "Exhausting" And "Satisfying" Art'. Online. www.npr.org/2014/02/03/270954011/philip-seymour-hoffman-on-acting-an-exhausting-and-satisfying-art (retrieved 8 February 2014).

Homer (1896). *Iliad* (A. Pope, trans., 1896). New York: American Book Company.

Homer (1938). *The Odyssey*, VIII (W.H.D. Rouse, trans., 1938). New York: Signet Classics.

Huizinga, J. (1955). *Homo ludens: A Study of the Play Elements in Culture*. Boston, MA: Beacon Press.

Isenberg, N. (2008). 'Review: Her Best Shot: Women and Guns in America by Laura Browder', *The Journal of Southern History* (Southern Historical Association) 74(1): 175–176.

Jaynes, J. (1976). *The Origin of Consciousness and the Breakdown of the Bicameral Mind*. New York: Houghton-Mifflin.

Jobs, S. (2005). 'Text of Steve Jobs' Commencement address (2005)', *Stanford News*, 14 June 2005.

Johnson, R.A. (1987). *Ecstasy: Understanding the Psychology of Joy*. San Francisco, CA: Harper.

Johnson, R.A. (1991). *Owning Your Own Shadow*. San Francisco, CA: Harper.

Johnson, R.A. (2008). *Inner Gold: Understanding Psychological Projection*. Kihei, HI: Koa.

Jordania, J. (2011). *Why Do People Sing? Music in Human Evolution*. Tbilisi: LOGOS Publishing Programme.

Jung, C.G. (1949). 'Foreword to Adler: Studies in Analytical Psychology', *Collected Works, volume 18: The Symbolic Life: Miscellaneous Writings*. Princeton, NJ: Princeton University Press.

Jung, C.G. (1957). *The Undiscovered Self*. New York: Mentor.

Jung, C.G. (1961). *Memories, Dreams, Reflections* (R. and C. Winston, trans.). New York: Random House.

Jung, C.G. (1990). *The Collected Works of C. G. Jung*, Vol. 17. Princeton, NJ: Princeton University Press (original work published 1951).

Kalshed, D. (2013). *Trauma and the Soul: A Psycho-Spiritual Approach to Human Development and its Interruption*. London and New York: Routledge.

Keats, J. (1817). Letter to George and Tom Keats, 22 December.

Keegan, M. (2014). 'Wembley Attendance: FA Must Act on Low Turnout, Warns Davies', BBC.com. Online. www.bbc.com/sport/football/29069804 (retrieved 3 January 2017).

Klein, M. (1964). *Love, Hate and Reparation*. London and New York: The Norton Library Press.

Kornfield, J. (2001). *After the Ecstasy then the Laundry*. New York: Bantam.

Langley, P. and Jones, M. (2013). *The Search for Richard III: The King's Grave*. London: Murray.

Leakey, R. and Lewin, R. (1992). *Origins Reconsidered*. New York: Doubleday.

Leonard, G. (2001). *The Ultimate Athlete* (first published in 1974). Berkeley, CA: North Atlantic Books.

Mandela, N. (1995). Nelson Mandela Children's Fund speech, 8 May, Pretoria.

Marcus, L., Mueller, J. and Rose, M. (eds) (2002). *Elizabeth I: Collected Works*. Chicago, IL: University of Chicago Press.

McGilchrist, I. (2012). *The Master and his Emissary: The Divided Brain in the Making of the Western World*. New Haven, CT, and London: Yale University Press.

Mithen, S. (2005). *The Singing Neanderthals: The Origins of Music, Language, Mind, and Body*. Cambridge, MA: Harvard University Press.

Mumford, G. (2016). *The Mindful Athlete: Secrets to Pure Performance*. Berkeley, CA: Parallax Books.

Naisbitt, J. (2006). In *Wisdom for the Soul: Five Millennia of Prescriptions for Spiritual Healing*, Larry Chang (ed.). Washington, DC: Gnosophia Publishers.

Nande, A. (2017). 'Lily Parr: The Gun Which Dodged Bullets to Pioneer Women's Football', footballparadise.com. Online. www.footballparadise.com/lily-parr/ (retrieved 12 February 2018).

Nehru, J. (1981). *Jawaharlal Nehru: An Anthology* (S. Gopal, ed.). Oxford: Oxford University Press.

Nesti, M. (2010). *Psychology in Football: Working with Elite and Professional Players*. New York: Routledge.

Newton, I. (1675). Letter to Robert Hooke, 15 February.

Nietzsche, F. (1982). Prologue to 'Thus Spoke Zarathustra', in *The Portable Nietzsche* (Kauffman, W., trans., 1954). London: Penguin.

Norretranders, T. (1991). *The User Illusion: Cutting Consciousness Down to Size*. New York: Penguin Books.

Novak, M. (1993). *The Joy of Sports: Endzones, Bases, Baskets, Balls, and the Consecration of the American Spirit* (rev. ed.). Lanham, MD: Madison.

Pankhurst, E. (1913). 'Freedom or Death', speech delivered in Hartford, CT, 13 November. *The Guardian*. Online. www.theguardian.com/theguardian/2007/apr/27/greatspeeches1 (retrieved 29 June 2018).

PBS (n.d.). 'Biography: Frank Butler'. Online. www.pbs.org/wgbh/americanexperience/features/oakley-butler/ (retrieved 28 December 2017).

Peters, S. (2012). *The Chimp Paradox: The Mind Management Programme to Help You Achieve Success, Confidence and Happiness*. London: Vermilion.

Piero, Angela and Piero, Alberto (1993). *The Extraordinary Story of Human Origins*. New York: Prometheus.

Pindar (1997). *The Odes and Selected Fragments, Pythian 8* (R. Stoneman, trans.). London: Everyman's Library.

Pinker, S. (2002). *The Blank Slate*. London: Penguin.

Plato (1899). *Apology* (S.T.G. Stock, ed.), 3rd edn. Oxford: Clarendon Press.

Plato (1989). 'Symposium', in *Plato in 12 Volumes*, Vol. 9 (H Fowler, trans., 1925). Cambridge, MA: Harvard University Press.

Riley, G. (1994). *The Life and Legacy of Annie Oakley*. Norman, OK: University of Oklahoma Press.

Rock, D. (2009). *Your Brain at Work*. New York: HarperCollins.

Rogers, C. (1961). *On Becoming a Person: A Therapist's View of Psychotherapy*. London: Constable.

Romanyshyn, R. (2004). *Technology as Symptom and Dream*. Hove: Brunner Routledge.

Rose, H.J. (1959). *A Handbook of Greek Mythology*. New York: Dutton.

Rowland, S. (2017). *Remembering Dionysus*. London and New York: Routledge.

Rubinstein, R.A. (2017). *Sports on the Couch*. London: Karnak.

Samuels, A. (1986). *A Critical Dictionary of Jungian Analysis*. London: Routledge.

Schechner, R. (1988). *Performance Theory*. New York: Routledge.

Schechner, R. (1993). *The Future of Ritual: Writings on Culture and Performance*. New York: Routledge.

Schopenhauer, A. (1840). *On the Basis of Morality* (E.F.J. Payne, trans., 1903). Oxford and New York: Berghahn Books (1995 edition).

Searl, S. (2016). *Homage to the Lady with Dirty Feet and Other Vermont Poems*. Kanona, NY: Foot Hills Publishing.

Selye, H. (1977). *Stress Without Distress: How to Survive in a Stressful Society*. London: Holder and Stoughton.

Shirl, K. (1992). *Annie Oakley*. Norman, OK: University of Oklahoma Press.

Simpkin, J. (2014). 'Dick, Kerr's Ladies', Spartacus-Educational. Online. http://spartacus-educational.com/Fdickkerrs.htm (retrieved 3 January 2018).

Singh, S.S. (2004). *Spirituality of Sport*. Cincinnati, OH: Saint Anthony Messenger Press.

Smith, E. (2009). *What Sport Teaches Us About Life*. London: Penguin.

Socrates Brasileiro (blog) (2014). '30 Great Quotes by Socrates'. Online. http://socrates brasileiro.blogspot.com/2014/03/30-quotes-by-socrates-give-my-goals-to.html (retrieved 15 January 2018).

Solomon, M. (1995). *Mozart: A Life*. New York: HarperCollins.

Stevens, A. and Price, J. (2001). *Evolutionary Psychiatry*. Hove: Brunner Routledge.

Sutton-Smith, B. (1997). *The Ambiguity of Play*. Cambridge, MA: Harvard University Press.

The Hamilton Spectator (2018). Boys' Team Identity, Meditation May Ease Stress in Thai Cave', Associated Press, 5 July. www.miamiherald.com/news/article214351339.html (retrieved 5 July 2018).

The Scotsman (2018). '25 of Spike Milligan's Wittiest Jokes and One Liners', April 16. Online. www.scotsman.com/read-this/25-of-spike-milligans-wittiest-jokes-and-one-liners/ (retrieved 29 June 2018).

The Times (1921). 'Women's Football Players: The FA's Boycott', 6 December, p. 10.

Toering, T. (2011). 'Self-Regulation of Learning and the Performance Level of Youth Soccer Players', University of Groningen. Online. www.academia.edu/2588854/SelfRegulation_of_Learning_and_Relative_Age_in_Elite_Youth_Soccer_International_versus_National_Level_Players (retrieved 20 February 2014).

Topping, A. (2017). 'More than 240 Clubs Now Involved in Football Sexual Abuse Scandal', *The Guardian*, 18 January. Online. www.theguardian.com/football/2017/jan/18/police-confirm-500-potential-victims-sex-abuse-football (retrieved 25 June 2018).

UEFA (2016). 'UEFA Report: Registered Female Footballers on the Rise', UEFA.com. Online. www.uefa.com/insideuefa/football-development/womens-football/news/newsid=2516070.html#/ (retrieved 1 January 2018).

UEFA (2017). 'Qualified Female Coaches: 17,550+, a 31% Rise Since 2015/16', UEFA. com. Online. www.uefa.com/insideuefa/football-development/womens-football/news/ newsid=2431355.html#/ (retrieved 1 January 2018).

van der Post, L. (1961). *The Heart of the Hunter*. New York: William Morrow and Co.

Virgil (1997). *Aeneid*, Book 6 (J. Dryden, trans.). London: Penguin.

von Franz, M.L. (1974). *Shadow and Evil in Fairy Tales*. Boston, MA: Shambhala.

West, R. (2005). *The Young Rebecca: Writings of Rebecca West, 1911–17*. London: Royal National Institute of the Blind.

Wilde, O. (1988). *The Picture of Dorian Gray* (J. Bristow, ed.). Oxford: Oxford World Classics.

Williams, J. (2003). *A Game for Rough Girls? A History of Women's Football in Britain*. London: Routledge.

Winnicott, D.W. (1971). *Playing and Reality*. London: Penguin.

Wohlleben, P. (2016). *The Hidden Life of Trees: What They Feel, How They Communicate. Discoveries from a Secret World*. Vancouver: Greystone Books.

Zdanowicz, C. (2015). '10-Year-Old Shooter: I Want To Be an Inspiration', CNN. Online. www.cnn.com/2014/10/17/living/10-year-old-competitive-shooter-irpt/index.html (retrieved 28 December 2017).

INDEX

For Product Safety Concerns and Information please contact our EU
representative GPSR@taylorandfrancis.com
Taylor & Francis Verlag GmbH, Kaufingerstraße 24, 80331 München, Germany